About this book

This book is a critical exploration of Isra
policy in the Occupied Palestinian Territi
CheckpointWatch, an organisation of Is⌐ _. ....g
human rights abuses. The book combines observers' daily reports
from the checkpoints and along the Separation Wall, with analysis
of the bureaucracy that supports the ongoing occupation. Keshet
demonstrates the link between Israeli bureaucracy and the closure
system as integral to a wider project of ethnic cleansing.

As co-founder of the group, Keshet critically reviews the organisation's transformation from a feminist, radical protest movement
to one both reclaimed by, and reclaiming, the consensus. Illustra-
ting the nature of Israeli mainstream discourse as both anodyne
and cruel, the book also analyses Israeli media representation of
CheckpointWatch and human rights activism in general. Keshet
contends that the dilemmas of these Israeli women, torn between
opposition to the Occupation and their loyalty to the state, reflects
political divisions within Israel society as a whole.

Critical praise for this book

'It is impossible to guess when and how the harsher Israeli version
of the Apartheid Pass System will collapse. When it does, CheckpointWatch will have had an important role in its collapse.'

Amira Hass, Israeli journalist

'This important book offers an insightful perspective of the system
of Israeli military checkpoints and blockades in the West Bank,
their devastating impact on the Palestinian population, and the
arbitrary use of a control mechanism for reasons which often have
little to do with security considerations. The first-hand accounts and
observations of the Watchers – Israeli women from all walks of life
– also provide an interesting insight into how different sectors of
Israeli society see – or fail to see – the impact of such a system and
its injustices.'

*Donatella Rovera, Researcher on Israel and the Occupied
Territories, Amnesty International*

About the author

Yehudit Kirstein Keshet was born in Wales and has lived in Israel since the late fifties, settling there permanently in 1974. With a background in both anthropology and film studies, she is now a full-time activist having dedicated her retirement to opposing Israel's occupation of the West Bank and Gaza.

As the daughter of refugees from Nazi Germany, Kirstein Keshet is adamant about the importance of speaking out and regards this book and the work of CheckpointWatch, of which she is co-founder, as the expression of her determination not to be silent. She is currently working on a political novel set in Jerusalem.

YEHUDIT KIRSTEIN KESHET

Checkpoint watch

Testimonies from Occupied Palestine

Zed Books

LONDON | NEW YORK

Checkpoint watch: testimonies from Occupied Palestine was first published by Zed Books Ltd, 7 Cynthia Street, London N1 9JF, UK and Room 400, 175 Fifth Avenue, New York, NY 10010, USA in 2005

www.zedbooks.co.uk

Copyright © Yehudit Kirstein Keshet, 2006

The right of Yehudit Kirstein Keshet to be identified as the author of this work has been asserted by her in accordance with the Copyright, Designs and Patents Act, 1988.

Cover designed by Andrew Corbett
Index: <ed.emery@britishlibrary.net>
Set in Arnhem and Futura Bold by Ewan Smith, London
Printed and bound in Malta by Gutenberg Press

Distributed in the USA exclusively by Palgrave Macmillan, a division of St Martin's Press, LLC, 175 Fifth Avenue, New York, NY 10010.

A catalogue record for this book is available from the British Library.
US CIP data are available from the Library of Congress.

ISBN 1 84277 718 1 hb
ISBN 1 84277 719 X pb

ISBN 978 1 84277 718 3 hb
ISBN 978 1 84277 719 0 pb

Contents

Maps

Acknowledgements

First and foremost my gratitude and appreciation to the women of MachsomWatch/CheckpointWatch who every day, year round, are there at the checkpoints, observing, reporting and testifying. Thanks too to Amira Hass, who was our inspiration both as a model of courageous committed journalism and for her harrowing descriptions of checkpoints that spurred us to start CheckpointWatch. Special mention must go to our first recruits, Maya Bluhm, Nava Eliashar Yehudit Elkana, Roni Hammerman, Ivonne Mansbach and Norah Orlow, without whom Checkpoint-Watch would never have happened. My apologies to the many Watchers who provided interviews and material; although it was not possible to use every one of them, each one has contributed to the fabric of this work. As I read, cut and pasted from the innumerable reports (over 10,000 to date), often with tears in my eyes at their eloquence, I was spoilt for choice and regret that more could not be included. Although this book is often critical, presenting a picture with which many will disagree, it never lessens my admiration for the courage and tenacity of these modest witnesses. Thanks also to my editor Anna Hardman of Zed Books for her support from the very first, very rough, draft and her helpful suggestions that contributed to the final manuscript. Esti Tzal and Elisheva Smith made available their superb photographs. Anat Caspi Kaivanto painstakingly prepared the photographs for press. Dr Ronit Lentin of Trinity College Dublin, Josephine Jaffrey and Dr Michal Nachman of Lancaster University read an early draft and made thoughtful comments incorporated into the text. Diana Martin, that rare being, a truly peace-full soul, made significant improvements to the Conclusion. Thanks to Dr Susan Einbinder of Princeton University, Professor Ruth Wodak of Lancaster University and Nimrod Amzalek of B'Tselem, Jerusalem, for their readings, to Ada Ravon for legal clarifications while Watchers Hagit Back, Hana Barag, Adi Dagan, Michelina Dank, Tzilli Goldenberg, Tamar

Goldschmidt, Dalia Golomb, Yael Lavie-Jenner, Aya Kaniuk, Susy Mordechay and Yael Na'aman, provided invaluable information; Deborah Jacobs edited two chapters for submission to publishers and Brian Sawyer helped prepare the final version. I am grateful to Jeff Halper of the Israel Committee Against Home Demolitions for use of the Matrix of Control map, to the United Nations Office for the Coordination of Humanitarian Affairs in Jerusalem and particularly to B'Tselem, the Israeli Information Centre for Human Rights in the Occupied Territories, for permitting the use of their maps and data.

There are others who contributed to this endeavour unawares: Hava HaLevi, Ruti El-Raz, Elliot and Veronica Cohen in Israel gave friendship and encouragement; Lynne Alexander and Jenny Foot in Lancaster provided walks and talks and an introduction to the delights of vegetarian cooking; the Lancaster 'Witches', Sandy, Liz, Tracy, Catriona and Mary, were a welcoming committee; weekly visits to Barsie the cat in quarantine gave time for the rethinking of many troublesome paragraphs.

Last but not least this book owes a huge debt to two women: Ronnee Jaeger and Adi Kuntsman, who together with this author made up the original 'Troika' of MachsomWatch/CheckpointWatch: Ronnee whose ebullient personality helped draw in, and hold, new members and whose energy and spirit kept us enthused when our spirits flagged. Adi, my partner, whose impact on my life in so many ways is for ever entwined with the founding of CPW, with the writing of this book to which she has so substantively contributed, and with the future we now share. In the small horizon of our lives, that future looks promising; let us hope that a similar promise will some day prevail in the big picture of Israel–Palestine.

In memory of my parents: Shimon (Siegmund) and Margot Kirstein.

For B & B and A & A and for Adi

Foreword by Amira Hass

In the five years of MachsowmWatch/CheckpointWatch's activity since it was established in February 2001, not a single checkpoint has been removed in the West Bank. On the contrary, the more activists joined its ranks, so too did the checkpoints erected by the Israeli army multiply: between villages and their neighbours, between village and city, between region and region. What CheckpointWatch has done is to serve as observer of and protest movement against these checkpoints: permanent checkpoints, temporary checkpoints, staffed checkpoints, unstaffed blockades. Watchers are witnesses to, and recorders of, the permanence of supposedly temporary major checkpoints allegedly erected in response to security needs, and have recorded their metamorphosis into well-fortified gates between walls and fences that create Palestinian enclaves, isolated from one another. Gradually, Watchers have become expert witnesses documenting the whole phenomenon of the checkpoints: the orders to halt all Palestinian movement from area to area, the barring of main roads to Palestinians, the bureaucratic system that issues pass permits, or, more accurately, usually refuses them. They have acquired expert knowledge about the types of permits, and the methods of harassment that prevail at the checkpoints.

Watchers have become the frustrated scribes and monitors of a particularly sophisticated Israeli policy: closure, that euphemism for the policy of denying Palestinians their right to freedom of movement. It is a delicate description of the Israeli Pass System, an understatement for the methodical sabotage of the Palestinian project to establish an independent, viable state within the borders of 4 June 1967 in the West Bank and Gaza.

The sophistication lies in its consistency and its dynamism, and in its managing to evade attention in Israel and internationally. Sophisticated because it is easy to present it as a collection of discrete decisions, uncoordinated and unplanned. Because its damage is singular and individual, it is hard to discern its totality and long-term implications for Palestinians, individuals and collective alike, from any one checkpoint visit or newspaper article. This policy is always presented as responsive to terror and, of course, as *ad hoc*, temporary, although it has been in place, with constant refinements, since 1991.

CheckpointWatch 'entered the picture' only ten years after Israel introduced the Pass System. In order to understand why – despite their daily presence – not a single checkpoint has been removed, it is necessary to dwell on the successful history of the Israeli policy of closure.

On the eve of the Gulf War in 1991 a military order cancelled a previous military order that granted Palestinian residents of the West Bank and Gaza a general entry permit to Israel, which had guaranteed them free passage between the two areas. The general permit was one of Moshe Dayan's measures for economically integrating the Occupied Palestinian Territory (OPT) into Israel with the aim of toning down Palestinian national aspirations and undermining the feasibility of an independent Palestinian state. Whatever the motives, that freedom meant a great deal for individual Palestinians, economically, socially and psychologically. From the 1970s onwards there were categories of people to whom Israel denied or severely limited freedom of movement, by various bureaucratic means. However, the general right of freedom of movement was respected. From January 1991 the situation was reversed: no more freedom of movement for many and denial to the few, but denial to many and freedom of movement for the few. It must be stressed that within those same territorial boundaries Israelis enjoy unlimited freedom of movement.

A right not granted to all is a mutilated right – that is, a privilege for the few. And thus, from 1991, Israel granted that privilege of freedom of movement only to certain categories, when and as it deemed fit and in numbers that it deemed fit, for instance, labourers, merchants, collaborators, officials of the Palestinian Authority, the sick, the dying, investors, artists. The first Intifada (1987–93) ended. There were talks on peace in Madrid, Washington and Oslo, the Oslo Process began, the Palestinian Authority was established, but the general rule did not change. The number of privileged categories, under conditions determined by Israel, were contracted or expanded. The numbers in each category changed, as did the areas for which an entry permit was required, but the general rule remained: Israel controls freedom of movement between the West Bank and Gaza through Israel, movement outside Israel's borders, and, since 2000, within the West Bank. The military evacuation from the Gaza Strip in 2005 has eased the draconian restrictions on internal movement for Palestinians there but, again, the control over exit from and entrance to Gaza remains in Israel's hands.

From 1991 onwards until March 1993, the new policy was imposed mainly on Gazans who found that they could no longer leave the Strip for Israel and the West Bank without special permits. From March 1993 residents of the West Bank also began to feel the pinch of closure: free 'entrance' to occupied East Jerusalem, in every sense their capital – cultural, religious, medical, economic and political – was restricted. Whoever was caught without an appropriate entrance permit was fined or sent for trial.

During the Oslo years, 1993–2000, the closure policy only became more refined: an elaborate bureaucracy was established in which Palestinian clerks served as couriers or subcontractors for requests for permits to Israeli representatives in the Civil Administration and the General Security Services (GSS), who then issued, or refused, the permits. The Oslo years, supposedly the years of a negotiation process based on the recognition that Gaza and the West Bank are one territorial unit that would constitute the future Palestinian state, were characterized by an ever-increasing severance between the two. This separation damaged family connections, education, culture, medicine, trade, and so on, and turned Gaza into one large prison for the majority of its inhabitants. Their horizons became more and more closed, until the majority ceased to aspire to leave their prison. Israel, which since 1967 has controlled the population register, also played with the human right of individuals to change their place of residence: Gazans were forbidden to move to the West Bank, and to change their address in their ID cards. During the five years of the Intifada, Israel even banished Palestinians living in the West Bank whose address was in Gaza.

What is more, during the Oslo period the physical infrastructure for this separation was established in the West Bank by means of the ceaseless expansion of the Israeli settlements/colonies and the building of a network of bypass roads whose purpose was to connect all the colonies, including the smallest and most isolated, to the larger colonies and to Israel proper. The roads cut off Palestinian villages from their area cities, villages from their lands and from other villages, and cities from their land reserves. On the eve of the current Intifada the jurisdiction area of the colonies spread over half of the West Bank. Since the end of 2000 the infrastructure of separation has been reinforced in the form of blockades, permanent and mobile checkpoints, watchtowers and tanks from which soldiers shoot at 'criminals' trying to bypass the blockades.

From October 2000 the restrictions on movement were expanded and were applied with ever-increasing severity to movement within the West Bank. In the five years that have elapsed since then the Gaza picture has been duplicated and multiplied: mini-Gazas have been established in the West Bank and Palestinian enclaves whose connections with each other are dependent on the policies of the Israeli army, and are gradually being blocked by the same logistical means that turned Gaza into a prison: fences, walls and military checkpoints with pretensions to being 'border crossings'.

Orders were issued that prevented Palestinians from travelling on main roads used by the settlers/colonists. With time, the orders elapsed, but even without them those roads are empty of Palestinians: the many blockades, military checkpoints and police harassment do not encourage Palestinians to try to travel.

In the spring of 2002 another bureaucratic layer of separation within the West Bank was introduced: it was announced that going from area to area via the ever-expanding, ever-increasing military checkpoints in the heart of Palestinian territory would be permitted only by means of special passes issued by the Israel Civil Administration in offices and command posts outside the enclaves themselves.

The military authorities rapidly discovered that the order was unenforceable: most people defied it; international organizations protested politely; and the Palestinian Authority forbade its employees, mostly teachers, to ask for permits while continuing to receive pass permits on preferential terms for its own executives. Specifically, the Israeli bureaucracy could not bear the volume of the tens of thousands who daily required permits in order to survive: to get to work, to school, to family events, to shop. The order did not disappear altogether and is still valid in certain areas, particularly those close to the Separation (Annexation) Wall and the Jordan Valley. There are also some major checkpoints where entry through them to the Palestinian enclaves is allowed only to those with valid permits, or often permitted only to those whose address in their ID cards indicates residence in those enclaves. While there are long and arduous bypass routes in some cases, mobile checkpoints and *ad hoc* blockades promise that the appearance of free movement is fragile. In fact, two parallel transportation systems have evolved in the same geographic area in the OPT: broad, well-paved highways for Jews, rough and twisted routes for Palestinians.

For Palestinians from East Jerusalem, who were compelled to accept the status of Israeli residents against their will, entrance to West Bank cities without special permits, sparingly granted, is forbidden. Until now the authorities had turned a blind eye to Palestinian Jerusalemites entering Ramallah, the *de facto* capital of the Palestinian Authority (PA),

xiii

due to outstanding publication and diplomatic pressure. However, the order stands: Palestinian Jerusalemites are considered 'Israelis' and they have Israeli IDs. Already at the beginning of the second Intifada, Israelis were prohibited by the army from entering the territory of the PA, ostensibly for their own protection. Thus, under the false pretence of 'equality between Jews and Palestinians', the natural connections of Jersualemites with West Bank society were severed.

Security is always cited as the reason for these measures and, indeed, terrorist acts (against civilians in Israel) and guerrilla activities (in the OPT) have always led to an intensification of the closure policy. It is easy, therefore, to present the closure and the checkpoints as a response, and to ignore the following facts:

- The policy of passage permits, that is, revoking the freedom of movement of Palestinians, began in 1991, long before the nightmare of suicide bombers became reality. (The first attack in Israel was in April 1994.)
- The permit policy and the prohibitions prevent freedom of movement not only into Israel but also within the OPT.
- The internal closure policy within the West Bank is intended to protect Israeli settlers/colonists who live in the Occupied Territory in defiance of international law. The policy protects a privileged minority, at the expense of the majority.
- In 1991 the closure policy was introduced as a bureaucratic/logistic measure in order to contain the first Intifada. It then developed as a means of demographic separation between Jews and Palestinians (and not a political-geographical separation between two political entities, as was wrongly assumed).

During the Oslo years, since 1994, the closure policy, which severely damaged the economic and social development of the Palestinian Authority, turned into a war of attrition against the Palestinians, and this at a time of political negotiations. The alternating severity and alleviation of the closure policy – that is to say the weakening and strengthening of the Palestinian leadership and its policy and the Palestinian economy – became a bargaining tool during the negotiations for the implementation of the interim agreements and the redeployment in the West Bank. Temporary political concessions were obtained in return for increasing the number of passes and work permits in Israel, and the contrary: the number was reduced if the Palestinians did not behave at the negotiating table. During the Oslo period the closure policy created the first, massive, significant long-term severance between the West Bank and Gaza. In that period the expanding colonies and the bypass roads in the West Bank began to perpetuate the division of the OPT into enclaves, surrounded by territory mainly under Israeli control – Palestinians were forbidden to develop or build on it. Thus did the 'Palestinian State' evolve: as a collection of detached enclaves, a concept contrary to that of a viable Palestinian state alongside Israel, ensuring that the emergent Palestinian entity would be weak, dependent on and controlled by Israel. This apart from the fact that extensive valuable territory and water sources would remain in Israel's hands.

The closure is considered the primary cause of the collapse of the Palestinian economy – in fact a string of collapses since 1992, with some recovery once the hermetic closure was loosened. Naturally, after 25 years of deliberately created dependence on the Israeli economy, preventing Palestinians from working in Israel caused a chain of economic disasters.

The colonies and the bypass roads devour Palestinian lands, and the permit regime, the checkpoints and the prohibitions also rob them of their space, with all that this implies: mobility, perspective, connections, relaxation and leisure. More than this, though, the checkpoints and the closure plunder time. Land can eventually be returned but the endless waiting at checkpoints, the vain wait for a permit, the long and exhausting bypass routes, the renunciation of simply moving from place to place, are all lost time that can never be regained. Time is a fundamental human resource, whether it is used for studies, work, family outings, voluntary idleness or travel. Day by day Israel's closure policy robs 3.5 million human beings of that precious resource, from each one individually, each a world unto themselves, and from the collective as a whole. With time, they are also robbed of the right to plan their lives. How can you plan when you don't know if you will wait at the checkpoint for one hour or four, if you will encounter three checkpoints or only two, if the permit will arrive or not? They are robbed of the right to spontaneity. Who can dare to do something on the spur of the moment, to hike in the hills, to visit family in a distant village, just like that, when in the middle of the way there is a checkpoint, or two?

And there at the checkpoints you will find the CheckpointWatchers, witnesses to the great time robbery, in real time. They are powerless in the face of the horrendous 15-year-old policy that has gone on, unrecognized, without world protest, and with no effective opposition from the Palestinian leadership.

Foreword

CheckpointWatch was born at a time when most of Israeli society fully supported its government and army in every action or attack against Palestinians. The founding members of the CPW came from the radical fringe of what is known as the Israeli peace camp. During the 1990s this peace camp totally ignored the closure policy and the despair engendered in Palestinian society by the limping Oslo Process. It was believed that an irreversible 'dynamic of peace' had been created. Thus with the outbreak of the second Intifada the Peace Camp felt betrayed and injured. How dare the Palestinians open war while we are already enjoying the peace? CheckpointWatchers, then, clearly established a distinct space of active dissent in an overwhelmingly conformist society. Not infrequently they suffer the anger of transitees at the checkpoints for their impotence, for their Israeliness. Not infrequently they must also suffer the hostility of the soldiers. They phone, plead, fume, call the press and lawyers when the inevitable arbitrariness of the situation delays a sick person, or prevents teachers from reaching their schools. Sometimes they manage to pass someone, despite initial refusal. More often than not they fail. Contrary to first impressions, the intervention is not intended to prettify the Occupation or to make the checkpoints more user-friendly. Rather it is the natural instinct of activists and only increases their awareness of the fact of the ever-intensifying closure policy.

What CheckpointWatch does do is to bring home, to Israel, all the appalling details that many prefer to ignore. The lies, the deviousness, the nastiness, the gap between security discourse and the real goal behind the checkpoints: dismembering the West Bank into disconnected Bantustans. They compel those around them to become aware of those details. They confront the security rationale that for years has been considered (and still is by many) the realm of men and the military. At the checkpoints they have become familiar with Palestinian society in a period in which Israel does all it can to keep the two peoples apart, to distance, to disengage. These women remind the Palestinians that there are Israelis other than soldiers and settlers/colonists. Paradoxically, then, these women, who are often presented by other Israelis as traitors, do a service to the Israeli society. They show that it has another face, has characteristics other than obedience, indifference and compliance. Often have I heard Palestinians comment that such Israelis and such activities give them hope for a change and at least ease their suffering under the occupation.

CheckpointWatch is one of several Israeli groups and movements

xvi

opposing the Occupation whose members devote a large part of their time and energy to this inexorable struggle: former soldiers testifying about army conduct, refuseniks, activists against the Separation (Annexation) Wall. Nevertheless, every Jewish Israeli, be s/he as active as possible against the Occupation, enjoys rights and privileges in comparison to the Palestinians. Against our will we are privileged, and against our will we collaborate with a new Apartheid regime in which we are ranked as the masters. All that we can do is to narrow the scope of that collaboration as much as possible. CheckpointWatchers are thus narrowing the scope of their imposed collaboration as Israeli Jews. Their existence and stubborn activity forces others to think about their own collaboration, and, if not to act to reduce it, at least to be aware and ashamed of it. It is impossible to guess when and how the harsher Israeli version of the Apartheid Pass System will collapse. When it does, the CPW will have had an important role in its collapse.

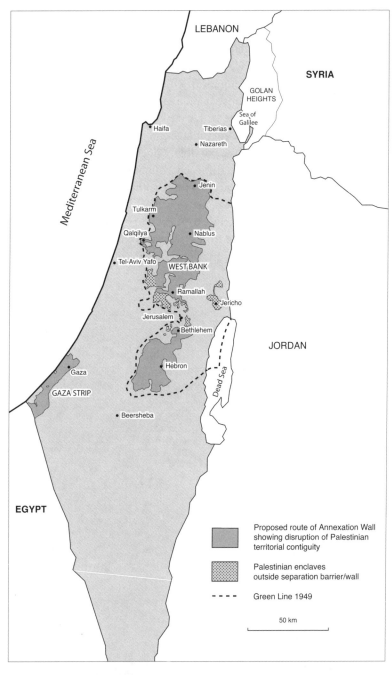

Map 1 Israel and the West Bank, 2005 (data courtesy of Israel Committee for House Demolitions)

LEBANON

SYRIA

GOLAN
HEIGHTS

Mediterranean Sea

Sea of
Galilee

• Haifa

• Tiberias

• Nazareth

• Jenin

Tulkarm •

Qalqilya •

• Nablus

• Tel-Aviv Yafo

WEST BANK

• Ramallah

• Jericho

Jerusalem •

• Bethlehem

JORDAN

• Hebron

Dead Sea

• Gaza

GAZA STRIP

• Beersheba

EGYPT

Proposed route of Annexation Wall
showing disruption of Palestinian
territorial contiguity

Palestinian enclaves
outside separation barrier/wall

- - - - Green Line 1949

50 km

Introduction

Why does a middle-aged woman, very much preoccupied with her
personal and professional interests, decide to spend three hours a
week at checkpoints around Jerusalem? It is rather easy to answer – I
cannot live in Israel if I do not somehow express my protest against
the Israeli occupation of Palestinians. I came to Israel in 1968 from
Poland following a wave of anti-Semitism that swept that country. I
was full of hope of finding a new identity and a place where I wanted
to belong. After thirty-five years in Israel, I have achieved only the first
goal. I have established my identity as a Jewish person and I am no
longer afraid of anti-Semitic remarks. But Israel is not a place I want
to belong to anymore. I have lost my love for Israel, which once was
very dear to me. I cannot love a country where the majority of Jews
support a Fascist government and turn their heads away in order not
to see the disaster imposed on Palestinians. This loss of love for Israel
is hard for me as if I had lost my love for a beloved person. I no longer
even enjoy its countryside, its views and its air. I am too old to leave
this place to look for somewhere where I can live in harmony with the
surroundings again. So I am doomed to stand at checkpoints and to
cry out my disagreement with the brutality, stupidity and lies of the
Israeli government. It is very difficult to witness the humiliation and
suffering of other people ... It is this very strong urge to protest against
... the occupation ... that leads me to go there [to the checkpoints]
nearly every week. (Dr Nina Mayorek, biochemist, Jerusalem, personal
communication, October 2002)

April 2005. Israel's military occupation of the West Bank and Gaza has
been going on for thirty-eight years, the El Aqsa intifada/uprising for
four-and-a-half. Since 2001, Nina Mayorek and other Israeli women
of MachsomWatch/CheckpointWatch have monitored human rights
abuses at the military checkpoints that not only bar Palestinian access
to Israel, but also cruelly restrict movement within the Occupied
Palestinian Territories themselves. This book is a testimony to the
oppression of the Palestinian people inherent in the checkpoints and
to the CheckpointWatchers who so faithfully record that oppression.

Borders and boundaries

When speaking to audiences about the work of MachsomWatch/ CheckpointWatch two questions always surface: why are you obsessed with checkpoints, and why don't you present an Israeli point of view? Where to begin with the answers? Perhaps with my personal odyssey.

Like Nina Mayorek, I came to Israel to find a place of belonging. Leaving my home in Britain in 1958, I dreamed of draining swamps, making the desert flourish and, above all, helping to build a model society. Well, the swamps were drained, the desert was doing fine without me and the issue of what constituted a model society was as hotly contested then as now. A rebellious teenager, I was sent to agricultural school at Ben Shemen near the Jordanian border. Everywhere in those days was near a border. Borders were a fixation. You couldn't approach the border for fear that 'they' would shoot you. Borders had to be constantly policed in case 'they' tried to sneak in. No one mentioned that 'they' had been driven from their homes, and that many snuck back to try and salvage possessions, or crops. 'They' were all killers, to be shot on sight. 'They' were the Palestinians who had allegedly opened war on the newly declared State of Israel. That war, Israel's War of Liberation (1948–49), is enshrined in Zionist historiography as a mythic moment of victory, a fight for survival. It is depicted as the triumph of the few over the many, the purity of arms over barbarians. The wholesale, deliberate, evacuation of the Palestinians ('they fled'), the destruction of their villages, the erasure of their culture and history from the land (Khalidi 1992; Morris 1989) are denied, or excused as acts of self-defence. In many ways, the wholesale collective punishment of the Palestinian people under Occupation is a continuation of that war.

At Ben Shemen I had my first encounter with Israeli reality, and the denial of that reality. The 1950s were the years of the great immigration of Jews from Arab lands, from Iraq and from North Africa. Many were housed in the homes left behind by the Palestinians as they fled from war. My peers were youngsters forced, as I was, to imbibe new norms, to abandon whatever cultural baggage we had brought from the East or the West (especially from the East) and become Israelis. Paramilitary training figured large in this scheme. School trips focused on *moreshet qrav* (battle heritage), scenes of military derring-do. Across from where I toiled in the chicken-coops were the ruins of – what? Villages? Military positions? The road to Ben Shemen lay past shells of houses, deserted fields grown wild and untended fig trees. The worst insult we used was

'Arab!' The use of Arabic among the immigrants was discouraged. No one admitted to coming from Casablanca or Baghdad, claiming instead to be from 'near Paris' or wherever in Israel. Fridays as we readied for the Sabbath we listened clandestinely to pop music on Radio Ramallah – perhaps 30km distant in the West Bank[1] but as inaccessible to us as the moon. The rest of the time we listened to Israeli songs, drenched in love of country and nostalgia for the days of battles won. These were patriotic times, ten years into the new state. The values were simple, the dichotomy clear: good Israelis/bad Arabs. Apart from their deserted fields and fig trees, the 'Arabs' merely lurked silently in the shadows of our nightmares. They were, and are, what is officially known in Hebrew as absentees (Khalidi 1991, 1992). Those who remained within Israel were *nifkedim nochachim* (present absentees).[2] These newly subdued citizens of the state lived under military rule until 1965 (Jiryis 1976; Benziman and Mansour 1992). That regime provided much of the practice that evolved into the curfew–closure–checkpoint policy which is the subject of this book.

Our house-mother, the late Shoshanna Lustig, belonged to Brit Shalom/Tahalof Essalam, the Jewish–Palestinian Peace Alliance, inspired by the philosopher Martin Buber. Brit Shalom favoured a binational state in which both sides, Jewish and Arab, would renounce their national claims and live in harmony and parity. I remember conversations with Shoshanna in which she expressed both her longing for a just peace, an equally passionate desire to impose her Western notions on what she considered to be the Oriental barbarism of her young charges and her anxiety about the 'Arab threat'. We never spoke about the fig trees across the way. This ambivalence lies deep in the heart of Israeli thinking and culture: the longing for peace versus entrenched militarism, the hegemony of European culture versus that of Jews from Arab lands and the denial of the persistent, ghostly presence of those absentees, the Palestinians, amid the ruins of their homes and their neglected fields.

A political awakening

The power of a good Zionist education is not to be underestimated, and although abandoning the chicken-coops for higher education, I returned to Israel permanently in 1974. As a declared left-winger I opposed the Occupation of 1967, but my commitment to the Palestinian cause *qua* cause merely revolved round the search for a common tradition, for righting individual wrongs. When Palestinian friends or colleagues spoke about humiliations suffered, lands lost, I commiserated, shrugging the accounts off as exaggerations, aberrations. I was concerned for their personal rights but gave no thought to their national rights. The mantra, common to so many Israelis, was, 'Why can't the Palestinians just let us get on with being here, stop killing us, live in peace?' My epiphany came during a conversation at a dialogue group in Beth Sahour,[3] near Bethlehem, early into the first intifada (1987–93). I was convinced that if properly presented, by me, the Israeli perspective would be accepted, the Palestinans would 'agree to live in peace with Israel' and the Occupation could end. Our host at the meeting, Ghassan Androni, retorted that Palestinians too feared annihilation, desired the Right of Return, wanted their national aspirations recognized. He didn't mention the Occupation; it was simply not the issue. The issue was Palestinian political, cultural and economic liberation. How banal, how profound, how illuminating, how Israelicentric not to have thought of it oneself. That moment marked the end of denial for me and resulted in a search for a new narrative of history, replacing that dearly held Zionist myth of victimhood and virtue. This did not mean relinquishing Israeliness, but resulted in a more liberated identity, one not bound by the constant need to defend the indefensible: the total erasure of Palestinian political rights in order to assert our own. I mention this rude awakening at length because it describes the dilemma of many CheckpointWatchers, as will be seen in Chapter 5.

Liberation brought loss. Like Nina, I too have lost my love for Israel, if not my identification with it. Even the landscape has lost its charm. I write these lines on the eve of Passover, the festival of freedom, 5675 (April 2005). In order that we Jews may enjoy our holiday free from alleged threats of terror, Palestinians throughout the West Bank and Gaza will be barred not only from entering Israel, but also from movement within their own areas for four whole days. They will be denied access to basic services within the West Bank/Gaza. Health, education, banking and employment access are suspended, to be negotiated with the military. So, too, the simple pleasures of life: family gatherings, a shopping trip. How can we as Israelis enjoy the privileges of freedom and security when on our doorstep a whole nation is oppressed, supposedly in the name of preserving those privileges? This is why checkpoints are an obsession. Both physically and symbolically they embody the Occupation, the absolute subduing of one nation so that the other may walk free. It is an illusory freedom, because the walls that keep 'them' out hem us in too. The contrast between the paralysis of Palestine and the virtual freedom of Israel must be seen to be believed. That is what we observe at checkpoints.

1948 and after

Oppression goes beyond preserving the privileges of life, liberty and the pursuit of happiness for one side, and their denial to the other. The oppression of the Occupation goes much further. It is aimed at maximum Israeli control of territory with a minimum number of Palestinians. There is no intention, nor has there been in successive Israeli governments, to end the colonization of the West Bank (Eldar 2004; Reinhart 2002; Kimmerling 2001). The measures cited in this book – the restrictions on mobility, the bureaucratic control of a civilian population, apartheid roads – are all integral to a policy of ethnic cleansing. In Israel's democratically elected parliament, the Knesset, there are parties that openly preach a policy of transfer, not only for West Bankers, but even for Israeli-Palestinians, citizens of the state. Statements such as this, appearing in a centre-right English-language newspaper, go unchallenged by the public at large.

> [I]t's going to be a human catastrophe. Those people will become even bigger animals than they are today, with the aid of an insane fundamentalist Islam ... It's going to be a terrible war. So, if we want to remain alive, we will have to kill and kill and kill ... If we don't kill, we will cease to exist. The only thing that concerns me is how to ensure that the boys and men who are going to have to do the killing will be able to return home to their families and be normal human beings. (Arnon Sofer, Professor of Geography, University of Haifa, and father of Sharon's Gaza disengagement plan, *Jerusalem Post*, weekend supplement, *Up Front*, 21 May 2004, p. 9)[4]

Sofer is speaking about Gaza, but his words apply as well, or as badly, to the West Bank. We find here three themes that have featured in government, military and public discourse throughout the current war: the threat to the survival of Israel by allegedly insane, bestial, Islamic fundamentalists; the need to kill or be killed; and concern for the Israeli soul (something we will encounter elsewhere in this work).

That is one Israeli perspective. This book presents another viewpoint, that of the opponents of Israeli government policy. These are Israelis like Nina Mayorek and the 500 Israeli Jewish women of MachsomWatch/CheckpointWatch who feel it is imperative to speak out against injustice and state terror. We struggle with our identity as

5

Israelis, with conscience and denial from a whole spectrum of political beliefs. We are no less Israeli than the voices of power, the army and the government, with their constant demonization of the 'Arabs'. We are no less Israeli than the confused, disappointed, frightened silent majority, simultaneously aggressive and defensive, trapped in denial. As this book will show, Watchers too are often confused, disappointed and frightened but, consciously or not, they are confronting those feelings. Every minute at the checkpoints calls them into question. That is why we are obsessed with these barriers. It is not only the abuse of human rights, although that is bad enough in itself. For many of us, the sight of the endless lines of civilians, standing at gunpoint, exposed to the vagaries of weather, climate and soldiers' whims, reminds of us other scenes in other places in our own not-too-distant past.

CheckpointWatch is about speaking out, about bearing witness, perhaps in future war crimes trials, at the very least in some future chronicle of the times. The testimonies of Watchers are not the first, nor the last to be published. Our witnessing, part protest, part resistance, part appeasement of our own consciences, is a strand in a tapestry of testimonies, from soldiers, human rights organizations, activists, press and media. One of the amazing things about Israel is what people know and what they choose not to know, or to excuse. For years the press and media have reported the abuses, the injustices of Occupation. Journalists Amira Hass and Gideon Levi, Tanya Reinhart, Uri Avneri and many others write outspokenly in the mainstream as well as the alternative press, criticizing government policy, exposing iniquities great and small. If future chronicles of these times refute the denial that accompanied the foundation myths of the Israeli state, it will be thanks to these testimonies and others.

The war of 1948 was a war for Israel's survival, or at least its political survival as a nation-state. It was a time of constituting the Israeli nation. It did involve acts of heroism, did forge a new Jew, one who walked free, who fought and overcame oppression. But there was also another side to the glory, a side that is concealed and denied. That side is the tragedy of the Palestinian defeat, the loss not only of their land and possessions but the deliberate erasure of their presence, culture and history by Israel. One of the great mistakes of 1948 was that Israel failed to recognize the need for magnanimity towards the enemy. That war, in all its drastic and unrelenting determinism, became the model for Israel's subsequent behaviour in the political arena; force became an ultimate virtue. That too is what we see at the checkpoints.

6

The book

This book was written in Lancaster, England, with frequent trips to Israel and daily readings of Hebrew newspapers, CheckpointWatch reports and the amazingly active online bulletin boards of Israeli opposition movements. In speaking out, both in my own words and those of CheckpointWatchers, I have given a picture of both the banality and the iniquity of Occupation. Setting these in the context of Israeli political discourse, I have also explored some of the dilemmas that confront anti-Occupation activists in Israel and their representation in the Israeli media. To be an activist in Israel is for many to be torn between loyalty and conscience in a culture that has little or no regard for human rights, unless of course the humans in question are Jewish, or victims of some distant natural disaster.

With regard to details: the situation in Israel-Palestine changes on an almost daily basis and this book should therefore be regarded as a diary of the times – from February 2001, when CheckpointWatch began its observations, to mid-2005 when this book went to press. For this reason, I have kept statistics and figures to a minimum, with references to appropriate sources throughout. Discussion of Sharon's Gaza disengagement plan and political developments since the death of Yasser Arafat have also been left aside. Many and various are the commentaries on those topics, as recourse to any newspaper will show.

The book has three sections:

1 The Context. This provides a background both to the history of the conflict, the curfew–closure–checkpoint policy and the bureaucracy that supports it. This is followed by a study of MachsomWatch, its *raison d'être* and mode of operation. I introduce three motifs that appear in many testimonies: courage, conscience and the desire to speak out.

2 The Checkpoints. Part II focuses on the checkpoints themselves, including those along the notorious Annexation Wall. Here, quoting from the daily reports of CheckpointWatchers, I show a wide variety of the situations in which the Palestinian civilian finds him/herself. There are reports of routine days, reports of violence, of deliberate delays, harassment, of the grotesque, the tragic and the frightening. Although these reports describe what happens to the Palestinians, the voice they feature is the Israeli voice. Once again, the Palestinian voice is not heard directly and we Watchers, with the best intentions, speak out on their behalf. It is yet another luxury of the Occupier to do so. While our activism brings the Palestinians little relief, to abandon them is unthinkable.

3 The Observers. This section looks at the internal dilemmas of

7

MachsomWatch, dilemmas fundamental to Israeli society as a whole. I
explore the organization's gradual transition from a cutting-edge protest movement to one ostensibly less politicized. This transition does
not minimize the importance of the protest, and the question remains
whether it increases or diminishes its effectiveness.

A final chapter deals with media representation of MachsomWatch
and how this both reflects and forms Israeli public opinion, a public
of which Watchers are an integral part. I raise the question of how this
representation will affect the future collective memories of Israelis. Will
new myths of heroism, humanitarianism and purity of arms emerge or
a more realistic picture be drawn, allowing also for a coming to terms
with the darker side of our collective past? Will the heroes of the future
be warriors with guns or warriors for justice? Be that as it may, the
testimonies of CheckpointWatchers will surely go some way to ensuring
a truer chronicle of the conflicted history of Israel-Palestine.

Quotations from reports are credited to their writers, with permission. Country of origin is stated where this is other than Israel. The
opinions expressed in this book are my own, not those of Checkpoint-
Watch, and so too are any errors and omissions.

Notes

1 The West Bank was under Jordanian control from 1948 to 1967.

2 The term applies to Palestinians banished or who fled during the hostilities of 1948 whose property was expropriated by the state. It includes internal
refugees – Palestinians forced to leave their villages but who remained in
Israel as citizens.

3 Dialogue groups, meetings between Palestinians and Israelis, enjoyed a
vogue during the 1980s and 1990s. Both sides would gather in a Palestinian
village or town and each try to convince the other of the justice of their cause.
The mere fact of Israelis and Palestinians meeting without an armed escort,
not to mention in the heart of 'enemy' territory, was a radical move. The Rap-
prochement Group, founded by Dr Veronica Cohen, Hillel Bardin and Judith
Green on the Israeli side, together with Ghassan Androni on the Palestinian
side, met regularly between 1987 and 1999 and hundreds of Israelis partici-
pated during those eight years.

4 Quoted on Kibush website, March 2005, see <www.kibush.co.il/index>.

ONE | **The context**

1 | Occupation

Preamble, Article 3. In the case of armed conflict not of an inter-national character occurring in the territory of one of the High Con-tracting Parties, each Party to the conflict shall be bound to apply, as a minimum, the following provisions:

Persons taking no active part in the hostilities, including members of armed forces who have laid down their arms and those placed hors de combat by sickness, wounds, detention, or any other cause, shall in all circumstances be treated humanely, without any adverse distinc-tion founded on race, colour, religion or faith, sex, birth or wealth, or any other similar criteria ... To this end, the following acts are and shall remain prohibited at any time and in any place whatsoever with respect to the above-mentioned persons: (a) Violence to life and per-son, in particular murder of all kinds, mutilation, cruel treatment and torture; (b) Taking of hostages; (c) Outrages upon personal dignity, in particular humiliating and degrading treatment; (d) The passing of sentences and the carrying out of executions without previous judg-ment pronounced by a regularly constituted court, affording all the judicial guarantees which are recognized as indispensable by civilized peoples. 2. The wounded and sick shall be collected and cared for.

Section III, Article 47. Protected persons who are in occupied territory shall not be deprived, in any case or in any manner whatsoever, of the benefits of the present Convention by any change introduced, as the result of the occupation of a territory, into the institutions or govern-ment of the said territory, nor by any agreement concluded between the authorities of the occupied territories and the Occupying Power, nor by any annexation by the latter of the whole or part of the occu-pied territory. (Fourth Geneva Convention, 1949)

The term 'occupation' is a loaded one. For Palestinians, occupation began in 1948, with the establishment of the State of Israel on 78 per cent of their land, the creation of the refugee problem and the oblit-eration of Palestinian history and culture from what is now Israel. For Israelis, 'occupation', in so far as it exists at all, refers to the military conquest of the West Bank and Gaza during the Six-Day War of June

1967.[1] I will use the latter definition since this implies recognition of the State of Israel within internationally sanctioned borders, those prevailing until 4 June 1967.

Since 1967, Palestinians[2] in the West Bank and Gaza have lived under Israeli military rule. They are a stateless people in their own land, disenfranchised and with no political and very few civil rights except the most basic as laid out in the Geneva Conventions of 1949. Israel has continuously evaded its responsibility to implement the Fourth Geneva Convention to which it is a signatory (Geneva Convention Protocols, Vol. 1, [1995], p. 559). An outstanding example is that of the colonies/settlements in the West Bank and Gaza despite the fact that these are illegal[3] under international law (Fourth Geneva Convention, Section III, Article 49).

The Convention deals most comprehensively with the obligations of an occupying power towards civilians in occupied territory, but Israel contends that since the West Bank was formerly under Jordanian occupation it cannot be considered a sovereign state, a prerequisite for application of the Convention. Nor is the legal status of Palestinians assured. West Bankers are subject to the directives and commands of the Israeli military commander. Criminal cases against Palestinians are tried by the State of Israel in military courts, with all that this implies. Early in the Occupation, the Supreme Court ruled that Palestinian residents of the Occupied Territories (OT) are eligible, in certain cases only, to appeal to the High Court of Justice based on the equity law system that differs from the regular court system based on rights. Israelis living in the West Bank are subject to Israeli civil and criminal law.

Much has been written about the Occupation and the endless series of plans and road maps that seek to bring 'peace' or 'end the Occupation'. One of the claims of this book is that Israeli interests, political, economic and strategic, are so bound up with possession of the territories as to make any viable, just solution to the conflict unlikely. A solution would imply recognition of legitimate Palestinian claims as equal to those of Israel. That recognition is sadly lacking at all levels of Israeli policy and discourse.

This chapter focuses on Israel's restrictions of Palestinian mobility as a primary tool for perpetuating the Occupation, for creating territorial facts on the ground, and for asserting Israeli supremacy and control. It will provide the reader with a guide to understanding how that system, of which the checkpoints are part, works.

Checkpoint policy

Immediately after the Six-Day War in 1967, a general permit for entry to Israel was conferred on Palestinians in the West Bank (for Gazans this came in the mid-1980s) with the exception of security suspects and criminals. This was part of a general policy of linking the economy of the Occupied Territories with that of Israel. An 'Open Bridges' policy also allowed freedom of goods and movement between the West Bank and Jordan. This 'freedom' often involved humiliating checks on entering and exiting the territories by the military, but nevertheless created a sense of openness and transparency, something that Israel could point to in its favour. Naturally, these concessions could be revoked at will. The open–close–open cycle, the carrot and the stick, created a sense of uncertainty and tension among the Palestinian population, a deliberate programme of psychological warfare (Gazit 1995). Apart from routine weaponry, the arsenal of this war was simultaneously complex and simple: closures, checkpoints, curfews backed up by a permit system that has become more Sisyphean and more draconian with the years. This is how the system evolved:

- 1967 General entry permit conferred on Palestinians wishing to enter Israel. Entry restrictions loosely applied.
- 1991 Continuous general closure imposed on the territories with outbreak of first Gulf War; a personal permit is now required for individuals wishing to enter Israel. Military checkpoints are erected at key points to monitor the system.
- 1991–93 In the wake of a series of stabbings of Israelis by individual Palestinians, the checkpoint-closure system is tightened. Passage between the northern and southern West Bank, between Gaza and the West Bank and East Jerusalem is subject to a permit from the Civil Administration.[4] Paradoxically, the Oslo Accords[5] signed in September 1993 result in further ramifications to the system. Israeli commitment to a safe passage route between Gaza and the West Bank is never fully implemented.
- 1996 Prime Minister Nethanyahu opens the controversial Hashmonean Tunnel under the Temple Mount in Jerusalem. Armed clashes break out between Palestinian policemen and Israeli troops. A first *internal* closure is imposed on the territories: restrictions on movement between Palestinian towns, villages and areas are accompanied by severe limitations on entry into Israel. The system is implemented by an ever more elaborate checkpoint system.

13

- 2000–01 With the outbreak of the El Aqsa intifada (2000–04) the closure–checkpoint policy is intensified and systematized by means of reinforcing all the measures outlined below: general closure, internal closure, curfew and, of course, proliferating and expanding checkpoints. At the same time the permit system is rigorously implemented and, since May 2002, extended to cover any and all movement of Palestinians within as well as outside the West Bank. Palestinian vehicles are totally or partially barred from travel on 700 km (350 miles) of roads within the West Bank. These roads are reserved for Israelis only. Palestinians may use only secondary or tertiary routes (B'Tselem 2004c).[6]
- 2004 There are some forty-eight staffed permanent barriers of which twenty-eight are on the Green Line (i.e. barring access directly into Israel) or deep within the West Bank. There are seven manned control towers at various points and 607 physical blockades around villages (B'Tselem 2005).
- 2005 Some checkpoints, mostly those between Israel and the West Bank, have undergone cosmetic upgrading such as rudimentary and partial cover against the elements and have acquired the appearance of permanence. Metal detectors and revolving gates have been introduced that limit access to one person at a time.[7] Some checkpoints have even been equipped with laptop computers to speed up the process of checking for security suspects. The upgraded checkpoints are strategically located to enable Israel to close off access to, and within, the West Bank at will.

A glossary of oppression

Blockades Physical obstacles to freedom of passage. Since September 2000 or earlier, almost every village in the West Bank has been blockaded, usually by means of concrete cubes and/or earthworks, rubble, mud or ditches. Some of these blockades are staffed, others are not. On a visit to the southern West Bank in July 2004, there was almost no visible sign of the military in the area, the blockades serving the purpose of preventing vehicular, and even pedestrian, access to and from each village. Palestinians too were noticeably absent. The blockades are usually waist high or more and residents must scramble across and over them. This is an obstacle even for the nimble and an impossible task for the disabled, heavily laden, sick or elderly. The individual arrives at her/his destination dusty or muddy in season, hot and bothered and, inevitably, humiliated. Worse still, access for emergency vehicles, ambulances, fire engines and so on is prevented by the blockades and I have personally witnessed several cases of patients being lifted or dragged across on makeshift stretchers in a way unlikely to improve their condition. Ambulances must make detours that considerably delay their arrival and departure, again to the detriment of those they are trying to reach. There has been increased resort to donkeys for transportation, something that had almost vanished from West Bank life. Unfortunately, donkeys and horses may not pass the checkpoints, so that even this form of travel has its limitations. Some activists have suggested that there is a deliberate policy of forcing the Palestinians back into a pre-technological age; but perhaps the donkeys are a form of resistance rather than the result of conspiracy.

Checkpoints Barriers between the West Bank and Israel, and between West Bank towns and villages. Here civilians must present proof of identity, transit/mobility permits to military personnel and submit to baggage and body checks on demand. Since checkpoints are the subject of this book and will be dealt with at length in Chapter 3, suffice it to say here that these may be permanent or temporary, fixed or mobile, staffed either by the army or the border police. Along the route of the Annexation Wall (see Chapter 4), private security guards are also employed.

Closure Prohibition on passage of Palestinian civilians wishing to enter Israel with the exception of humanitarian cases permitted at the discretion of the security forces. Closure may be declared without warning on suspicion of a forthcoming terror attack, or in the wake of such an attack, and on all Jewish and Muslim festivals and public holidays. Closure may last anywhere from hours to several days.

Curfews Military prohibition on civilians leaving the confines of their homes. Possibly the cruellest plank in the oppressive structure of curfew–closure–checkpoint is the curfew itself. From the early years of the state until 1965, curfews were used as a regular security measure, or collective punishment, for Palestinian citizens *within* Israel under military government. During the years of Occupation since 1967, curfews have become a regular weapon in Israel's arsenal of oppression in the West Bank and Gaza.

A curfew can be imposed by the army at any time and in any location, often prior to a planned military operation. Residents of the unlucky town or village in question risk being shot on sight if they leave their homes during the curfew (B'Tselem 2002c). A curfew may last anywhere from a few hours to several weeks, with only short, erratic, breaks for replenishing stores, not to mention living one's life. In the tight confines of West Bank homes, it is not difficult to imagine the pressure on whole families trapped with frequent electricity blackouts and dwindling supplies, in all weathers, not knowing when their siege will end. Nor are the short- and long-term effects of this stress difficult to foresee.

Between June 2002 and December 2004, Nablus recorded 4,688 curfew hours; Hebron suffered 5,828 hours, respectively 25 per cent and 35 per cent of the entire period.[8]

Encirclement Whereas a 'closure' imposed on the territories prevents Palestinians from coming into Israel, 'encirclement' totally closes off every town and village in the West Bank; nobody comes in, and nobody leaves. As one checkpoint commander reportedly said: 'They know there's an encirclement, so it's better if they all stay at home' (MachsomWatch 2005: 106).

The integrated curfews–closure–checkpoint system expedites the Occupation. Curfews facilitate military operations such as the rounding up of suspects/militants to take place supposedly with minimum civilian casualties. Closures and encirclement bar not only access to Israel but also movement within the West Bank itself, effectively isolating a city or area from its surrounding satellites, paralysing all activity. The checkpoints control the lives of the thousands of individual Palestinian civilians attempting to go about their daily tasks, and, together with the blockades of villages, and the complex ID/permit system (see below), enable the security forces to monitor the movement and whereabouts of every Palestinian man, woman and child in the West Bank. Israeli settlements and their residents are never subject to curfew or mobility restrictions.[9]

Amira Hass has written that the curfews, closures and checkpoints are a plunder of time as much as they are a theft of space (Hass 2002a: 10). One might say without exaggeration that they represent a theft of freedom, the freedom to control your own life in its most intimate and minute details. The effect not only on the individual but also on Palestinian society as a whole is physically, economically, socially and psychologically devastating. For Israel, it involves an enormous expenditure of funds, troops and materiel with no real security benefit. As we shall see, there is also growing concern in Israel about the morally corrupting effects of Occupation on the occupier although without the concomitant of concern for the denial of Palestinian rights (*Ha'aretz*, 24 November 2004).

Bureaucracy

> Freedom of Movement and health are inseparable ... the dismem-
> berment enforced by the encirclement–curfew–closure policy on
> [Palestinian] geography, economy and society serves one central idea:
> control of all areas of life of the occupied group in order to prevent
> any chance of realization of its rights to political, social and economic
> independence. (PHR 2003: 2)[10]

The winning combination of curfew–closure–encirclement–checkpoint used to such effect by the Israeli military in suppressing the Palestinians was not born overnight, but like many invidious systems developed slowly, each step preparing the way for the next. As we have seen, it evolved from the curtailment of movement of Israeli Palestinians in the early years of the state, through the supposedly temporary closures during the first Gulf War of 1990–91, to the total paralysis of the West Bank during the current conflict. It is backed up by an elaborate, dysfunctional, system of passes, permits and privileges administered by the army in its guise of the so-called Civil Administration's District Coordination and Liaison Office (DCL). The very concept of the permit system is a priori iniquitous, turning a basic human right into a grudgingly granted, by no means universal, privilege (Hass 2002a, 2002b; PHR 2004).

The process of acquiring a permit may be likened to a game of snakes and ladders. The applicant scores one success, only to be plunged back to the beginning of the process by refusal at the next. Several accessories are required for this game, a game whose outcome is never assured, one that can become a matter of life or death.

§

> If your brother was killed by the IDF ... then you will probably be pro
> hibited on security grounds, because you are more likely to be involved
> in a terrorist attack. (Tzadoq Yehezkeli, *Yediot Achronot*, 23 January
> 2004)

> People sit for hours ... At the end of the day, if the gate does not open,
> they return to the hatch for magnetic cards to get a chit for another
> day. (CPW Report, 1 January 2004)

17

The Palestinian civilian wishing to move around the West Bank or cross into Israel must first acquire a magnetic card, indicating that s/he has no security crime or misdemeanour on his/her record. Each application must be filed with the local Israeli DCL office in coordination with the General Security Services (GSS) office on the premises. Ideally, cards take ten days to process, after which the applicant is notified as to whether or not the request has been granted. No reason is given for refusal nor for what constitutes a security offence. Rejected applicants are often at a loss to understand of what it is they are accused or suspected.[11]

Identity cards are compulsory for all Israelis and Palestinians from age eighteen upwards. The numbered cards, blue for Israelis, orange or green for Palestinians, have a photograph of the bearer, and show name, place and date of birth, religion, sex, place of residence. A separate slip lists children up to age eighteen.

Any Palestinian losing his/her ID, or having it confiscated by the army or border police, must try to acquire a new one. This is usually done via the Palestinian DCL, to which the applicant must pay a sum rumoured at several hundred shekels (around $200), an enormous sum by local standards. The Palestinians then coordinate with the Israeli DCL (IDCL) or Civil Administration that issues, or refuses, the new ID, so far as is known, at no charge. Only the Civil Administration can grant or refuse permits, the Palestinian DCL acting merely as a conduit. Even that shaky symbol of Palestinian autonomy has been weakened since 2002 since application can now be made direct to the IDCL (PHR 2004). The recruitment of a vast network of collaborators by means of the granting or withholding of permits has been a mainstay of Israel's intelligence-gathering activity in the West Bank and Gaza during all the years of Occupation (Hass 2002a, 2002b).

Possession of a magnetic card indicates that the bearer has security clearance from the GSS and is not wanted, suspected or otherwise listed for some misdemeanour, real or imagined. A friend of one of our observers had his application refused, presumably because he had spent two weeks in an Israeli prison for working 'illegally', that is, entering Israel without a permit, and was apprehended during one of the frequent hunts for such infiltrators. He cannot reapply for a card for another two years.

Having overcome the obstacles and acquired the magnetic card, the fortunate holder is now in a position to apply for a long-term *tasrich* (permit). Bearers of this permit can enter Israel to work, conduct busi-

1 Beth Iba checkpoint, 2004 (photo: Esti Tsal)

ness, visit family. The process of acquisition is equally long, arbitrary and uncertain. Furthermore, permits are issued for different, often very short, periods of time and cease to be valid whenever there is a closure of the West Bank cities and villages, as in October 2003 when, as a collective punishment for a suicide bombing in a Haifa restaurant, all three-month permits were declared invalid and Palestinians were ordered to take out permits with a date of issue after 7 October (see Appendix 2). In such cases, the whole application process must be repeated, with no guarantee of success. In order to acquire a work permit in Israel, the applicant's employer must also submit a request on his/her behalf.

As for those needing medical treatment:

> Whether a situation is an urgent medical emergency is left to the discretion of the checkpoint commander. The checkpoint commander will consult with a medical official, where time permits ... In the event of doubt whether an urgent medical emergency is involved, the resident shall be given the benefit of the doubt. (IDF, 'Procedure for the Handling of Residents of Judea and Samaria who Arrive at a Checkpoint in an Emergency Medical Situation', 2002)

It is these cases that are frequently encountered at checkpoints, pleading to be allowed to pass even in the absence of official permission. If you are suddenly taken ill or suffer an accident, you are at the mercy of the discretion and good-will of soldiers at the checkpoint near your home. The benefit of the doubt is seldom granted. The Palestinian Red Crescent Society reports that between 28 September 2000 and October 2003:

- 991 cases were denied medical access
- 25 medical personnel were killed , 425 injured
- 83 patients died at checkpoints due to denial of access
- 121 ambulances were damaged
- 57 women were forced to give birth at the checkpoint; over 32 of these cases resulted in the death of the infant.[12]

Watchers have frequently encountered a contemptuous attitude towards the sick and towards medical personnel on the part of soldiers who refuse to believe, or even investigate, the urgency of their cases (see also B'Tselem 2003a; PHR 2003, 2004).

The mechanism of oppression

Tamar Goldschmidt of CPW has videotaped the application process at two West Bank IDCLs. Each video, shot in real time, documents the trying physical conditions: endless waiting periods, lack of adequate shelter, toilets and refreshment facilities. Clerks sit behind narrow slits of the unreceptive reception counters at which the plaintiff has no redress, no agency and very little hope. Applicants must be constantly on the alert to spot the rapid opening and closing of the counters. If missed, the opportunity is lost for the day. Complaints usually result in the closing of the DCL for several hours, or for the remainder of the day. The waiting seems the longer because of the uncertainty as to when it will end and what its results will be. The very request for a permit is regarded as suspect, as insolence.

Nor are there concessions to the needs of the chronically sick: Y, who is disabled, requires frequent treatment in Bethlehem which is outside his residential area. His request for a blockade permit to move between his home and Bethlehem has been serially rejected allegedly on security grounds. With the help of CheckpointWatchers, whom he encountered at the IDCL, he was granted a permit for internal travel in the West Bank but for one day only. In desperation, he subsequently set out without a permit, was stopped at a checkpoint and as a punishment made to stand for an hour by his car, supported by his crutches (CPW Report, 5 February 2004).

Many Watchers speak of the fear, fatigue and boredom of young soldiers forced to do the unpleasant work of guarding checkpoints, seeing them as much sinned against as sinning. In cases like the one above and the thousands of others like it, there can be no excuse. They are the product of a culture in which brutality and licence are tolerated with impunity (MaschomWatch 2005). I will venture to say that the punitive attitude of many, though not all, soldiers is very much part of the Israeli ethos, simultaneously defensive and oppressive.

No dry description can do justice to the frustrating experience of even the most routine procedure of application for a permit. Not content with the many second-hand reports heard at checkpoints, some of our observers decided to see for themselves. At the time, this was a pioneering step, although the monitoring of DCLs has since become a CheckpointWatch routine.

23 November 2002

The issue of Palestinians being refused passage at Qalandia CP for not holding a valid permit and instructed by the soldiers to go to the DCL in Beit-El,[13] supposedly 'no big deal', has been bothering us for a long time. We keep getting reports from Palestinians about the ordeal they face in order to get this much cherished permit, if at all. Having followed the reports of an acquaintance of ours who for the past few weeks has been trying to get himself a permit in Beit-El, and was given the runaround there, we decided to accompany our friend as a test case. His problem is as follows: he lives in Bir Naballah (south of Qalandiya) and works in Ramallah, bears an [Palestinian issue] ID and, hence, needs a permit to pass the Qalandiya CP to get to work and, what's more important, to come back through there.

This Sunday, then, our friend M travelled to Beit-El early in the morning to queue for a magnetic card, which did not take very long, as he had already handed in his application beforehand and is 'clean'[14] ... He then returned to Qalandiya checkpoint ... and together we took a taxi to Beit-El. When we got there around 10.30, we saw a crowd of a hundred people (mostly men) waiting for their names to be called out over a loudspeaker. This enables them to get to one of the four small windows outside the barrack and hear the verdict: request granted/rejected/come back next week ...

I was approached by several people, who were all at their wits' end and were hoping for some help from me. I explained that I would probably not be able to help, but wanted to hear their stories, in order to understand [what was going on].

Here are a few examples:

A man originally from Gaza, listed in his ID as residing in Tul-Karem, who works in Ramallah and wants to visit his family in Gaza is continuously refused a permit – the reason: closure.

A man who three years ago was in administrative detention for eighteen days (he does not know why) is now on the blacklist of the GSS and has no chance of getting a magnetic card.

A young man was told by the GSS that he is 'clean' … but at IDCL Beit-El they claim to have no information about him and keep telling him to come back the following week. The GSS does not provide documentation for those cleared and the DCL claims they have no record.

Several people apply for a permit to get to Ben-Gurion airport for a journey abroad – among them are four elderly women (the youngest being 68) and one old man – who want to fly to the US to visit their children there. They come from the village Zar'ha-el-Sharkiye and have to pass four checkpoints, in order to get to Beit-El – they have been sitting there since early morning, waiting for their names to be called out and seem very lost.

A Palestinian, who returned from Kuwait through the Gaza strip during the Oslo heydays had Gaza listed as his residence. He now lives in Dir Naballah, and wants the address changed in his ID. The IDCL sent him to the PDCL who sent him back again.

… Our achievements: extremely poor. Roni called [a friendly officer] about M and was told to enter the barrack from the back gate and talk to the soldiers in charge there, which we did. It turned out that there was a mistake in the application of M's employer which was in Hebrew. M had not realized that the location 'Ramallah' had not been specified – and nobody had so far explained to him [during his several visits], that this was the problem. Had it not been for us, this could have gone on endlessly. M raced over to his employer and came back with the correct specification [sic]. By then the soldiers were having their lunch-break, and M was told to wait. We appealed to the officer in charge and asked for 'special treatment', as the man was with us. M eventually came back with the wonderful permit – VALID FOR 1 MONTH ONLY! All this hassle for ONE month! But M was happy as a lark!

We also succeeded in having the above-mentioned old people get first in line and at 14:00 they were extremely happy just to get a summons to return some time next week ... We had saved them a wait of several hours during the Ramadan fast, that was all!

Contrary to what the soldiers say, it [going to the DCL] IS a big deal! (Norah Orlow, Swiss-born translator, Jerusalem)

We are not speaking here about visa applications between one sovereign state and another but of licences for civilians to go about their daily business within their own territory. The two Watchers were able successfully to exercise 'pull', albeit limited, by virtue of their being Israeli. They were even invited back by the DCL commander who agreed to answer their questions and explained the necessity of the procedures for 'weeding out terrorists'. This is consistent with the desire of the military to appear responsive to humanitarian concerns, while silencing criticism by pleading security needs.

The struggle involved in getting to the IDCL offices are such as to deter all but the most determined. As the roads of the West Bank empty of Palestinians, it can be assumed that many people simply don't bother to apply for permits, remaining within their villages or towns unless urgent business or illness compels them to leave. This reluctance is probably coupled with the fear that the price of a permit will be the agreement to collaborate, or that it may be perceived as such by friends and neighbours. Nevertheless, labourers, hardest hit by loss of income, will risk arrest and try to circumvent the checkpoints (see also Chapter 3). There is no route too circuitous or dangerous for people desperate for a day's wage, for the economic and social effects of the Occupation are devastating, as the following quotation indicates:

> The second year of the *intifada* witnessed a further steep decline in all Palestinian economic indicators. By the end of 2002, Real Gross National Income (GNI) had shrunk by 38 percent from its 1999 level. Unemployment stood at the end of 2002 at 37 percent of the workforce, after peaking at 45 percent in the Third Quarter. With a 13 percent growth in the population of the West Bank and Gaza over the past three years, real per capita incomes are now 46 percent lower than in 1999, and poverty – defined as those living for less than US$2 dollar per day – afflicts approximately 60 percent of the population. (World Bank 2002: xi)

Refinements The permit system is constantly being refined and streamlined. In January 2005 a regional brigade commander, Colonel Mickey

Edelstein, personally confirmed to Norah Orlow that East Jerusalem Palestinians are to be denied freedom of movement into Ramallah; the Qalandiya checkpoint that falls within his bailiwick is being upgraded to a terminal and a series of tunnels will serve the villages around Ramallah. Israelis will have the privilege of using overhead passes – us on top, them down below. The restriction on movement into Ramallah is a severe blow for East Jerusalemites, separating families and preventing access to cultural and educational facilities.

A new ID system for Palestinians is being introduced using biometric identification techniques: faceprints, handprints and fingerprints. As of mid-2005, the implementation of these measures is still unclear. The cards will take minutes to issue and will be used along the Annexation Wall where seven access points are planned. Transitees will be able to swipe their new cards, minimizing contact with the soldiers, according to *Ha'aretz* (29 March 2005).

Even without these controlling technologies, the permit system reaches a preposterous nadir in Jerusalem.

Jerusalem

From the beginning Israel saw the Palestinians in Jerusalem as a demographic problem and a threat. Israel's failure to restrict the number of the Palestinians in the city broke the taboo over dividing sovereignty in Jerusalem but also increased Israeli fears of 'the other' ... Neither could Israel agree to the transformation of Jerusalem into an open, equal and bi-national city which belongs exclusively to neither side. This would run counter not only to Israeli policy since 1948 but also to the self-determination of the state of Israel and the Zionist movement as Jewish entities. Moreover, Israel could not agree to the creation of a city which would be neutral, civic, nationally 'blind'; and would have an orientation toward providing the needs of the residents, a part of which are, of course, religious. After so many years of Israeli dominance, it would also be difficult to expect the Israeli authorities to relate to the Palestinians as equals, be it on the municipal or the national level. (Klein 2003: 1)

In the article quoted above, Professor Klein, an adviser to the Israeli team at Camp David and a sharp critic of government policy, emphasizes the link between a demographic threat, real or imagined, and the policies implemented against the Palestinians by military force, economic strangulation and bureaucratic harassment. Nowhere is this connection more clear than with regard to Palestinian residents of Jerusalem (Eldar 2003).

East, or Palestinian, Jerusalem was included as part of the extended municipal boundaries of the city in 1967[15] and officially annexed to Israel in 1981. At that time Palestinian residents were offered special residency status – that is, the right to live and work in the city and enjoy certain social security benefits, as well as the right to vote in municipal, but not in national, elections, a right mostly rejected. This rejection is a means of passive political protest, since bearers of the coveted Jerusalem ID have a lot to lose: they may work in and around the capital, move freely within the confines of the city, and, with less freedom, around Israel generally, privileges that their West Bank compatriots can only envy. As will be shown, these benefits are grudgingly granted and conditional. Municipal taxes are perhaps the only area in which Palestinians enjoy equal obligations, if not rights, with their Israeli neighbours.

Since 1967 Israel has pursued a divisive policy of increasing the Jewish population of Jerusalem while minimizing the Palestinian presence in the city. Tactics include:

- Building a series of Jewish urban settlement-neighbourhoods that surround the city in all directions, the most recent being Har Homa to the south. These settlements, built largely on expropriated Palestinian land, prevent the natural expansion of Palestinian neighbourhoods.
- Cutting off East Jerusalem from the rest of the West Bank and erecting the Annexation Wall (the Jerusalem 'envelope') to prevent West Bank Palestinians having access to the city.
- Land expropriation, discrimination in the granting of planning and building permits, and the demolition of houses built without permits.
- Discriminatory allocation of budgets and of services between Jewish and Palestinian areas of the city.
- Revoking residency and social benefits of Palestinians unable to prove that their centre of life is in Jerusalem or who stay abroad for at least seven years.

Until 2003, a West Banker marrying a Jerusalemite (and there is a premium on Jerusalem brides for West Bankers) could apply for residency on the basis of family reunion. The process took seven years and involved a multi-stage process of reapplication each year. In between

Occupation

25

there were unannounced spot checks by inspectors to make sure that the candidate actually had the 'centre of his/her life' in Jerusalem.

In August 2003, the Citizenship and Entry into Israel Law came into force, bringing with it a sweeping cancellation of the process of family reunification. The Ministry of the Interior has taken a stringent position in this regard and interprets the law to exclude as Jerusalem residents minor children born in the West Bank to Palestinian Israelis (Moked 2004: 22–3; B'Tselem 2004b).[16]

Not only is this policy geared to the dispossession and expulsion of Palestinians from Jerusalem, the very procedures for registering residency, family reunification, the birth of a child, the death of a parent, the application for a passport or *laissez-passer* are designed as a deterrent.

These procedures, long predating the current intifada, are carried out at the Ministry of the Interior, East Jerusalem branch.[17] Here, as at the checkpoints and the DCLs, chaos and contempt rule. Only a limited number of people are seen each day. Applicants must line up on the pavement outside the building from as early as 2 a.m. to ensure their place in line. Those who can, pay a tout to hold their spot in the queue. There are no facilities, no shelter or seating. Young and old, women with babes in arms and small children must wait their turn in all weathers. Some people faint; some just lose it. Access is never assured and one may be called upon to repeat the process several times before reaching one's goal. The Ministry's application form is printed in Hebrew, a language not spoken by the majority of applicants. This has given rise to a brisk trade in interpreters who squat on the sidewalk armed with ancient typewriters and, for a consideration, fill out the forms.[18] Once inside, applicants report that there are too few clerks and an atmosphere of harassment and bullying. It is a dehumanizing situation, ignored or deliberately fostered by the authorities.[19]

The fate of one Jerusalem family sums up the plight of many: MA was born in Jerusalem and married a West Banker. Until 1997 the family alternatively lived in Qalandiya refugee camp and in Abu Tor, a mixed Israeli-Palestinian neighbourhood of Jerusalem. In 2000 they moved to Kufr Yacub, inside the (ridiculously expanded) municipal boundaries yet beyond Qalandiya checkpoint[12] on the Ramallah side. Over the years seven children were born and in 2000 MA applied to have them registered in the city census and for a family reunification permit for her husband. In 2001 the application was rejected, as was a subsequent appeal, on the grounds that the couple's life did not centre on Jerusalem. The process of rejection and appeal continued throughout 2002, and

2003 when the Citizenship Law made all such reunification applications invalid. As of 2003, the three eldest children (twelve, thirteen and fourteen years old) could not leave their neighbourhood because the soldiers at the nearby Qalandiya checkpoint would not allow them passage since they were not listed in their parents' IDs. MA's family were thus forced to live in a bureaucratic limbo (Moked 2003: 20).

In yet another turn of the screw, in January 2005, the government announced that the Jerusalem property of West Bankers would be declared state property (*Ha'aretz*, 20 January 2005). The rationale for this land grab is the fact that West Bankers are no longer allowed access to Jerusalem, regardless of the fact that the city has been the administrative, educational and religious centre of their lives for generations.

It takes little imagination to think what would happen if Britain, France or the USA were to take similar discriminatory action against its Jewish, black or Asian citizens. Palestinians, however, are not citizens of any state, they are subject to a military occupation, deprived of rights. They have no redress, no possibility of appeal against the political, physical and bureaucratic punishments that the Occupation puts in their way. In this context it is important to mention the untiring efforts of Israeli human rights NGOs such as B'Tselem, the Israeli Information Centre for Human Rights in the Occupied Territories; the Moked, Centre for the Defence of the Individual; and Physicians for Human Rights who monitor and protest these abuses, and others, through legal channels such as appeals to the High Court of Justice of the Israeli Supreme Court. While the latter almost invariably accepts state claims of security requirements over human rights considerations, the persistence of the appeals keeps these issues on the public agenda, and has some, limited, influence.

This chapter has demonstrated both the gradual development of the checkpoint policy, first as a simple means of controlling a population under occupation and subsequently as an ever more sophisticated, if brutal, means of creating territorial facts on the ground, dismembering the West Bank in such a way as to make a viable Palestinian state an impossibility. The Palestinians are left with a clutch of Bantustans, isolated, and often inaccessible, one from another.[21] The combined measures of mobility restriction and land grabs have not only facilitated military action but have literally de-structured Palestinian society. At the individual level, the humiliations, the restrictions, the constant threat of military incursions, the economic crisis, the numbers killed and injured, and the traumas of life in a war zone are an excellent

27

recipe for 'encouraged departure', in other words, ethnic cleansing. The measures are neither accidental, nor defensive, but deliberate and well thought out (Kimmerling 2001; Reinhart 2002).

Notes

1 The Six-Day War of June 1967 between Israel, Syria, Egypt and Jordan. The latter, then the occupying power of the West Bank, entered the war late and half-heartedly. In the counter-attack, Israel occupied that territory and has imposed its military rule there ever since.

2 Throughout this work, 'Palestinians' refers to residents of the West Bank and Gaza. 'Palestinian-Israelis' refers to Palestinian citizens of Israel living inside Israel proper and who are not the subject of this book.

3 'Settlements' refers to Israeli colonies established in the West Bank and Gaza since 1981. Israeli references to illegal settlements/outposts relate to those few not authorized by the Israeli government (Eldar and Zartel 2004).

4 The Civil Administration (CA) is actually a military body responsible for civilian affairs in the West Bank and Gaza since 1981. It was suspended between 1994 and 2002 when the Palestine Authority took responsibility for civilian matters in parts of the West Bank (Areas A, total Palestinian control and Area B, under Israeli control but declaratively civilian Palestinian control). The CA was reintroduced in 2002 when Israel reoccupied areas A and B. It controls every aspect of civilian life from infrastructure to health. As the representative of the occupying force it is responsible under international law also for health, welfare and economy (Fourth Geneva Convention, Section III, Article 50), responsibilities that it does not fulfil, serving instead largely as the executive arm of the military. Many staffers, military and civililan, are themselves settlers (Eldar and Zartel 2004: 402).

5 The Oslo Accords or Declaration of Principles on Interim Self-Government Arrangements (DOP) were a series of agreements negotiated between the Israeli government and the Palestinian Liberation Organization (PLO) acting as representatives of the Palestinian people in 1993 as part of a peace process. The DOP included provisions for building mutual trust and a series of limited Israeli withdrawals from the Occupied Territories. The DOP did not specify the establishment of an independent Palestinian state at the end of the process, which in fact collapsed in 2000 with the outbreak of the Al Aqsa intifada (Pundak 2001).

6 B'Tselem, the Israeli Centre for Human Rights in the Occupied Territories (1989), endeavours to document and educate the Israeli public and policy-makers about human rights violations in the Occupied Territories, combat the phenomenon of denial prevalent among the Israeli public and help create a human rights culture in Israel. B'Tselem in Hebrew literally means 'in the image of' (Genesis 1:27), a synonym for human dignity.

7 The revolving gates are purportedly for more efficient monitoring of individual transitees. The system does not take into account the disabled, heavily laden or those with children. Watcher Naomi Lalo reports several

28

instances in which children, forced to enter the revolving gate alone, panicked and got stuck, anticipating the day when a real disaster will occur (personal communication, September 2004).

8 Palestinian Red Crescent Society (PRCS) on line, 26 December 2004, <www.palestinercs.org/>.

9 For instance, following the massacre of twenty-nine Palestinians during morning prayers by a settler in Hebron in February 1994, the Palestinian residents of the city were placed under curfew while the Israeli settlers walked free (Eldar and Zartel 2004).

10 Physicians for Human Rights (PHR), an Israeli NGO (1988) monitors human rights abuses relating to medical care. PHR runs five projects: the Occupied Territories Project, the Prisoners and Detainees Project, the Migrant Workers and Refugees Project, the Project for the Unrecognized Villages of the Negev, and the Residents of Israel Project. In addition, it operates a mobile clinic in the Occupied Territories, and an open clinic in Tel Aviv providing services for those with no legal status and therefore no health insurance.

11 The alleged potential of the individual to commit a terrorist act is sufficient to deny him clearance. Security offences range from illegal entry into Israel to contacts with organizations such as Hamas or the left-wing PFLP, having family ties to a known terrorist/militant to actually organizing or carrying out terror attacks. There is no statute of limitations so that a boy who threw a stone in the first intifada (1987–93) may as a married man find himself denied a permit in 2005. The denial of a permit to someone committing an actual act of militancy/terror is irrelevant, since such an individual would be unlikely to apply, being either on a list of wanted suspects, in prison or dead.

12 <www.palestinercs.org/>, accessed 26 March 2005.

13 Beit-El is a large settlement some twenty minutes' drive from Jerusalem and some five minutes from the outskirts of Ramallah. A large, eponymous, military base is situated close to the settlement, including a military courthouse. The HQ of the West Bank Civil Administration is close at hand. Beit-El settlers object to Palestinians driving past the settlement, ostensibly for security reasons. Palestinians must therefore walk to and from Ramallah and nearby villages. The dusty pedestrian route is demarcated by a high wire fence that protects the settlers, whizzing by in their cars along their parallel paved road, from the sight of the weary Palestinians trudging along on foot.

14 That is, he has security clearance.

15 During the Six-Day War in 1967 the eastern, Jordanian, sector was captured and annexed by Israel. The municipal boundaries were expanded to include areas to the north, south and east of the city. We speak of East Jerusalem as Palestinian, West Jerusalem as Jewish, although the situation on the ground is much more confused. At the heart, figuratively and literally, of the city lies the 1 square mile walled Old City: the historic area sacred to Jews, Christians and Muslims. It is divided into four quarters, Muslim, Christian, Armenian and Jewish. At the heart of the walled city is the Temple Mount/ Haram es Shariff, site of the great mosques of Omar and El Aqsa. The Mount

29

is buttressed by the Wailing or Western Wall, last remnant of the outer wall of Herod's Temple. It is also the place where Muhammad's winged steed, Al Buraq, was tethered on the Prophet's legendary journey to Jerusalem. This ancient history makes for an inevitable arena of conflict.

16 Ofir Pines-Paz, Minister of the Interior, has declared his intention to alleviate the stringencies of the Law (*Ha'aretz*, 25 February 2005) but Israel's National Security Council has prepared the groundwork for more general legislative amendments 'that will make it more difficult for non-Jews to receive Israeli citizenship or permanent residence in Israel. The move is aimed against granting legal status to Palestinians and other foreigners who have married Israeli citizens.' Giora Eiland, head of the NSC, has declared that the legislation was determined by the need to preserve the Jewish character of Israel as a state in which the Jewish nation realizes its right to self-determination. He notes the distinction between granting equal individual rights and granting national rights to minorities (Yuval Yoaz, 'Eiland Proposes Citizenship Limitations for Palestinians', *Ha'aretz,* 3 March 2005).

17 Israelis and non-Palestinian foreigners use the Ministry building in West Jerusalem. Here too the process is deficient and waiting interminable, albeit within a building with seating and other facilities. When waiting becomes intolerable clients can complain, loudly, with relative impunity, something that for Palestinians would incur a penalty such as arrest, or worse.

18 The situation described predates the current violence and, in fact, is a standard practice in relation to Palestinian Jerusalemites. For instance, a major banking chain until recently maintained a special branch office for Palestinians where clients were forced to queue outside the building and allowed in only in twos and threes. Similar conditions pertain at other Israeli institutions in East Jerusalem, the more so since 2000, always with the blanket excuse of 'security'. Here, as elsewhere, to be Palestinian is to be suspect and presumably not heir to all the ills the flesh is heir to.

19 Repeated complaints and appeals to subsequent Ministers of the Interior from human rights organizations and from individual Israelis have brought no alleviation of the situation. Although a new building has been under construction for years there seems to be no haste on the part of the authorities to move into it. As of November 2003, the High Court of Justice gave the Ministry of the Interior nineteen months (!) to deal with the problem of its East Jerusalem branch and to increase the number of staff there (High Court of Justice appeal 2783/08). As of December 2004, the matter was still not resolved.

20 Qalandiya is the checkpoint for entry to Jerusalem from Ramallah. Kufr Yacub is north of Qalandiya but included in the Jerusalem boundaries.

21 Another important element in this policy, but beyond the scope of this book, is the Israeli colonies or settlements across the West Bank, strategically sited to prevent territorial continuity for any future Palestinian entity that may be established (Eldar and Zartel 2004).

2 | Bearing witness

On the Street of the Prophets, Jerusalem: It seemed to have come from another place, another, darker time ... a few metres away from me stood two policemen from the Special Unit for the Prevention of Terror, with guns pointed at a young Palestinian woman ... Her personal possessions ... were strewn on the wet pavement ... The policemen were yelling at her to lift her shirt ... [she] refused to strip in the street and the policemen shouted more ferociously than ever ... The young woman seemed frightened but determined not to submit to the violent, masculine intrusion ... I don't know how I found my voice to ask the policemen what they were doing. They got angry and cursed me, as did many of the passers-by on that Jerusalem street, that Israeli street. [The police] responded rudely and explained that they were ... protecting my safety, and how ungrateful I was to 'the security forces' ... In the end, after a few minutes that seemed like an eternity, they let the girl go. Are we really like that? Is this what we look like? Me and them – is that us? (Michal Sagui, educator, Jerusalem, personal communication 2004)

What moved me to join [CheckpointWatch] was the horrifying story of a Palestinian woman who became pregnant after nine years of fertility treatments ... When her time came she arrived at the checkpoint with the pangs of labour already upon her and she with twin boys in her womb. Soldiers prevented her from reaching hospital and she gave birth in great suffering to one son who died immediately. Her family beseeched the soldiers to allow her to get to hospital but the second [son] also died at the checkpoint. At exactly that time my daughter-in-law gave birth ... to my grandsons who are a source of great joy to me ... I can't forget those [other] boys ... whose grandmother cannot hug them ... If I had been there at that checkpoint, perhaps it would have ended differently. (Daniella Yoel, university librarian, Jerusalem, personal communication)

Is it because of my past as a young child in Holland, now sixty years ago ... hidden to escape extermination camps? Is this experience still influencing my life to such an extent that I constantly seek ways to help those people who are less fortunate than I am? Somehow the activities in my life have always centred on the underdog, the persecuted and the unprotected. (Ilana Drukker Tikotin, Dutch-born retiree, Jerusalem, personal communication)

These personal statements by CheckpointWatchers – Israeli women monitoring human rights at *machsomism* (military checkpoints) – present themes of conscience and commitment that are paradigmatic not only for CheckpointWatch (CPW) observers but for many of those who oppose and protest Israel's occupation of the West Bank and Gaza.[1] These are the voices of women whose compassion has a political as well as a humanistic significance, in the context of the consistent and overwhelming dehumanization of Palestinians in Israeli public discourse. Their concern for the dignity of Palestinians is also a concern for the moral stature of Israeli society, while the motif of the Holocaust is a constituting Israeli experience, both personal and collective. The connection to the Holocaust made here by human rights activists, one herself a survivor, is both reassuring and subversive. It confirms a self-image of Israelis as moral and humane but also subverts that image by opposing, and exposing, the immoral deeds of the Occupation. I shall return to those motifs later in this chapter and throughout the book. But first let me introduce CheckpointWatch. Who are these women and why is this movement so significant?

§

Machsom: (Heb) obstacle, barrier, block, barricade, muzzle, gag. A checkpoint.

As outlined in the previous chapter, 3.5 million Palestinians, residents of the West Bank and Gaza, live under Israeli military occupation. The Occupation began in June 1967[2] in the wake of the Six-Day War, leaving the Palestinians stateless in their own land. They have no political rights and few civil rights; although some hold Jordanian passports, most are not citizens of any state. One of the most grievous infringements of human rights during the Occupation is the restriction on freedom of movement. Since 1991, although with increasing vigour since the mid-1990s, this limitation has been enforced by a series of closures and checkpoints that restrict the movement of Palestinian civilians not only into Israel but also within the West Bank itself.

The curfew–closure–checkpoint syndrome is both a sophisticated tool for ethnic cleansing and a brutal means of daily oppression. Backed by a labyrinthine bureaucratic system and an apartheid policy banning travel to Palestinian traffic on major West Bank roads (B'Tselem 2004c), the curfew–closure–checkpoint system has become the principal tool for perpetuating Israel's occupation of the Palestinian territories, herding the population into ever tighter enclaves disconnected one from another. A flashpoint for violence, closures and checkpoints engender insupportable hardship, frustration and rage among the Palestinian population; surely stimulating an inevitable desire for revenge.

CheckpointWatch[3] monitors human rights abuses at military checkpoints in the West Bank, along the Green Line (the pre-'67 armistice line) and at the municipal boundaries of Jerusalem. A non-party-political volunteer organization, CPW began, as do so many important ideas, with a small group of activists, almost casually with a chance meeting at a demonstration and a few determined people.

A decisive factor was a talk by journalist Amira Hass, who provided chilling descriptions of checkpoints she herself had encountered. Most harrowing were the accounts of women forced to give birth at checkpoints when soldiers refused them passage. Yet in those early days, we activists had no real idea of the quotidian hardships faced by ordinary Palestinians, or of the terrible vulnerability of transitees.[4] We could not imagine the paralysis, the desperation that has affected every aspect of Palestinian life: society, economy and even the personal spheres of family and worship:

> Each afternoon, the trip home with my children takes 1.5–2 hours depending on how difficult the Qalandiya[5] checkpoint is. Without these 'security' checkpoints, this trip takes a maximum of 15 minutes.
>
> Painfully enough for the civilians involved, these checkpoints are for harassment only, and add absolutely nothing to 'security', as suicide bombers still manage to cross [into Israel] in spite of them. After a difficult day at work, this extra time wasted only adds to our frustration and anger. By the time we get home, we are all on each other's necks. (letter to CPW from Mr Bassem Khoury, pharmacist, Ramallah, 9 February 2002)

We naively believed that our presence at the checkpoints and our resulting testimony would quickly do away with checkpoints! We had no idea, in those hesitant first moments, that we were spearheading what would become a nationwide women's movement and the largest opposition activist group in the country.

It was after much deliberation that five of us[6] set out for the Bethlehem checkpoint, known as Checkpoint 300, just 2 miles south of my own home (February 2001). It was a bitterly cold morning. We subsequently developed procedures for improving teamwork, but on that first morning we arrived at the checkpoint as a collection of individuals without having clearly decided on our tactics and mode of operation. Nor had we any identification to mark us as legitimate observers. The idea of armbands was rejected outright as too reminiscent of Nazi Europe in the 1930s. Only later did we decide on large pin-on badges. When challenged by the very young and very sleepy soldier on duty, we were struck speechless. It was a face-off.

I looked across towards the desert and the Dead Sea, invisible behind the hills to the east. The sun was just starting to make its way above the neat concrete cubes and building cranes of the massive settlement of Har Homa jutting up on the horizon. Inspiration. 'We've come to look at the sunrise!' The soldier demurred that this was no place to watch a sunrise. We retorted that it was a perfect spot – and, moreover, that it was quite outside his jurisdiction to prevent us. Whether because of the bizarre request or fatigue, he turned away with a warning that we not stray beyond the point where we stood.

The minute his back was turned we marched across the checkpoint, leaving the sun to rise alone. That day, and during our early observations, we were consistently surprised by the comparative ease with which we were able to access checkpoints, transitees and even detainees.[7] In the course of our work, soldiers have tried to obstruct Watchers, and as the political situation deteriorates they increasingly voice hostility towards CPW's work. But except for isolated occurrences, the 'civilian invasion' has not been seriously hindered or challenged.

That first morning we chatted to passers-by, and tried to observe and make sense of what we saw. Much of it was mystifying, even patently absurd. Why were people standing around with their backs against a wall? Who passed and who returned from whence they came? Most surprising was the sight of large numbers of people bypassing the checkpoint and soldiers by going through the valley to the east or the orchards to the west. Except for periodic onslaughts to drive the offenders away, the soldiers ignored them. At their approach the 'by-passers' would stop in their tracks, scramble to hide behind a rock or tree until their pursuers moved away, at which point they simply continued their passage. It was like some cruel schoolyard game. Subsequently we learned that these were people denied entry to Israel permits, most of them trying to get to work, school or medical appointments in Jerusalem. As the months went by, these manhunts came to involve more and more violence, with soldiers using tear-gas, rubber-tipped bullets, or even live ammunition. On that first morning, though, the harassment was half-heartedly nasty, and, to us, simply bewildering. Was it an attempt at deterrence, a show by the soldiers for our benefit? Who passed, who remained and who was turned back on their tracks? After a couple of hours we said goodbye to the guards, who enquired civilly enough if we had seen our sunrise.

We came away that morning with a confusion of impressions: the harshness and the indescribable ugliness of the checkpoint setting, the evident distress and anxiety of those waiting to cross, the desperation of those using the bypass routes. For our part we had experienced the exhilaration of successfully 'challenging the military' and the empowering sense that we were going to succeed in our chosen role of observers. We felt no fear as lone Israelis amidst a Palestinian crowd. We were wary, though, of the potential threat presented by the edginess of the soldiers.

One thing was very clear: the checkpoint served no real security purpose but was rather a means of control, harassment and humiliation for those wishing to cross. This impression has only been confirmed by time and the forty or so checkpoints that Watchers now visit on a regular basis.

Witnesses to the Occupation

From the outset it was clear that CPW would be an all-women's activity. Because of Israel's almost universal military service requirements and the role this plays in the identity of Israeli men in particular, we sensed that the latter would be both disadvantaged and obstructive in engaging non-confrontationally with the security forces (Lomsky-Feder and Ben-Ari 1999). Subsequent experience, as for instance when groups have been accompanied by male guests, has borne out this intuition. We also sensed that, as had happened in other protest movements, a male presence would diminish women's role as bearers of knowledge (Sasson-Levy and Rappoport 2003). We three founders, coming from activism in the women's movement, had a definite agenda, part of which was to challenge military assumptions and practices by means of our civilian presence at the checkpoints. This was not an essentialist claim for women as peace-makers, but rather the intention to take agency in a male-dominated arena. An incidental outcome of CPW's activity has been the empowerment that came from that agency.

Watchers have acquired a voice and expertise countering that of the military. For some women it is the voice of resistance, for some protest, for others a reaffirmation of humanitarian concerns.

Initially, new members of CPW came from the veteran Women in Black movement (1988). This was the first Israeli all-women protest group whose members stepped outside the traditional role of wives, mothers and Home Front supporters. Women in Black is a weekly silent vigil of Israeli Jewish and Palestinian women, dressed in black, holding placards in Hebrew, Arabic and English calling for an end to the Occupation. Participants are subjected to considerable heckling and abuse, both verbal and physical, from passers-by. Women in Black's revolution was to 'use the body as an agent of social and political change' (Helman and Rappoport 1997: 188; Shadmi 2000). CPW's revolution was to go one step further and take the body into the arena of conflict (Ginzburg 2003).

There is a profound difference between urban demonstrations and being active on the ground in the dangerous field of the West Bank. Yet women rallied to the call and membership continued to increase, expanding within weeks of our sunrise foray from five to thirty, and by December 2004 to over 500 women. Much of the recruitment has been by word of mouth, while media coverage, which has been considerable, has always resulted in new volunteers. New members are not asked for political or feminist credentials. It is assumed that anyone joining both opposes the Occupation and has a concern for human rights.

Although not clearly articulated, witnessing, providing testimony for the future, whether in war crimes trials or in the formation of collective memory, was another element in our programme. However, our initial stated goals were modest:

- To monitor the behaviour of soldiers and border policemen (BP)[8] at checkpoints
- to ensure the protection of the human and civil rights of Palestinians attempting to enter Israel and travelling within the West Bank
- to bear witness from our observations and report our findings to the widest possible audience from the decision-making political and military levels to the general public in Israel and abroad, including media coverage

§

There are CheckpointWatch branches in Jerusalem and Tel Aviv, and, as of November 2003, in the north and south of the country. Organizationally, CPW is a non-profit company with little organizational hierarchy. With no paid positions, an elected coordinator, her deputy and an all-important work scheduler run each chapter. The decision-making body, known as Org, is open to all members. Those women who show leadership and wish to take on extra tasks beyond their checkpoint shifts are able to do so. This is particularly evident in the enormous task of editing, translating and circulating the daily reports that are issued after each shift. Some members work or study full-time, others are retirees, many have family obligations. Some, particularly the few religiously observant women involved, have paid the price of being distanced or even excluded from their community. The lack of hierarchy has proved problematic in establishing an efficient decision-making process and has led to inevitable friction, dealt with at length in Chapter 5. Yet each and every one exhibits great dedication and devotion to 'duty'. The checkpoints, and the people trying to cross them, have irresistible drawing power, with all the real anguish and suffering embodied there.

Practices and tactics

What do we actually do? We conduct three or four observations a day, 365 days a year, at checkpoints throughout the West Bank and around Jerusalem. Most women commit to at least one shift a week. The observations are explicitly non-violent. We observe, intervene when necessary and report after each shift. Arriving at the checkpoint, we don our identifying badges. We address the soldiers civilly, informing them that we have come to observe. If the soldiers are unfamiliar with CPW they are offered an explanatory handout. A similar handout is available in Arabic for Palestinians. The nature of our interventions is dealt with at length in Chapter 3.

Reception by the soldiers varies from indifference to obstructive opposition, and only very occasionally are there words of welcome. Soldiers may insist that we not disturb their work and require us to 'stand 50 meters away', something that of course limits the effectiveness of observations. Watchers may be ignored, our questions refused reply; on occasion there have been harassment and arrests. Every woman has her own strategy for coping, and a repertoire of tactics she employs. Some take notes during their shifts; others make demonstrative use of mobile phones to contact officers or human rights organizations or the press. Intervention, that is a direct appeal to the soldiers on duty, takes place in cases where someone is arbitrarily refused passage, when access to medical care is prevented, or in incidents of verbal or physical

37

abuse. Some women intervene only in cases where a valid permit-holder is denied, others will try to gain passage even for those without permits. Tactics include cajoling, pleading, appealing to reason, insistence, bluffing or 'pulling rank', perhaps by calling a senior commander on the phone, or by alerting the media. One never knows what will work or what will boomerang.

New members are given only a brief orientation and are assigned to shifts with more experienced Watchers. Each woman also receives a checkpoint 'toolkit' (Maymon 2004). Beyond this, there is little preparation that can be given to women in advance, not for the overwhelming awfulness of the checkpoints, and not for the constantly changing, challenging and often threatening circumstances one finds there. The toolkit contains:

- an identifying badge, clearly marked in Arabic, Hebrew and English with the CPW logo and name
- a list of telephone numbers of human rights organizations,[9] including real-time hotlines run by the Moked, Centre for the Defence of the Individual,[10] and that of the army. Also included are telephone numbers of field officers, commanders, military liaison officers, and any other official who may be able to help in case of emergency
- handouts in Hebrew and Arabic for soldiers and Palestinians respectively
- CPW business cards with contact information (in Hebrew and Arabic) as well as those of the Moked; in this way, people wishing to lodge complaints or receive assistance can make direct contact with the NGO
- an emergency contact number for use by Watchers if arrested or harassed

To these tools must be added the on-line group bulletin board and discussion forum <MachsomOrg@yahoo.com> where experiences, views and news are shared and argued over.

Sometimes the calls to the military and agencies work, and sometimes they do not. Sometimes the bluff is enough to change a soldier's decision.

The process of reporting is no less important than the observations themselves. Circulated twice or three times daily by e-mail to all CPW members on <machsomwatch@yahoogroups.com>, the reports provide succeessive shifts with an up-to-the-minute account of what is happening in the field, such as overlong holding of detainees or medical emergencies not speedily dealt with by soldiers. More than this, the reports are an invaluable testimony of life under the Occupation as well as providing an opportunity for debriefing after arduous and distressing shifts.

In addition to internal circulation, the reports are posted in Hebrew and English to the CPW website <www.machsomwatch.org> as is a monthly digest, *MachsomWatch Matria*/CheckpointWatch Alerts (see Appendix III), indicating specific problems in the field. Digests of reports are distributed weekly to a mailing list in Israel and abroad, including human rights organizations, journalists, political figures and interested individuals.

Complaints against soldiers abusing Palestinians, or Watchers, are issued to the relevant authorities such as the army, the border police or Members of Knesset, at the rate of two or three a week. Some 5 per cent of these were merely acknowledged and no further action was taken; 30 per cent elicited an inadequate or inappropriate response and 52 per cent of the complaints were simply ignored (MaschomWatch 2005: 80).

The reports are direct testimony from the field. These, and the many other testimonies that are accumulating from soldiers, human rights organizations and, not least, from Palestinians, mean that no one will be able to deny Israel's imprisonment of an entire population in a web of closures and checkpoints. No one will be able to say that the accounts of humiliation and oppression are merely enemy propaganda. No one can claim that the Occupation was enlightened, or that the war against the Palestinians was a war of self-defence. By our presence, Watchers bear witness to that Occupation and its attendant evils.

A case of conscience

CheckpointWatch offers no financial rewards, no glory and – as the following chapters will show – much frustration and heartache. What motivates these middle-class, mainly middle-aged women, none of whom is a professional civil rights worker, to undertake this truly gruelling and often thankless task?

> Once a week it is a punishment for me to get up early in the morning. The morning of my CheckpointWatch shift. Right afterwards I treat myself to the best cup of coffee in town. I have a home that is in no danger of demolition [by the authorities].[11] No tanks drive around my neighbourhood, leaving complete chaos, physically or socially

[sic]. There is no Border Police jeep, its doors banging open and shut, farting around. No soldiers order me to show my ID, on the way to ... university, grocery, hospital. I don't have to send my little children off to school through the checkpoint, and they don't cling to my dress afraid to leave me, and I don't have a guilty conscience because I cannot protect them from the arbitrary behaviour of the Border Police. No soldiers come to my home, not in the middle of the day and not in the middle of the night to take my sons for investigation. Nobody shouts at me to lift my shirt or to hold my hands up; nor shoots me if I don't react fast enough. I am free to go whenever I like: to a movie, to a concert, to the theatre, to Tel Aviv or Netanya. I am free to visit my neighbours, friends and family. I sit in front of my home and feel privileged; I am a Jew. (Magdalena Hefetz, Jerusalem, personal communication, 2002)

Magdalena Hefetz, a Berlin-born ceramicist and a long-time peace activist, sums up the dilemma of many CheckpointWatch observers. She knows that the 'best cup of coffee in town' with which she rewards herself after the rigours of checkpoint duty is a luxury of the Occupier. It is, of course, also an indicator of class, as are some of the freedoms that she appreciates: to attend cultural events, for instance, or to visit cafés. Her freedom of movement, a family visit, or the freedom from military pursuit and persecution – these are things that Palestinian women and men can only dream of. Magdalena exemplifies the unease felt by so many activists while protesting Israeli government policies. On the one hand, challenging the prevailing consensus, while on the other, remaining part of the privileged (Jewish) community, enjoying rights and freedoms that include the liberty to protest. It is this dissonance, as much as political ideology, which brings Magdalena and others like her to activism, and particularly to the role of observers at checkpoints. For it is at these checkpoints that Palestinian civilians engage the Occupation at its most tangible. It is where their humiliation is most constant and the disruption in their daily lives most strongly experienced. It is at the checkpoints, too, that the disparity between Israeli privilege and Palestinian disadvantage is most clearly seen and felt.[12]

There are also other reasons for women to join CPW: the sense of outrage that human rights abuses should be perpetrated 'in our name', and the empowerment offered by being active in the field. The motifs in Michal Sagui's account of the experience (quoted at the head of this chapter) that led her to join CPW are paradigmatic: questioning the

2 Blockaded village, West Bank, 2003 (photo: CheckpointWatch)

authority of security forces, speaking out against the consensus – in this case against those who ignore what they see in broad daylight on a Jerusalem street – and her sense of affront, of moral indignation. Two other elements also appear. One is the anger of the policemen and passers-by over Michal's intervention. As a civilian she has dared to challenge the military instead of being grateful for the protection supposedly provided by their 'investigation' of the young woman. The latter, if not engaged in an immediate act of terror, is certainly perceived, by virtue of being a Palestinian, as containing in her person all the potential for terror that threatens to disrupt that Israeli street. Secondly, Michal describes the scene as gendered: masculine, invasive, threatening the exposed body of the girl. Militarism, racism and sexism, the heady mix of much of Israeli discourse, are all present here in very vivid form. We will encounter these elements at the checkpoints themselves.

An Israeli savant, an orthodox Jew, once reportedly said that he could not talk with those with whom he ate and could not eat with those with whom he talked.[13] Daniella Yoel finds herself in a similar predicament. She is one of a very few religiously observant women in a group that is predominantly (sometimes militantly) secular, while the majority of the Jewish orthodox community are politically right-wing. This has created tensions with family and friends who do not share her views and are perplexed by, or hostile to, her CPW activity. Her statement, quoted above, echoes the language of the Hebrew Scriptures: 'her time came'

41

and 'twin boys in her womb' recall the stories of Tamar and of Rebecca the Matriarch in the Book of Genesis. Daniella foregrounds her personal and emotional connection to the death of the Palestinian twins, taking as given the value of children in both Israeli and Palestinian culture. However, the significant point here is her feeling that her presence at that terrible moment might have made the difference between life and death. She, both personally as Daniella and more generally as a Jewish Israeli, might have persuaded the soldiers where the Palestinians failed. Indeed, it may be so.

> Therefore [it is] correct to focus on the Holocaust from the point of view of the victims, and not to give equivalent importance to the process ... by which a nation with an enlightened culture turned into a nation of murderers ... Every display of Jewish vitality in the post-Holocaust world is a victory over Hitler. But it is also clear that the need for a sovereign state – in which Jews can both defend themselves when necessary and also develop their culture within a national context, and not only as a minority group – was and will remain the principal lesson of the Holocaust. (*Ha'aretz*, 15 March 2005)[14]

This quotation expresses both the tropes of victim[15] and victor, contradictory as they are, so intrinsic to Israeli discourse and its manipulation of the Holocaust for political ends. While the Holocaust is also a major theme in the motivation of Watchers, they approach it from a different perspective. For some, like Ilana Drukker-Tikotin, quoted above, it was a first-hand experience. For others, like Michal Sagui who is too young to have lived through the Nazi period, the awareness of that 'darker time' is very much present. For Ilana, Michal and many others, this perception leads to the very different conclusion that ethnic persecution and genocide must never be allowed to happen again, not just to 'us' but to anyone.

The politicization of the Holocaust as a constituting factor in Israeli national identity, and in justifying any and all actions as necessary defensive measures, is contested by Watchers' activism. Infused with the awareness that one step in the process of delegitimizing a nation leads to another, the fear is that Israel may eventually do to others that which was done to the Jews. Remembering the silence of the majority during the Nazi/fascist period impels many of us to speak out, now, while there is still time. The thought of Jews as perpetrators of evil is highly charged for Israelis, and any analogy with the Nazi period in particular is tantamount to sacrilege.[16]

In Israel the Holocaust is invoked in support of a variety of political positions, such as the false correspondence often drawn between Palestinians (or Arabs generally) and Nazis. The current stage of the Israel–Palestine conflict is thus widely perceived both as an existential threat and, at some subliminal level, as the opportunity to hit back at oppressors, past or potential (Eldar and Zartel 2004). The slaughter must be pre-empted – as in the mythic moment of the Six-Day War.[17] One may object profoundly, as I do, to the manipulation of the Holocaust at various levels of Israeli culture and politics, the illusion of perpetual victimhood and its concomitant implication that victims can never be perpetrators; however, it is also impossible to deny the genuine impact of the Holocaust trauma on the national psyche.

'We dwell among our own people'

Watchers are integrally part of Israeli society or its liberal-left elite. In the Tel Aviv branch the majority of members are Israeli-born, while in Jerusalem the proportion drops to roughly 50 per cent, others coming from Western Europe, the USA, and South and Central America. The northern and southern branches include kibbutz members as well as city dwellers. This breakdown refutes the contention that the Left is foreign (Westernized) espousing values and concepts of civil rights that 'may work in Holland' but are deemed inappropriate to harsh realities of the Middle East.

'Left' in Israel is a very loose term, including anyone with even a minimal commitment to human rights or a negotiated solution to the conflict, regardless of political affiliation. It has traditionally little class solidarity or much of a common language with Israel's own disadvantaged: residents of development towns, the poor neighbourhoods of the larger cities and Palestinian Israelis.[18] There is a tendency to defer urgent internal issues until 'after the Occupation'. The connection between the oppression of the Palestinians and the deliberate marginalization of, and hostility between, Jews from Arab lands, Palestinian-Israelis and other minority groups is largely ignored (Shohat 1988; Shenhav 2003).

The mainstream, Zionist, Left – what is known as the 'Peace Camp' – has not succeeded, or perhaps has not tried, to step outside the colonialist mentality that has always characterized Israeli policy towards the Palestinians (Kimmerling 2001). True, demonstrations and protests were organized against this, that or the other aspect of the Occupation, but the fundamental problem – the denial or dismissal of Palestinian national rights – was scarcely addressed. The opposition to the ills of Occupation or the support for 'Peace' always centred on Israeli rights, needs and desires, including, of course, security. A case in point is the mainstream Peace Now movement. Founded in 1978 during the Israeli–Egyptian peace talks, when a group of 348 reserve officers and soldiers from combat units published an open letter to the prime minister calling for the opportunity not to be lost, Peace Now emphasized a moderate, Zionist, message and was careful to disassociate itself from 'illegal activities' or any radical stance. Despite success in the 1970s and '80s in organizing mass demonstrations in favour of peace with Egypt, ending the Lebanon war or opposing settlement in the Occupied Territories, the movement did not succeed in significantly changing public opinion in relation to the conflict with the Palestinians, perhaps because of its own ambivalence. Peace Now has largely disappeared from the streets, except for a weekly vigil in Jerusalem, but continues to run an important settlement watch project, monitoring and protesting settlement expansion in the Occupied Territories.

The Zionist Left/Peace Camp includes not only intellectuals and professionals but also a cadre of generals, former heads of the General Security Services and other establishment figures. The discourse is peppered with militaristic terms, debates about how much 'to let them have', how much to 'concede' and demands for promises of Palestinian good behaviour.

The non-Zionist, or critical, Left has a long and honourable history of opposition to the Occupation and concern for Palestinian national aspirations (Kaminer 1996). It includes extra-parliamentary protest groups, such as Gush Shalom (Peace Bloc) and Ta'auysh (Arab Jewish Cooperation) and issue-specific groups like the Israel Committee Against Home Demolitions. They call for recognition of the national aspirations of the Palestinian people, a return to the 1967 borders and the uprooting of all settlements. Many favour the concept of 'a state for all Israel's citizens'; that is, one redistributing power more equitably between all citizens, including Palestinian Israelis, whether in a two-state or a bi-national framework. Needless to say, there are any number of variations and a whole spectrum of views, vigorously aired, within these groups and a heated debate regarding the nature of Zionism, post-Zionism and anti-Zionism (Kimmerling 1983, 2001; Silberstein 1999).[19]

Despite no little jockeying for prominence, there has been a good degree of cooperation and considerable overlap between the radical organizations in the period of the El Aqsa intifada. Hardly a day has passed without its demonstration, petition, food convoy to besieged Palestinian villages or anti-wall protest. This is very different from the situation prevailing during the Oslo years when the Left was silenced and paralysed, unable to take up the challenge presented by the well-organized, highly motivated and often very violent Right (Eldar and Zartel 2004). At the same time, this issue-oriented approach leads to fragmentation. There is a need for an overall strategy of opposition-resistance beyond intensive activism. It is at this point that ideological disputes such as the one-state versus a two-state argument erupt and prevent the development of a coherent programme.

This is also opposition *de luxe*. While most radical extra-parliamentary groups, including CPW, are monitored and probably infiltrated by the General Security Services (GSS), harassment is usually limited to phone-tapping and sometimes intrusive body-searches upon leaving or entering the country.[20] A notable exception is the case of Tali Fahima, a young woman with no previous record of activism, who was arrested in August 2004 on suspicion of involvement with the military arm of the PLO in Jenin, after having spent time in the company of Zakharia Zubeidi, a militant leader in the northern West Bank city. The charges against Fahima are unclear, and she has been interrogated under torture and held in solitary confinement. The charges against her have changed over time and, at the time of writing, she was still awaiting trial.

Since mid-2003, police brutality at demonstrations has also increased, particularly at demonstrations against the Annexation Wall (see Chapter 4). Many activists were shocked, calling out 'Don't shoot, we're Israeli!' (January 2004) when they were fired on by troops during a joint demonstration with Palestinians. Previously, the Israeli presence at such demonstrations elicited more restraint from police or army, such is the privilege of the Occupier. Perhaps this more even-handed military violence creates a more genuine solidarity between Israelis and their Palestinian comrades.

How does CheckpointWatch fit into this picture? The profile of the average Watcher is that of a middle-aged, middle-class, professional with a university education. The overwhelming majority are 'white', that is of Western (Ashkenazi) origin, and their age and class background mean that they enjoy certain innate advantages such as self-confidence and access to power centres, as well as more mundane benefits such as free time, independent transportation and resources. With a kind of unintentional inevitability, friend bringing friend, the movement

45

preserves this class and ethnic unity and CPW meetings have a club-biness discomfiting to those from different backgrounds. It doesn't break through the political and social barriers that, since the inception of the state, exist between the Ashkenazi elite and Mizrachim[21] from development towns[22] and peripheral urban neighbourhoods. The commonly held view that Mizrachis are generally rightist and nationalist elides leftist Mizrachi (Jews from Arab lands) with groups such as the feminist Achoti (My Sister) and the Keshet HaDemokratit Ha Mizrachit (Mizrachi Democratic New Rainbow-New Discourse) which address both political and social concerns, on the traditional leftist model. This stereotype shifts responsibility for the Occupation from 'us' to a group perceived by the hegemony as 'other' (Shenhav 2003; Lavie 2002, 2005). CheckpointWatch has very few Palestinian-Israeli members, partly because they are more vulnerable to military harassment. Then, too, they have their own political battle as subordinated second-class citizens (Lentin 1998). Nor are relations with West Bank Palestinians devoid of ambivalence (see also Chapter 5).

Ideological non-conformity and social homogeneity are part of the secret of CPW's success. Women from across the political spectrum – or at least the centre-left – can participate on a broad platform of opposition to the Occupation. Although not all members are feminists, CheckpointWatch is a member of the feminist Coalition of Women for a Just Peace, a coalition of nine women's organizations with an agreed platform of principles relating to the conflict and to social and feminist issues within Israel itself.[23] This is not to say that all coalition members fully subscribe to these principles, or that their interpretation of them is uniform. Within CPW itself, some women have demurred at coalition activities such as signing petitions with radical organizations, or in support of *refuseniks* (conscientious objectors) facing trial or jail sentences (Kidron 2003). In this way, the less radical members have the potential to depoliticize CPW by requiring consensus on political issues. As will be seen in Chapter 5, the ideological differences within the organization have, as of late 2004, become difficult to contain, awakening the possibility of a change in CPW's orientation, and perhaps even a split along ideological lines. This division is integral to Israeli society as a whole.

The modesty of witnessing

The constant confrontation with the military, the unwavering challenge to army and police decisions, the need endlessly to badger, complain and pressure and, yes, even beg, to allow a detainee to be released, for an alleged 'hot suspect' to be freed or simply for a more humane and respectful attitude towards the transitees at the checkpoints, require tremendous energy. There is a relentless demand to be creative, assertive, and also to keep matters from becoming violent. The innate tension in the engagement of observers and the military in the hostile war zone that is the checkpoint requires both diplomacy and no little courage.

Courage, perseverance and tenacity are all qualities of Checkpoint-Watchers, but has the movement fulfilled its stated goals?

The initial modest goals – monitoring checkpoints, recording and reporting – have certainly been met beyond expectation. Galvanizing the Israeli public, despite widespread press and media coverage in Israel and abroad, seems to be a slow process, with only moderate success. Lobbying efforts have worked well and CPW is widely known and respected. A parliamentary committee to monitor checkpoints has been set up by MK Roman Bronfman of the Yahad Party, avowedly in response to CPW's activities. While not particularly effective, the existence of this committee at least keeps checkpoints on the public agenda. There are ongoing contacts with senior figures in the security establishment, reminding them that they, too, are under civilian scrutiny. I will address the dilemmas involved in courting the establishment in Chapter 5. The significant growth in politically mainstream members has proved a double-edged sword, but this is also a measure of success. Internationally, CPW has gained both recognition and respect from other NGOs and from the media.

Unfortunately, the goal of protecting the human rights of Palestinians has not been achieved. The curfew–closure–checkpoint policy radically curtails freedom of movement and access to the basic necessities of living: work, education and health care. The deliberate destruction of infrastructure and the economy, the demolition of homes, mass arrests, so-called targeted (extra-judicial) killings and similar assaults, are in themselves fundamental violations of international agreements that Israeli is signatory to. Israel has turned the West Bank, and even more so Gaza, into virtual prisons. The prospect of territorial continuity for any future Palestinian state has been disrupted. Seen in this perspective, the harassment and humiliation observed at the checkpoints are only a small part of the picture. Perhaps, though, they are the proverbial straw intended to break the camel's back.

CPW's activity declares the value of Palestinian life and dignity and in the Israeli context this is an outstandingly political act. Our most significant achievement has been in pioneering a protest movement that is powerful not only in content but also in form. It does not rely on sporadic demonstrations but has created an identity between opposition and taking action on the ground. Watchers have placed themselves as civilians in the front line at the war zone of the checkpoints, by our physical presence contesting the military ethos that security is a paramount virtue. Without that presence, the violence and abuse at the checkpoints, so near and yet so far from the Israeli public eye, would probably be far worse. Our observations and reports have exposed the military at its most vulnerable. The sheer iniquity, oppressiveness and absurdity of the closure–checkpoints system is revealed for all to see.

Why 'modest witnesses'?

> Modest Witness ... A man whose narratives could be credited as mirrors of reality was a modest man: his reports ought to make that modesty visible. (Shapin and Schaffer 1985: 25)

The 'modest witnesses' of this book are, of course, not men but women, women who have breached a man's world (the Israeli military) by documenting its encounters with a civilian population under occupation. Watchers have challenged the military image of an untarnished knight, defender of the nation, and demanded accountability for the actions of the security forces.

Donna Haraway, a noted feminist historian of science, has questioned the concept of modest witnessing by pointing out that, 'the witness whose accounts mirror reality is deemed to be invisible ... an inhabitant of the potent, unmarked category ... constructed by the extraordinary conventions of self-invisibility' (Haraway 1997: 39). Of course, there is no such thing as 'self-invisibility', none of us is neutral. But I want to give Haraway a slightly different reading. As women, as non-combatants, Watchers are part of that large and invisible community not credited with the capacity to bear witness: women, children and, in the specific context of the Middle East conflict, Palestinians. On the contrary, it is the military, men, who are credited with presenting the 'mirror reality'. The word of the Israel army spokesman acquires the status of a sacred text, or a scientific body of knowledge, and is uniquely endowed with the authority to speak on the mysteries of security, despite the fact that its mendacity is well documented.[24] The great achievement of our modest checkpoint witnesses is to have acquired an alternative authority, one rooted in a civilian perspective.

In the arena of the checkpoints, this perspective is not only challenging, it is revolutionary.

Notes

1 Since Gaza is inaccessible to Israeli civilians, including human rights activists, this book refers only to the West Bank.

2 Palestinians regard the establishment of the State of Israel in May 1948, the Naqba or Disaster, the loss of 78 per cent of Palestine, and the expulsion/ flight of 750,000 Palestinians as the beginning of Occupation. In Israeli terms this is a very threatening definition, one that challenges the existence of the State of Israel.

3 MachsomWatch: *Machsom*/checkpoint and Watch, subtitled 'Women for Human Rights' in tribute to Human Rights Watch. In 2005 'Women Against the Occupation' was added to the title.

4 For want of a better term this refers to Palestinians attempting to cross a checkpoint.

5 Qalandiya is the major checkpoint between Ramallah and A-Ram checkpoint, monitoring entry to Jerusalem.

6 Founding members Ronnee Jaeger, Adi Kuntsman and this author, and also Yael Lavie-Jenner, a former judge from Germany, and US-born social worker Stephanie Black.

7 Individuals detained for checking by security forces because they attempted to cross the checkpoint without the appropriate permit, or tried to use one of the bypass routes, or for some arbitrary reason. Detention may last anywhere from minutes to several hours, a whole day, and even, on occasion, all night.

8 The army (IDF) and the border police (BP) are two distinct forces (see Chapter 3).

9 B'Tselem, the Israeli Information Centre for Human Rights Abuses in the Occupied Territories, established a checkpoint observation team in the summer of 2003. This NGO team, which includes Palestinians and Israelis, accesses checkpoints deep in the West Bank, using a bulletproof vehicle. CPW was pleased to cooperate with B'Tselem on that project and to provide information regarding our own modus operandi.

10 The Moked – Centre for the Defence of the Individual is an Israeli human rights NGO based in Jerusalem with the objective of assisting Palestinians of the Occupied Territories whose rights are violated due to Israel's policies. The Moked runs a hotline that aims to provide real-time assistance to individuals at the checkpoints through liaison with the security forces and other bodies.

11 The demolition of Palestinian homes in Gaza, the West Bank and the Jerusalem area is part of a deliberate Israeli policy. Ostensibly either a punitive measure (the homes of accused terrorists or their families) it may also be an administrative tool. For instance, wholesale denial of building permits to Palestinians to build on their own land in and around Jerusalem forces many

families to build illegally. In West (Jewish) Jerusalem, where illegal building is very much the norm, offenders are merely fined. Since October 2001, 558 houses of families of terror suspects have been demolished, and since 1987 2,500 structures were demolished for administrative reasons (B'Tselem 2004d). In January 2005, a special committee established by the Chief of Staff, Major General Moshe Ya'alon, declared that the policy of demolishing the homes of terrorists had been ineffectual as a deterrent and would be suspended (Israel Committee Against Home Demolitions, 18 February 2005).

12 For example, in October 2003 the West Bank was under total curfew for several days while Israelis celebrated the Succoth (Feast of Tabernacles) festival. This closure was repeated during the carnival festival of Purim in March 2004, in the same year from the Passover festival in early April to Independence Day at the end of that month and subsequently for a major sports event in Israel. In March 2005, in an age of supposed alleviations, a four-day closure accompanies Israel's Purim celebrations.

13 Attributed to the late Professor Ernest Simon, who could not eat with secular Jews who don't observe the Jewish dietary laws, and could not talk politics with observant Jews, who do, owing to their disregard for the civil rights of non-Jews.

14 On the occasion of the opening of a new Holocaust memorial complex in Jerusalem, the final phase of a $56 million development.

15 There is ambivalence here, since Israel is also at pains to stress the heroism of those Jews in the ghettos who resisted the Nazis.

16 On 25 November 2004, our observers witnessed a young Palestinian man playing his violin for soldiers at the Beth Iba checkpoint near Nablus. There is some controversy over whether he volunteered to play when his violin case was checked, or was asked to do so by the soldiers. The incident caused a furore in Israel, awakening memories of Jews forced by the Nazis to play in the death camps. Yet for many, the issue was not the humiliation of the young Palestinian but, as author Yoram Kaniuk put it, the dishonour done to the memory of the Holocaust (Akiva Eldar, *Ha'aretz*, 27 November 2004).

17 At the start of the war, after weeks of uncertainty as to who would strike first, Israel destroyed the fighter planes of both Egypt and Syria on the ground. This was widely regarded in Israel as a war for physical survival and the victory was seen as almost miraculous.

18 At least one NGO, Rabbis for Human Rights, addresses both human rights and social issues.

19 It should be pointed out that, colloquially, the term Zionist is used in many ways, as indicating a desire for a better Israel, or as a synonym for dedicated commitment.

20 The harassment is selective and seems limited to those who have had contact with radical Palestinian groups such as the Democratic Front for the Liberation of Palestine, or contacts with suspected militants.

21 Mizrachi – from the Middle East and North Africa. The distinction is cultural and class-based as well as geographical (Shenhav 2003).

22 Towns established in the 1950s and '60s to develop (or Judaize) under-populated areas such as the Negev or the Galilee. New immigrants, mostly those from Arab lands, were sent to those towns which remain as examples of underdevelopment in terms of infrastructure, services and education invested there by the state (Shafir and Peled 2002).

23 Member organizations of the Coalition of Women for a Just Peace: Bat Shalom – the Israeli side of the Jerusalem Link – A Women's Joint Venture for Peace (est. 1993); Women in Black – holding weekly vigils throughout Israel (est. 1988); Women and Mothers for Peace; Women Engendering Peace; New Profile (est. 1998); WILPF – Women's International League for Peace and Freedom, Israeli chapter; TANDI – Movement of Democratic Women for Israel (est. 1951); *Noga* feminist magazine; NELED – (acronym) Women for Coexistence; MachsomWatch (est. 2001).

The principles of the coalition are as follows: an end to the Occupation; the full involvement of women in negotiations for peace; the establishment of a Palestinian state, side by side with the State of Israel, based on the 1967 borders; the recognition of Jerusalem as the shared capital of two states; Israel to recognize its share of responsibility for the results of the 1948 war and cooperate in finding a just solution for the Palestinian refugees; equality, inclusion and justice for Palestinian citizens of Israel; opposition to the militarism permeating Israeli society; equal rights for women and all residents of Israel; social and economic justice for Israel's citizens and integration in the region.

24 See for instance Gideon Levi, 'Sacrificed on a Feast Day', *Ha'aretz*, 31 March 2000; Amos Harel, 'IDF Gave False Information on Nusseirat, for "Operational Reasons" ', *Ha'aretz*, 2 November 2003; Amira Hass, 'A Story About Generals', *Ha'aretz*, 24 May 2004.

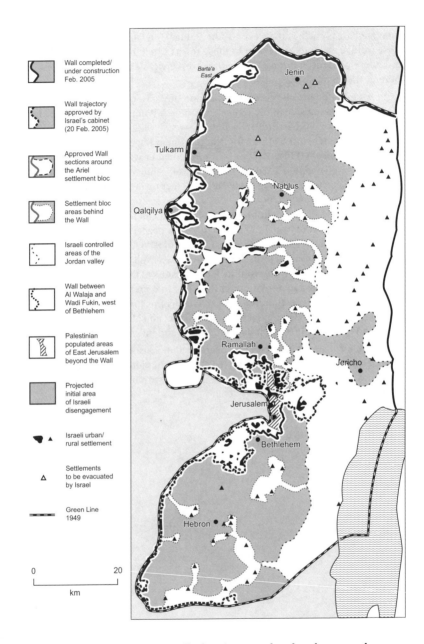

	Wall completed/ under construction Feb. 2005
	Wall trajectory approved by Israel's cabinet (20 Feb. 2005)
	Approved Wall sections around the Ariel settlement bloc
	Settlement bloc areas behind the Wall
	Israeli controlled areas of the Jordan valley
	Wall between Al Walaja and Wadi Fukin, west of Bethlehem
	Palestinian populated areas of East Jerusalem beyond the Wall
	Projected initial area of Israeli disengagement
	Israeli urban/ rural settlement
△	Settlements to be evacuated by Israel
	Green Line 1949

Barta'a East

Jenin

Tulkarm

Nablus

Qalqilya

Ramallah

Jericho

Jerusalem

Bethlehem

Hebron

0   20

km

Map 2 Annexation Wall, showing completed and proposed sections, May 2005

TWO | The checkpoints

3 | The Gateway to Hell

Welcome to the Gateway to Hell! (Young Palestinian to Watchers at the Qalandiya checkpoint, September 2002)

We don't know what will happen next. Don't know what the rules are. Standing there, hoping it's the right thing. That's the worst of it, not knowing what will happen next. (Nuha Ahmed Musleh, Palestinian antiquarian, Jerusalem)

The checkpoints are not designed to improve the security of Israelis, but rather, to oppress Palestinians. In order to understand this, there is no need to visit the checkpoints every day for two years. One visit is enough ... They don't separate Israel from Palestinians; rather, they separate Palestinians from Palestinians. The aim is to prevent their freedom of movement and to disrupt their everyday life. Israeli politicians have succeeded in convincing most Israelis, including soldiers, to regard every Palestinian as a potential terrorist. A pregnant woman is suspect. An ambulance bringing a sick person is suspect. A witness told us how soldiers spilled the contents of school bags of six-year-old girls ... A Palestinian cannot be declared 'clean', that right is never accorded to one [who] is always transgressing some law, and therefore is subject to harassment by any soldier who feels like it ... With guns and gas grenades they also chase elderly women carrying children ... There is no limit to the creativity of the soldiers to teach ... a lesson [to the Palestinians]. You can make [them] jump rope. You can beat [them] ... make them undress and stand for hours in the cold ... Spilling oil on the rickety Abu Dis[1] passage and watching people slip and fall is another highly entertaining option ... Come and see. You will see that the checkpoints do not prevent terror. Rather, they create it (Nina Mayorek, excerpt from speech at a Peace Now demonstration in Jerusalem, 22 March 2003, in memory of Rachel Corrie, International Solidarity Movement volunteer killed in Gaza by an Israeli army bulldozer on 16 March 2003 while protesting the demolition of a Palestinian home)

In the preceding chapters we encountered the bureaucracy of Occupation and met CheckpointWatchers, the Israeli women who bear witness to it. This chapter deals with the bizarre world of checkpoints, where reason, and hope, are abandoned by all who enter. The situation described in this chapter is that pertaining between February 2001 and February 2005. In the wake of political developments during that period, the checkpoint situation was extremely fluid and changed from day to day. These reports from the field should therefore be read as a diary of Occupation for the given period. Although details may change, the humiliation and oppression remain.

In the quotations that open this chapter, Nuha Musleh expresses the anguish of uncertainty, the inability of Palestinians to plan for the simplest tasks of life. Nina Mayorek and Susy Mordechay (below) introduce, from an observer's perspective, the cruelty innate in even routine checkpoint days. Although subsequent reports in this chapter do not lack for drama, it is the banality of routine that erodes hope.

Thursday, 15 May 2003
'Twas a good day at Huwwara.

The checkpoint was 'open' when we arrived a little after 9 a.m.

Only 50–60 people were waiting in line.

No soldiers intimidated waiting folks with cocked rifles.

We didn't hear stories of grave abuse occurring in our absence.

We didn't witness a reserve unit headed by a brigade commander perform the illegal 'Neighbour Procedure', in which a [Palestinian] civilian is forced to check a suspicious bag as the soldiers step back to relative safety.

We didn't see a long line of men taken off a bus, standing in the burning sun, arms stretched out in front and a soldier checking their hands (or IDs) like a kindergarten teacher checking for cleanliness.

The checkpoint wasn't closed even once during the three and a half hours we were there, except unofficially when the soldiers had their breakfast or had a bit of a chat regardless of the waiting crowd.

Part of the time there were two soldiers on duty instead of only one.

Even at peak time there were no more than 100 people waiting; most of them were let through, including those who didn't seem confident enough to face the soldiers without seeking our support first.

The average time people had to wait in the scorching heat was no more than 1 hour and 30 minutes. (Susy Mordechay, mathematician, Tel-Aviv)

January 2005. In the crowded landscape of Israel-Palestine, an area approximately the size of Wales, there are forty-eight manned checkpoints preventing freedom of movement of Palestinians into Israel and within the West Bank. Seventeen checkpoints are in the heart of the West Bank far from the Green Line. Another twenty-seven checkpoints block Palestinian movement between the West Bank and Israel. In the West Bank city of Hebron there are twelve internal checkpoints (B'Tselem 2005). These figures do not include the hundreds of block-ades consisting of unmanned mounds of earth, rubble and refuse blocking access to almost all Palestinian villages and towns, separating them one from another. Not only do these restrictions limit personal freedom of movement, they interfere with territorial continuity, creating isolated ghettos encircled by Israeli controls. In addition to checkpoints and blockades, 'flying' or 'mobile' checkpoints operate: military patrols that hunt down would-be 'infiltrators', civilians attempting to bypass the checkpoints.

Checkpoints are not border crossings, although they may mark a border, real, imagined or potential. They are frequently shifted to de-marcate territorial boundaries, an imaginary line between 'ours' and 'theirs', with advantage always on 'our' side (Ginzburg 2003). At check-points there is only the rule of the moment, always shifting, always changing, sometimes responsive to pleading, sometimes not. There is scant shelter, no seating, no toilets, no facilities fit for human beings.[2] No Palestinian civilian can move, for any reason whatsoever, no matter which way s/he turns, permit or no permit, without encountering a checkpoint of some kind. This is not to say that there are no byways for those bent on mayhem, for they will always find their way to their goal. Checkpoints are not about security. They cannot provide hermetic closure, nor can they prevent terror. As Nina Mayorek points out, they ac-tually inspire it. Their true purpose is threefold: collective punishment, visible military control of the civilian population, and the disruption of territorial continuity that makes any prospect of a viable Palestinian state impossible. In 2005 checkpoints are being dismantled, re-erected, moved and changed, yet their potential to disrupt Palestinian life in the future remains. For Israel they are a weapon not to be renounced.

The checkpoints we examined in this chapter are fully fledged war zones, complete with watch towers, screaming jeeps, armoured vehicles and even tanks. Heavily armed and equipped soldiers check coincident civilians at gunpoint, demanding to see their identity cards and the precious, hard-to-come-by, permits.

Procedure Arriving at a checkpoint, the would-be transitee/observer[3] is confronted by soldiers with cocked guns facing the line of waiting pedestrians. People wait in stoical silence. If the crowd gets impatient and begins to surge or straggle forwards, it is herded back with shouts and curses to some arbitrary point, sometimes encouraged by shots in the air, sometimes by tear-gas and stun grenades. If soldiers feel provoked or threatened, they may respond with live fire, not infrequently with fatal results. At Qalandiya near Jerusalem, several youths have been killed over the last four years, some of them as young as ten years old, when soldiers reacted to stone-throwing with live fire.[4]

Advancing to the examination point, documents are checked. Checks may be cursory or thorough. The transitee may stand 10–20 metres from the soldiers, or suffer close examination. Men may, or may not, be asked to bare their chests and bellies and execute a pirouette to prove the absence of weapons or explosives. Women may, or may not, be required to undergo a more discreet body-check. Women and children may be passed ahead of the crowd, or forced to wait in line. The variations are unpredictable and endless.

Petty extortion and blackmail have their place here too. Palestinian men avoid carrying packages to speed up the checking process, carrying their cash in their ID card folders. When this is returned to them after checking, it is often minus the cash. Cigarettes, lighters and mobile phones are also common currency in checkpoint bribery. At Qalandiya, a major crossing, six soldiers were found guilty of extracting tangible favours from Palestinians in return for allowing them to cross (*Ha'aretz*, 31 January 2004). At the same checkpoint, taxi drivers were forced to collaborate with the military by chasing away children from the nearby refugee camp. In return the soldiers promised to reopen the checkpoint, closed as a 'punishment' for stone-throwing by the children (CPW report, 1 December 2003).

Detainees A common sight is the groups of detainees, held while their documents are checked by radio with some distant General Security Services (GSS) computer. Detention is part instrumental as a search for suspected terrorists. It is also part harassment and punishment, whether for daring to desire passage, or supposedly for cheeking a soldier, or to alleviate boredom. Officially, it is illegal to detain people as punishment for longer than three hours, but actual waiting periods may last a whole day, or even overnight, in blazing heat or freezing cold, with little or no shelter. Detainees may be forced to stand facing a wall, hands on head, or be allowed to stand or sit at ease, at the whim of their captors or on the intervention of Watchers. The majority are released sooner or later, but young men are particularly vulnerable to detention. Not only are they seen as likely militants/terrorists, they are also considered ripe for recruitment to the vast web of collaborators and informers that Israel has nurtured during the years of Occupation.

Suspects The term covers a multitude of possibilities, from a fully fledged militant or minor political leader to a potential source of information or a relative of another suspect. A serious militant/political leader will of course be on a list of wanted persons to be hunted down in military raids or on the hit list of targeted killings, as were peace activist Dr Thabet Thabet in January 2001 and Sheikh Ahmed Yassin, the spiritual leader of Hamas, in March 2004.

There is also a list of those who should be 'apprehended if encountered',[5] that is, those not specifically suspect but fair game for detention and even arrest. Curiously enough, just as the majority of checkpoint detainees are sooner or later released without being charged, so too are most of the thousands throughout the West Bank arbitrarily arrested and imprisoned.[6] Once arrested, on whatever grounds, an individual has a 'security record', ending all hope of obtaining a permit of any kind from the authorities.

Having run such gauntlets, the lucky individual passes the checkpoint, perhaps only to be stopped on the other side by the civil police, ostensibly settling old scores or seeking new ones. Do you have unpaid parking or speeding fines? Crimes and peccadillos not accounted for? This is the opportunity to atone for your sins. There is a truly unbearable lightness with which any Palestinian can be fined, detained, arrested or killed.[7]

On the roads of the West Bank, an apartheid system prevails, with the fast, well-paved highways restricted to Israelis. West Bankers must use a series of roundabout secondary or tertiary roads, such as the treacherous Wadi Naar that winds precipitously between Bethlehem and Abu Dis. They must make do with byways, often little better than cart tracks, that circumvent the Israeli-imposed obstacles – blocking the entrances and exits to their villages (B'Tselem 2003c). The roads are both a deliberate dismemberment of Palestinian territory and a message to the Palestinian civilian: you are not wanted here; you are as dust.

Since few cars are allowed to pass, the majority of those trying to cross the checkpoints are pedestrians. Young and old, the healthy and the sick, with burdens and without, must march considerable distances to reach the control area and then beyond it to transportation points. Imagine attending a business meeting after climbing over earthworks to leave your neighbourhood, walking a considerable distance to have your papers checked, waiting endlessly in line and then walking again to where a battered, crowded *servis*/taxi[8] can eventually take you to your destination. People often carry dusters to wipe their shoes after their enforced hike, an attempt to maintain a semblance of dignity.

Checkpointspeak

The time we have spent at the checkpoints has sharpened our senses. Today, we see more clearly, we hear more acutely. We have become more sensitive to the routine lies that have become part of our daily lives, to the laundering of language that is so integral a part of the checkpoint reality that attempts to hide the injustice, the arbitrary treatment, the negation of human rights. This is what we wish to expose to the full light of day, to comment on and explain. (CheckpointWatch 2005: 101)

Although incredibly noisy, checkpoints are not about communication on any level. The confusion and uncertainty of transit are compounded by problems of language and culture. Although District Coordination and Liaison (DCL) officers charged with problem-solving at checkpoints are supposed to be Arabic-speakers, the majority of Israelis don't speak Arabic, officially the country's second language. Soldiers are no exception. Their Arabic vocabulary, if it exists at all, is usually confined to 'stop', 'come', 'go' and a few insults or curses. Orders are often signalled by a beckoning hand, fingers turned towards the body or by a hand outstretched to repel, or the threatening movement of a weapon. Many Palestinians, especially women and older people, don't know Hebrew. Those who do often resent using the language of the oppressor.

Another favourite ploy of officers and men alike is the silence, the refusal to answer questions or to acknowledge a greeting, whether from Palestinians or observers. The refusal to answer is, of course, accompanied by the refusal to look, for instance at a medical certificate supposed to guarantee passage, or at the fear in the face of a child. It is the ultimate denial of another's existence.

Checkpointspeak assumes the right of the oppressor to oppress and the obligation of the oppressed to accept the situation.

Qalandiya, 6 August 2002
Watchers: Aya K, Nora O, Adi D, Roni H

... the armoured personnel carrier (APC) ... set off after its prey, roaring down the road; it splashed dirt (intentionally?) on a woman who had been standing on the side of the road and was just taking her baby out of the baby carriage, while another child was standing beside her. Ilana, angry, asks O, how could he threaten [the woman] scare her? O answered: they signalled her to move and she stopped deliberately.

The language with which we describe the world is intertwined and inseparable from the reality it creates. Just as the Occupation derives from, justifies itself and is maintained through usage such as 'liberated' territories rather than 'occupied' ... For O, the natural thing was the roaring APC. The woman was the aggressor, stopping the vehicle in its natural course. For us the opposite is true, her right to stand was the natural thing while the roaring machine was the aggressor, the unnatural force. And those two [opposing] concepts are inseparable from the language through which and with which these narratives are related. (Aya Kaniuk, writer, Tel-Aviv)

'Checkpointspeak', elsewhere termed by Aya Kaniuk *machsomism* (checkpointism), describes not only the spoken language but the whole panoply of elements that make up this cruel theatre of the absurd (Ginzburg 2003). These include speech, gesture, body-language, attitude, environment, and 'props' such as the APC. The press and media are very much part of this 'language laundry', using the terminology of occupation in their reporting. For instance, although the expression 'West Bank' in itself elides the reality of occupation, TV and radio presenters are obliged, by edict, to use instead the more loaded 'Judaea and Samaria', the biblical names for the area. In this way, it becomes definitively 'ours', Jewish-Israeli, eliminating the Palestinian presence and claims.[9]

In checkpointspeak, the generalized possibility of a terror attack becomes an 'alert', a signal for the checkpoint to close, whether for minutes or for hours. Rumours are a 'hot alert'. Relying on the widespread network of informers, details can be so precise as to be surprising outside of a film script. I was once told to abandon my shift because 'three dark-skinned men with guns in a green Peugeot are headed this way'. The three never materialized, deterred perhaps by my insistent presence? Hot alerts cause the checkpoint to close for

61

longer, more hermetically, and with an increase in the numbers of detainees, arrests, beatings and shootings. A hot alert, on orders from above, brings about the so-called 'stop all life' procedure, the sudden closing of the checkpoint to all movement for an indefinite period. In no instance is any explanation offered to the waiting transitees. The alerts have not prevented suicide bombings at the checkpoints themselves, such as that at A-Ram, Jerusalem (18 May 2003), and others.

Golda Meir is rumoured to have said: 'We may forgive the Arabs [sic] for murdering us, we can never forgive them for forcing us to kill them.' In checkpointspeak, Israelis are murdered, Palestinians are killed. Extra-judicial executions of Palestinian leaders are targeted killings. Palestinians are terrorists, never militants or guerrillas. Israel can only 'regret' that the targeting in these cases causes significant 'collateral damage' – the deaths of civilian bystanders, including children.[10] Collateral damage is considered to be the fault of the victims themselves, for harbouring terrorists in their midst, or the fault of the terrorists who disobligingly hide out among civilians. The Israeli army, allegedly the world's most humanitarian army, is, supposedly, careful to avoid such damage (Hass 2003a).

Although Palestinians outnumber the military at the checkpoints, it is the latter voice that dominates, determining the daily, even momentary, agenda and its implementation. When present, CheckpointWatchers may serve as a kind of chorus of protest, but our voices are muted, an echo of civilian conscience amid the din of war.

> We don't see the faces [of the Palestinians]. Because if we did, see the person, their humanity, know them by name, unique and separate not just as defined by 'race', if we didn't just look through a prism of racism that locates the Palestinian further from his human origins than the Jew ... we wouldn't be lending our hand to this, we wouldn't be silent, choosing not to know. Because then we couldn't. (Aya Kaniuk, 1 March 2003)

The 'prism' of racism evokes the 'gaze' – the right to look, to see and to categorize the Other (Ginzburg 2003).[11] The military, hidden behind camouflage gear and often behind dark glasses ('distance glasses' in the jargon), are exclusively accredited with the right to 'gaze'. Yet their physical and emotional distance from the object of the gaze limits their vision. They see only the enemy, not human beings.

Conversely, not only do Palestinians not dare to 'look' back, they *cannot* return the 'look' to the faceless, impersonal representative of

3 Bethlehem checkpoint, 2003 (photo: Elisheva Smith)

the Occupation confronting them. They must see themselves as they are reflected in the eyes of the beholder-oppressor: as potential or actual criminals. Though by no means quiet, they are silenced. They have no say in what goes on, both at the immediate, personal level and in the wider political context. They are robbed of agency as individuals and as a people. Their persistence in attempting to reach their places of work, education, health care and such services as still exist in the West Bank, is a silent, persistent, form of resistance. It is not only the determination, but also the necessity, to survive (Rosenfeld 2003–04).

A people's army

> The Israel Defence Force is a people's army and its activities represent the people of the state and are conducted on behalf of the people.
> (Reuven Rivlin, MK, Speaker of the Knesset, June 2004)[12]

The Israel Defence Force (IDF) is indeed a citizens' army in which most able-bodied Jewish males[13] from the age of eighteen serve for three years, followed by three or four weeks of annual reserve duty until the age of forty-two or, for non-combat units, fifty. Women serve for two years and are usually exempt from reserve duty. By law, an increasing number of combat roles are now open to women. The IDF is patently an army of occupation, the Israel Occupation Force (IOF). In order to avoid using either of these contested terms, I refer throughout to the army or the military. This term also includes the border police who figure prominently in CPW reports.[14]

Army service is perhaps the most significant rite of passage in Israeli culture.[15] Not only is it the moment that separates the men from the boys, the supposed crucible for forging nationhood, it also to a large extent determines issues of status and prestige in subsequent civilian life (Ben-Ari 2001). The successful soldier or officer from an elite unit will find many doors opening for him in any career he may choose. Israeli corridors of power are crowded with ex-generals; Prime Ministers Rabin, Barak and Sharon, were respectively Chiefs of Staff and a senior general before entering politics. A retired five-star general wishing for a political career finds that he is spoilt for choice among parties competing for his services. The implications of this glorification of the hero, both for the politicization of the army and for the militarization of Israeli policy, are all too clear (Kimmerling 1993).

Notwithstanding Israel's militaristic ethos, Israeli youth is as spoilt as its Western counterparts and the transition from schoolchild to soldier is abrupt, despite a process of conditioning that begins even before the last high-school year. From hedonistic pleasures and matriculation pressures, youngsters are thrown into a world where toughness, force and disregard for physical or emotional limitations are encouraged and rewarded. Costume plays a significant part in the transition: the sloppy olive-green battle duds and accessories reduce the soldiers, men and women alike, to clones, anonymous, faceless, almost indistinguishable from one another. Their cumbersome weapons are slung across their chests or point threateningly at the world. Battle gear, including 15 kg bulletproof vests, both magnifies and denies the body within. A paradigm for the Occupation itself, this protective uniform is a warning to the troops that although supposedly invincible by virtue of superior technology, they are still easy targets for a sniper or suicide bomber.

Orders from the senior echelons are vague and inconsistent. Conscripts must rely on their own interpretation of the rules, every man and woman a king. He/she may decide to obey rigorously the edict of the moment: today, only men over thirty-five may pass, tomorrow only men over forty; detainees may be held for hours, or minutes. Or magnanimity may win the day and, with a toss of the head or a dismissive wave, an 'illegal' may get through. There are surely soldiers whose inclination is more humane, but the social pressure to conform is great. Very few will risk being branded as weak, or reported for dereliction of duty by enabling passage. There is considerable indoctrination regarding the nature of the enemy and soldiers' own role as defenders of the homeland. As one, anonymous, conscript wrote in response to a report of abuses in his unit that he discovered on the CPW website:

> You ladies ... don't have to take the security of the State of Israel into account; you only have to protect one individual. I as a warrior must consider not only the man at the checkpoint but also the man on the bus ... you do not know better than me, my commander, my area commander, my chief of staff and my prime minister. In fact you know a whole lot less and even what you know you don't understand. (communicated 2004)

This warrior, with the received wisdom of his superiors, accepts responsibility for the whole nation, represented here by the image of the vulnerable bus, lurching towards the next terror attack. The presence of Watchers suggests a different responsibility – that of military accountability to the civilian estate.

Women soldiers adapt themselves to the security ethos either by matching the harshness of the men or by playing the classic feminine role of willing subaltern. Men are the army, women are in the army (Enloe 1983). As Orna Sasson-Levi has pointed out, women soldiers suffer the worst of all worlds. They 'may transgress gender boundaries [but] internalise the military's masculine ideology and values and learn to identify with the patriarchal order of the army and the state' (Sasson-Levi 2003a: 440). Even the prestige that women in combat roles acquire is individual. It does not net them the social and professional rewards, nor the 'glory' accorded to men, both during service and in civilian life (Lentin 2000; Sharoni 2000). Our encounters indicate that women are frequently no less aggressive and lacking in compassion than their male colleagues, whether because of desire to prove themselves as 'warriors' or simply because, as in any group, some are hard and cruel individuals.

§

> The daily killings of Palestinian civilians, the wholesale demolition of homes, the despoiling of infrastructure and agricultural land, the destruction of crops and uprooting of trees, all signal to the soldiers (and to Israeli citizens as a whole) that the lives, [the] private and collective property of Palestinians, are up for grabs. This is the reason for the absolute contempt ... for their work, studies, health, time,

and existential needs. The constant escalation of military aggression is therefore the basis and the framework for the gradual sliding ... from 'obeying orders' to dedicatedly executing them as an 'obligatory pleasure'. (Rosenfeld 2003–04)

These warriors and defenders are also depicted in Israeli discourse as the nation's sons, requiring protection and caring. Israeli culture is obsessed with its soldier-boys and, to a lesser extent, -girls. For parents there is a whole ritual of involvement in their children's army service, pride and anxiety mixing. There is also a considerable culture (and industry) of bereavement centred round the fallen sons (Maoz 2000). Ambivalence towards the defender-child finds expression in the relations between soldiers and CheckpointWatchers. The latter often ask whether we have sons – it is always sons – in the army, or whether we ourselves have served, as indeed many Watchers have. Some conscripts need to assert themselves by determining where we may stand or refusing to speak with us. Others show a need for approbation, asking 'Did I do all right?' In one case a youngster who had violently cursed both Watchers and Palestinians had to be comforted:

Qalandiya, 24 July 2002
Watchers: Daniella Y, Aya K, Ivonne M
    Daniella has a conversation that moves her. The soldier who cursed her earlier, came up to her: 'Write down my name and number, file a complaint' ... then he says emotionally, 'I don't want to be here' ... Later he tells how he was left alone, and that's why he burst out ... he had applied for transfer ... he is dying to leave, that it all has been ceaselessly getting on his nerves ... I may be petty, and not benevolent enough, but why did he [need] Daniella's ... forgiveness ... and understanding and not the forgiveness of those he had hurt, those [Palestinians] he had been rude to? Why did he feel the need to excuse himself in our eyes rather than theirs? ... As Daniella said, she represented a symbolic mother figure ... [We see] soldiers joking with CheckpointWatchers ... no one seems monstrous, but ... a few metres away, Palestinians are forced to stand in line, at the mercy of children, who decide whether or not they will pass, whether or not they will work, eat, study, live or die ... for no other reason than their being Palestinians. (Aya Kaniuk)

It is important to stress again that it is not my intention to portray soldiers *ipso facto* as sadists or brutes. The army is a reflection of the whole spectrum of Israeli society in all its diversity. However, the system by its massiveness and totality, as well as by the veneration it enjoys, corrupts. Youngsters are brainwashed into believing themselves bastions of defence and that force is the only language Palestinians understand.

During three years of observations, CheckpointWatchers have witnessed very few moments of kindness by the military, the kind of moments that might build a bridge of reconciliation between enemies. When these occur, they are often hard-won.

A-Ram, 19 March 2003
Watchers: Ruthy B, Daniella Y, Aya K

A young woman – drenched, shivering, it was pouring rain – is not allowed through. She explained that she lives in A-Ram but her ID was issued in Ramallah, that she must pass because her child in nursery school was waiting for her to come and pick him up. That morning she had gone to Ramallah to visit her mother in the hospital, and now she must get back. She was desperate. The soldier would not relent: '*How do I know she is from A-Ram ... Why didn't she get a permit ...? They all say this ... I know her, she is a liar ... They are all liars ... If I give in to everyone, what would happen then? Do you know that they caught a suicide bomber here? If she knew she couldn't come back without a permit, why did she leave in the first place? She knew ... It's her fault ... and no, no, no ...* ' He won't let her through ... Finally there was a different soldier, so we pleaded and explained, while all this time we were all getting wetter and wetter, especially the woman who wouldn't accept our offer of an umbrella. Finally the [second] soldier said, '*I wish they would throw this checkpoint away!*' (said it and meant it), and let her through. And she ran. (Aya Kaniuk)

Soldiers eventually return to civilian life at the end of their service. What kind of neighbours and colleagues will they make and what kind of society will they help to build in the future? The prospect, alas, is not encouraging. The problem goes beyond the morals and morale of conscripts and reservists, to the ethos of necessary evil – where evil comes to be seen more and more as desirable, as an end in itself (Rosenfeld 2003–04).

Qalandiya, 10 December 2003
Watchers: Ilana H, Aya K, Ivonne M. Deborah L

One of the soldiers, Tzachi, was particularly rude and vile to the Palestinians and also to us. A few shining examples: 'So, you are from

"Let the Animals Live?"[16] ... We are here to harass [the Palestinians]. Let them wait ... These Arabs, they're all terrorists, all animals. The State of Israel? I don't give a damn about it, I'm here to bash people. Talk to them nicely like I do to my mum? If that was my mum, I'd cut her throat.' (Dr Ilana Hammerman, Austrian-born writer and translator, Jerusalem)

Reservists Reservists also do checkpoint duty and are considered by popular wisdom to be more patient with transitees than the conscripts. Many regard reserve duty as an evil to be borne, a disruption of their civilian lives or see service in the territories as going against their conscience.[17] Others find that the donning of military uniform liberates them from the norms of civil society and gives them licence to vent racist or merely aggressive impulses.

Gush Etzion and environs, 7 February 2004
Watchers: Vivi S, Rachel H, Nina M

A few minutes after our arrival ... four reserve soldiers in a jeep arrived ... They asked who are we and after we described ourselves as human rights activists the response of three of them, including one with the rank of major, was: 'There are no human rights beyond this checkpoint. They ... are animals and do not deserve any human rights.' These representatives of the Israeli army [had no qualms about asserting] the complete dehumanization of the Palestinians. (Vivi Suri, Baghdad-born laboratory technician)

No longer primed for action, many reservists also feel a lack of confidence in their ability to handle danger or attack, something that may result in a nervously light finger on the trigger. Like conscripts, reservists represent the whole spectrum of Israeli society, and maturity is not an inevitable guarantee of wisdom or patience.

This is true, too, for the so-called humanitarian volunteers, a project initiated[18] just after the reoccupation of Palestinian areas of the West Bank in April 2002 and continuing for a year thereafter. Conceived as reinforcement for beleaguered conscripts, the volunteers were to be mature, fatherly, men, no longer eligible for reserve duty.[19] Following a sketchy induction, they were charged with handling humanitarian cases such as medical emergencies while the checkpoint commander, usually a conscript with the rank of sergeant or staff sergeant, retained operational control. The project eventually foundered both because of conflicts between the 'humanitarians' and the very young NCOs but also because a lack of coordination and perhaps commitment to the project within the army itself (H. Agmon, personal communication, August 2003). Like a similar volunteer venture, Kav HaTefer (Seam Line, see Chapter 4), the humanitarian project attracted both men and women reservists, some of whom were genuinely concerned for humanitarian values while others were fired more by patriotic sentiments and eagerness for action. Some had their own tragedies.

Qalandiya, 18 September 2002
Watchers: Ruthy B, Aya K, Michal Z, Ivonne M

There is a new [humanitarian] volunteer officer who would not tell us his name ... He wants to understand why we think the checkpoints are damaging Israeli society more than benefiting it. From his not very explicit conversation, we gathered that his daughter had been killed in a terrorist attack. He asked ... about our group: motivation, whom we represent. In the middle of our discussion we heard that there had been a suicide bombing in the north of the country (Wadi Ara), and the volunteer became very upset and hostile. I reiterated that the checkpoint only creates more desperation and lack of hope and he agreed with this but became very silent ... we parted with a handshake and wishes for better times for everybody. (Dr Ivonne Mansbach, Guatemala-born epidemiologist)

Part of the attraction for volunteers was the potential for action. For instance O, a major in the reserves, was for almost a year (2002–03) the self-appointed sheriff of Qalandiya. On good days O bestowed favours, on bad ones he enforced, or invented, more stringent rules. He would, when so moved, turn a blind eye and allow passage to those without permits, write notes that served as permits for lost, stolen or strayed IDs, banish those he considered to be malingerers. Day after day, he could be found sitting tirelessly in judgment, cellphone in hand, calling in favours, using connections. He affected exaggerated politeness to Watchers, not hesitating to rebuke us when, to his mind, we got out of line. Even some Palestinians admitted that he made the checkpoint work 'better'.

O was the quintessential Israeli, forceful and arrogant, a wheeler-dealer. Regardless of personal motivation and flamboyant style, he wanted 'his' checkpoint to work more smoothly with fewer crowds, fewer detainees and fewer violent incidents. He revelled in his power, often clashing with the checkpoint commander of the day, a young cock of the roost favouring a hard-line policy. O finally left Qalandiya under something of a cloud, rumoured to have accepted favours from transitees in exchange for passage. He subsequently surfaced again as a DCL officer at Huwwara checkpoint, with less panache than in his glory days, but still a force to be reckoned with. His story serves to highlight the anarchy that prevails at all checkpoints, enabling his individualistic leadership to be indulged. Had O terrorized transitees, or Watchers, the same indulgence would have prevailed, as it has in so many other cases.

In meetings with senior echelon officers, Watchers are told that although the former are personally committed to the protection of human rights they have 'no control' [sic] over their troops in the field. The truth is that the political climate in Israel is such that military brutality and licence are largely tolerated with impunity both by the army command and by the public at large (B'Tselem 2001, 2002a, 2002b, 2002e, Human Rights Watch 2005).

This brief introduction to the military is but one side of the checkpoint picture. How do these obstacles impinge on Palestinian life?

An 'invisible' people

The restrictions of the permit system reported in Chapter 1 explain not only the disappearance of thousands of Palestinians, once the primary source of cheap, manual labour, from the Israeli scene, but also their apparent absence within the West Bank itself. At the beginning of the El Aqsa intifada in September 2000, Palestinian villages were besieged by the army through the simple expedients of earthworks and concrete blocks closing off all access roads, staffed checkpoints at strategic points, and roving checkpoints on highways and byways. Thus, day labourers, making their way 'illegally' into Israel, must traverse these and other obstacles even before their day's work begins. Often the trip takes several hours, beginning at dawn, repeated again at dusk, on foot and by means of a succession of the *servis* taxis that have replaced most public transportation, paralysed by the ban on Palestinian travel on Israeli roads. The circuitous routes mean increased fares that eat up a substantial part of a day's wage. The taxis can ply their trade only on very limited stretches of road, so that Palestinian movement is virtually at a standstill, as the following report shows:

15 December 2002
Watchers: Maya R, Lauren E, Chaya O
    Arriving at Etzion checkpoint at approx. 7.15, we were soon to

witness one of the Occupation's latest innovations, intended to circumscribe Palestinians' movement even further: as of last week, several dozen Palestinian (green-and-white) plated buses and mini-buses from the Hebron district are back on the road, but of course under infinite restrictions: drivers must hold permits from the Civil Administration (month-long permit); vehicles are not allowed to depart from Hebron (regardless of whether or not the town is under curfew), but rather from the roadblocks near Halhul; buses are not allowed to enter any Palestinian town or village; buses and passengers are subjected to lengthy checks at Etzion junction (about halfway from Halhul to Bethlehem) as a consequence of which the journey will be cut even shorter. (Maya Rosenfeld, sociologist, Jerusalem)

From June 2001 to September 2003, Dr Maya Rosenfeld and her team, Dr Lauren Erdreich and Chaya Ofek, documented Palestinian absence in the southern West Bank, where some 29 per cent of all West Bankers live. Maya and Lauren are both Arabic-speakers, enabling them to make personal contacts with the few people encountered on the roads and at checkpoints, as well as with teachers and pupils at the El Khader School near Bethlehem.[20] The reports trace the gradual disappearance of the Palestinians as the permit system intensified and the checkpoints increased in number and size.

A favourite game of soldiers is to take IDs for checking, a process that should last only minutes, and then disappear leaving the detainees to wait until it pleases their tormentors to return the documents, or not. In many cases, the IDs simply vanish. The holder must pay a considerable fee to the Palestinian Authority for its replacement. Yet, without the ID s/he cannot leave home to apply for his/her mobility permit and will risk imprisonment by the Israeli authorities if caught (CheckpointWatch/Physicians for Human Rights 2004).

Yet another popular prank/punishment is the hounding of *servis*-taxi drivers who throng major checkpoints waiting for passengers. This persecution includes expropriating IDs and/or licences, impound-ing vehicles or keys for longer or shorter periods, breaking windows, shooting tyres, detention and beating of drivers for arbitrarily defined misdemeanours (*Human Rights News*, 2001). At Abu Dis near Jerusalem (December 2002), I encountered drivers obliged to police their own passengers and to pay a penalty for transporting passengers without permits.

Many of the taxi drivers and labourers trying to reach Jerusalem or other destinations are middle-aged men, enjoying respect and standing in their own community and family. The circuitous routes, the need to sneak and creep, to beg for work or peddle goods to survive, the threat of capture, the detention in front of family or passers-by, are deeply demeaning – a metamorphosis from respectable working man to hunted criminal.

Etzion, 20 July 2003
Watchers: Maya R, Lauren E, Haya O

At 8 a.m. the sun is already high in the sky and there is not a single shady spot ... Suddenly, ten of the labourers – some who had just retrieved their IDs, others with IDs still confiscated – make a move and start walking in the direction of the forest. A soldier immediately chases them with drawn weapon. We chase the soldier. The aborted mini-rebellion collapses into a heated verbal exchange. A soldier screams: 'Are you out of your minds?' One labourer shouts back (in Hebrew): 'I want you to know that I was prepared to continue walking, knowing that you may shoot me in the head. You should be ashamed of yourself!' Another joins: 'This is your government's deliberate plan to drive us all crazy.' And a third one adds: 'We are heading to Bethlehem, not Jerusalem; we don't want Jerusalem, the hell with Jerusalem.' The soldier finally retreats. (Maya Rosenfeld)

Bethlehem, 9 September 2001
Watchers: Maya R, Lauren E, Adi K, Chaya O

We were in the wadi between 7 and 8 a.m. in the company of labourers who already know us well and even wait for us to appear. In one of the 'pockets', dozens of men were huddled surrounded by three soldiers. A discussion ensues. The workers, some of whom had left home at 4: 30 a.m. ... had not lost their sense of humour and tried their luck with the soldiers. One said: 'Soldier, you probably didn't sleep all night did you?' The soldier concurred ... 'So get some sleep now ... it's better you should sleep.' And another phenomenon from the wadi experience: the moment the soldiers start the chase, the wadi is filled with the voices and echoes of voices of the labourers. Some imitate sheep, others crows, some whistle while others 'Indian call'. [Yet] the tension and despair gnaw at them. The almost daily cat-and-mouse with soldiers forces them to return home, often without having managed to earn a penny, at the same time having paid the costs of the long journey to the checkpoint. (Maya Rosenfeld)

Watchers: Maya R, Lauren E, Chaya O

Arriving at the Etzion checkpoint at 7.25, we were immediately confronted with the complete absence of Palestinians: no buses, no passengers, no detainees behind the fence, only soldiers at their posts. Shortly after, a group numbering approx. ten men, all in their thirties and forties, approached the checkpoint compound. Recognizing us from a distance ... they waved and called out our names. They then recounted their story: all the men, except for one, are residents of a village 4–5 km south of the checkpoint, who, despite unimaginable difficulties, managed to stick to jobs in West Jerusalem. Some return home only once or twice a week, and spend other week nights in rented [rooms]. Others make the risky journey to Jerusalem on a daily basis. Today they left [home] at 4 a.m., walked several kilometres, then managed to find a ride through side roads ... they were stopped by soldiers and forced to return. However, in the near absence of cabs, the way back proved to be extremely difficult. Now they still faced the journey from Etzion to their village, short in terms of absolute distance, but exhausting with no transportation in sight. (Maya Rosenfeld)

The paralysis of civilian life has of course huge implications for the economy and structure of Palestinian society. Nor are allowances made for children. El Khader School, including primary, secondary, boys' and girls' wings, is located on a rise at the entrance to the township of El Khader, west of Bethlehem. Since September 2000, a checkpoint has been erected beneath the school walls. The principal has been compelled by the army to seal off the windows on the south (checkpoint) side of the building in order, allegedly, to deter stone-throwers and prevent observation of military movement. Pupils must often make their way to their classes at gunpoint; tear-gas and other forms of harassment are frequent. The visits of Watchers seem to have been something of a high point for the beleaguered staff, a chance at least to air their difficulties, if not to receive redress.

Southern Checkpoints, 9 March 2003

Watchers: Maya R, Chaya O, Lauren E

All at the teachers' room [at El Khader School] seem to eagerly anticipate our visits these days. The issue at stake today was the shutting down by the military of the elementary boys' and girls' school on Monday last week (March 3rd). At about 8 in the morning, shortly

The gateway to hell

after school day began, an officer arrived at the school compound. The supervisor [from the Palestinian Ministry of Education], who speaks good Hebrew, welcomed him ... only to be ordered to evacuate the school in ten minutes. The pretext: a stone that was supposedly thrown at soldiers by children shortly beforehand. The supervisor and other staff members tried their best to persuade the officer that this was an illogical measure, but the officer went on saying that he wants this to be perceived as a collective punishment. 'You are not in a position to argue or debate a matter which is within my, and solely my, capacity and control.' Nonetheless, he noticed how frightened the children were ... and asked the supervisor to calm them saying, 'They will not be harmed.' 'How can I calm the little girls', replied the supervisor, 'when I myself am terrified of what you are doing?' (Maya Rosenfeld)

Israelis speak passionately about the fear generated by the terror attacks, the sense that there is no safe place. Even in the brief excerpts quoted here, one can see how pervasive fear is for Palestinians, subject to systematic and constant state terror, a fear compounded by economic hardship.

Due to the siege of Palestinian villages and towns and frequent closures, there is considerable malnutrition, especially among children. Unemployment is assessed at higher than 50 per cent, while over 60 per cent of West Bankers live below the poverty level of US$2 per day (Dugard 2005; OCHA 2005). Physical and verbal abuse by soldiers and/or border police can fall to the lot of almost any Palestinian. However, the 'illegal' labourers, arriving from afar on the off-chance of finding work, are a vulnerable target for kicks, blows and curses, even death. In spite of this they bear the manhunts and humiliation stoically. *Tzummud* (lit. clinging to and relentless attachment to the land, the determination to survive, to keep bread on the table) is a powerful incentive to continue trying to get to work against all odds. Like the clerks, the medical personal, the students and the teachers, the persistence of the labourers is in itself an act of resistance to the Occupation.

Even if a soldier is allotted to every labourer, a warrior to every clerk, an officer to every teacher and a Border Policeman to every sick person, if a jeep pursues every student, an APC blocks the path of every farmer, and an obstacle course of barricades is erected at the entrance to every educational institution – and this is not far off the reality of the current situation – as long as the Palestinians continue living in their land, the obligation of *tzummud* continues. (Rosenfeld 2003–04)

The banality of evil

[The means of controlling] the Palestinian population is to FORBID everything. Palestinians are not allowed to exist. Since this is an impossible situation, Palestinians [cannot help but] constantly trespass every rule. (Nina Mayorek, 8 June 2002)

For all Palestinians, regardless of class or rank, every aspect of the checkpoint is a collective punishment, an accumulation of stress, humiliation and real physical suffering. You leave home in the morning for work, errands, school, family visits, and within a short time you are scrambling over barriers, playing hide and seek with the armed forces in fields, and arrive at the checkpoint hot, dirty and clutching your ID card. Will the masters of your fate smile and wave you through? Will they add injury to insult by name-calling, beatings, tear-gas, shots? Will the checkpoint suddenly close for no apparent reason, leaving you stranded on the wrong side, even overnight perhaps? You never know what will trigger which response, and yet there is no choice but to pass through this gauntlet of hostility and contempt to in order reach your goal. Your time, your space, your life are no longer yours to call your own. You yourself have become a suspicious object.

In the heart of the West Bank between villages relying on access to the nearby Palestinian city of Nablus for services, there is a whole slew of checkpoints. Nablus is the site of the biblical city of Schem. Both because of its religious associations and for the political purpose of 'Judaizing' the area, many Israeli settlements have been established there, among them some of the most ideological and radical (Eldar and Zartel 2004). Like most Palestinian towns and villages in the West Bank, present-day Nablus predates modern Israeli settlement.

Dr Ilana Hammerman, a frequent guest on our shifts, has written this elegy to the cruel daily grind of checkpoint experience. Her account subverts the Israeli claim of historical right to the land as justifying all iniquity.

On the edge of Route 60 ... is a large signboard commemorating those who fell in defence of 'The Land of Schem' and alongside it a quotation, 'Open my Eyes that I may See the Wonders of Your Torah' (Psalm 119:18) ... yet any one of those few who read the sign correctly and who respond by opening their eyes in the fullest sense will look and see the iniquity – whether to God or towards their own common sense – that has covered that land and its environs with the concrete checkpoints, earthworks, ditches and improvised structures. Here, little bands of soldiers wander around sweating in their helmets, like strange mushrooms under the brownish-green nets that cover them and camouflage them from goodness knows who. If you want then to join those few, you will see that at that crossroads a sign points you in the direction of Itamar and Elon Moreh [settlements]. Go a few miles up a smooth road beyond the road leading to Itamar and before long you will see an Arab [sic] village, Beit Furiq, not signposted in any way. To your left, in the heart of a desolate stretch of land, you will see concrete cubes, an Israeli flag on a small rocky hilltop and on either side cars and hundreds of people desiring ... to go from Beit Furiq to Nablus/Schem or vice-versa. After many minutes during which you will not see any movement in the empty zone that separates each group, perhaps a solider will pop up and gesture with his hand to someone or to a car to approach for checking. One by one, very slowly, one from this side, one from that side. It is the misfortune of Beit Furiq that the road from there to Nablus intersects with the road leading to Itamar and Elon Moreh. Residents cannot therefore come and go from their village without getting stuck at this out-of-the-way checkpoint for untold periods of time. With them too are trapped the residents of other nearby villages [Sa'alim, Dir el Hatab and Azamut] that from here look deserted, bordered at either end by uneven dirt tracks, only metres from the fine asphalt road that serves the settlements. And if you have already decided to look, perhaps you would also like to listen to some of what is said at one of these checkpoints in the Land of Schem. For instance, at nearby Huwwara:

'You, what do you want in Amman?' scolds a skinny soldier, his very young face streaming with sweat, to a plump man with a large suitcase. 'What's wrong with Schem?' And to a woman holding a large bag: 'Tell me, what have you got here, you?' and he draws from her bag a small plastic object of uncertain purpose, waving it around for all to see, just a joke. He laughs and sticks it back in the bag. With that, the security check is over. 'Git off', he hurries the woman who has frozen for a moment. Then he waves a finger in the face of someone who seems to have got into an argument with him, 'Don't bug me, d'you hear?' He doesn't see a few people sneaking by from the side. Suddenly he does notice the infiltrators, who in the meantime have become shadows in the distance, brings some of them back and closes the checkpoint as a punishment ... Till the checkpoint opens again, even if only to alleviate boredom, look down at what seemed until now to be a solid cube and you'll discover that it's a tiny hollow space formed by concrete slabs and in it a young man is crouching, barred from crossing but not sent back and, instead, detained. All this time he has been packed into this space too small to hold him, hidden from your eyes ...

These are just a few of the things that I saw one Saturday in the month of August 2003. No abuse, and no atrocities but the routine of military and police activity so that anyone coming here, just 40 minutes' ride from Jerusalem, will find themselves more concerned for their security than they were before. Maybe there are no explosive belts here but the disruption of the lives of tens of thousands of people, day in day out, creates a whole stockpile of explosives. 'Open my eyes that I may see the wonders ...'

The following reports reflect the tensions found at these internal checkpoints:

Beit Iba and Saara, 21 January 2004
Watchers: Orit B, Michal P, Edna K, Ada R, Anat G, Shira Kh, Dafna B

Summary: Tzara is now closed to people coming to and from Nablus; only those from the immediate neighbourhood may pass. Anyone unaware of the new permanent order will be sent on foot (there are no taxis) to Beit Iba, some 15 km away.

Beit Iba: There is now a metal detector for those approaching from Nablus. People pass one by one; bags are not checked ... close to one thousand people stood there in an appalling crush, in a narrow enclosure awaiting their turn. There is no way of speeding things up, and people stood there for between four and six hours. It was impossible to see beyond the first rows of transitees, and humanitarian cases were stuck without any possibility of passing through the dense mass of people or being able to ask the soldiers to be allowed to pass.

A woman with labour pains, an amputee, a blind man, old women, and women with children all stood for hours swallowed up among the crowd. Nor could the soldiers be aware of cases in need of assistance.

Detainees – including women and children – were held for several hours, some since the morning. One woman and her family were still there when we left at nightfall. Later we learnt that she at least had been released but we couldn't make contact with the father. Horrendous!!! (Dafna Banai, Welsh-born tour consultant, Tel-Aviv)

For one of the observers in that same shift, this was her first encounter with checkpoints:

A man ... tells us that the checkpoints 'breed 1,000 martyrs'.[21] At that moment a father with his son, aged about six or seven, pass. Understandably, the boy is panicked by the screaming soldiers with their weapons; he ... breaks away from his father running back into the dense crowd of waiting people. The soldiers yell: 'Bring back the kid, where is he?' One of them dives into the crowd with his weapon and shortly emerges with the quietly crying child. It's not clear if he was struck by the soldier or not. The father points to a red patch on the child's head, but refuses to speak and passes quickly. It's clear the child cannot contain his rage, shame and pain. From sheer fear he's wet his pants and must face the world with stained trousers. That child is an example of the raw material of terrorism fashioned by the checkpoints. No drama of life and death, just the banality of evil, endless humiliation and almighty fear. (Ada Ravon, attorney, Tel-Aviv)

§

Holidays and religious festivals are times of particular stress since, despite the closures that accompany all festivals, at these times many people try to reach the numerous holy sites in and around Jerusalem, particularly the great mosque of El Aqsa. Paradoxically, easing of mobility restrictions is always declared by the military on such occasions; it is usually not felt on the ground.

It was the first Friday in Ramadan.[22] On our way to the checkpoint, we heard reports that in honour of the festival the authorities were going to ease the restrictions imposed on the movement of Palestinians. We were hopeful that this would be so, and anticipated a lively flow of traffic.

On reaching the checkpoint, we discovered that these promises were false. The place was swarming with policemen, volunteer police, Border Police and army reservists. They surrounded the area and blocked every possible access route. At the checkpoint itself, several dozen people were already waiting, mainly elderly country folk in traditional dress. They had made the long trek in order to attend the special Ramadan prayers in Jerusalem. Now, to their dismay, they were told by the military that the way was barred. However, the would-be worshippers did not give up and continued to wait in impressive, stubborn silence behind the metal barriers that blocked their route. It was clear that they were not going to budge. The soldiers were becoming increasingly tense. The silence of the crowd may have been impressive but it was also threatening; it was clear that their patience would soon give out. One soldier confided that he couldn't remove his sunglasses because he could not bear to look the waiting women and men in the eye. We, for our part, pleaded with the men to contact someone of higher rank and demand that the crowd be allowed to pass before it was too late.

After a seemingly endless wait, without apparent coordination or warning, the crowd simply moved across the barrier. As one body, they began to march towards the soldiers who blocked their way to the main road and transportation. One soldier fired in the air, while others simply stood there ... helpless. To their credit, the soldiers, mostly ... reservists correctly gauged the ... situation and tried to prevent it deteriorating into mayhem.

The crowd, whose numbers had now swelled to over a hundred, formed a line across the width of the road. Opposite them, the soldiers too formed a line, trying to close ranks, but finding themselves pushed ever backwards. Once again, in a single wave, the crowd simply strode past the soldiers and resolutely marched onwards. The police, to our surprise, rolled back the barriers, and the crowd passed on towards Jerusalem and the great mosques.

It is hard to describe the power of that moment. We Watchers who have witnessed the daily humiliation and abuse, the despair and impotence of Palestinians at checkpoints could only stand in wonder at this display of courage and non-violent resistance. We avoided the eyes of the humiliated and embarrassed soldiers, not only because of being trounced by the 'enemy', but because of the system that had placed them in that impossible position. Who knows – hopefully, some 'refuseniks' were born that day.

However, that is not the end of the story. At the checkpoint itself, yet another group of would-be worshippers had gathered and their way too was blocked by the military. After a short wait, they too crossed the barrier and marched towards the soldiers. Only this time the army was prepared and behind the soldiers was a row of jeeps, nose to tail, blocking the width of the road. The increased tension and violence in the air were palpable. One false move by either side and bloodshed would surely ensue. Just then, an officer with the rank of colonel arrived on the scene, presumably the reservists' commander. We begged him to try and bring about a change in the orders and to let the worshippers through. He called his superiors and after a short, nerve-wracking wait, the redeeming order to permit passage to adults over 40 was handed down. (Yehudit Oppenheimer, Director of the Kol Ha-Isha Women's Centre, Jerusalem, personal communication, November 2001)

Unfortunately, that must have been a rare moment of grace. I myself witnessed what happened on the following Friday at the same checkpoint. The military once again closed the barriers and, once again, the place swarmed with men and matériel. While a crowd of Palestinian pilgrims was kept waiting for over two hours, a busload of Jewish worshippers appeared headed for prayers at Rachel's Tomb just one half-mile across the checkpoint on the Palestinian side. The barriers were pulled back. The crowd of Palestinians parted, like the waters of the Red Sea, and the bus was tenderly escorted through by an armed jeep and a posse of soldiers. The inviolable right of the oppressor to worship in the heart of the territory of the oppressed. The barriers closed again behind the bus. The Palestinian worshippers remained trapped on the wrong side. In our checkpoint observations we have witnessed many instances of cruelty and brutality, but that moment of unabashed discrimination was an outrage in a class of its own.

Days of violence

6 August 2002
Watchers: Nora O, Adi D, Roni H, Aya K

One of the Palestinian drivers says: 'Look at the soldiers.' 'Where?' 'There.'

He points again, and there, in front of us, 50 metres up the road, children around 7 to 10-years-old were throwing stones at a few soldiers (crouching probably because of the stones). Suddenly they rose with pointed guns and started shooting live ammunition at the fleeing children while chasing them ... The soldiers turned back to the checkpoint, one of them clearly wounded [by a stone], holding his face ... [he] didn't seem to need any help. Then there was more shooting ... None of us could see what caused this ... right away the checkpoint was closed, a lot of soldiers had gathered, the big guys too of course ... When a soldier is hurt, they close the checkpoint, it's the 'procedure' ... [one] soldier points his gun towards the quiet crowd of the waiting Palestinians. 'Move back or I'll shoot!' he says ... The waiting queue of cars and pedestrians was getting longer ... Then an

APC (which looks like a juvenile tank) appeared, and roared down the street towards the place where it all began, outside the refugee camp, a jeep in its wake. On approach, the driver began shooting ahead of himself ... Soldiers jumped out, crouching and bouncing in ... combat positions. Then they started shooting all around; it seemed like for ever. Other than the shrill piercing sound of bullets, the other 'disturbance' was of a terrified flock of birds which burst out of one of the roofs ... The APC moved to its right, which wasn't its natural course, and [deliberately] crushed a parked car. Then it returned 'home' ... When [they try] to arrest a random kid we interfere: 'It wasn't him.' 'It doesn't matter,' answered the soldier. 'They all throw stones.' But he allowed the child to go.

His answer is a paradigm: one child throws stones, the other will be caught, and pay the price ... they are all the same ... all guilty a priori ... someone has to pay ... so why not he who is guilty by definition, he who is Palestinian.

While all the shooting occurred, some Palestinians stepped out of their cars and watched; they weren't afraid, or surprised ... they watched with detached curiosity, most wouldn't leave their place in the queue. In the midst of the mad, irresponsible shooting they cannot allow themselves to miss their place in line. This event didn't just happen, it was created – the soldiers created it. (Aya Kaniuk)

Qalandiya, 31 May 2002
No movement south ... only few people and few cars allowed north ... the checkpoint looked nearly deserted when we arrived ... We were told that the night before there was shooting and tear-gas and about 150 people, men, women, and children, were held in the checkpoint area all night ... it was not allowed to bring them food ... As we were talking, we heard shouts and screams and sounds of beating ... A young man was held there and something was happening between him and the soldiers ... We saw them beat him and heard shooting ... We started screaming at them to stop ... It went on and on for about half an hour until a military ambulance came [to take him to hospital]. (Yehudit Oppenheimer)

A major problem at all checkpoints is the lack of access for ambulances and the plight of medical cases in general. According to protocol, medical emergencies are to be allowed passage, with the benefit of the doubt given to the patient. However, this relates to emergencies, defined at the discretion of the checkpoint commander, usually a conscript with the rank of sergeant or staff sergeant, hardly a qualified source (Physicians for Human Rights 2003; Physicians for Human Rights 2004; Palestinian Red Crescent Society 2005). In practice, ambulances are invariably delayed for a security search and, worse, are often forced to wait until the soldiers condescend to check them at all. Because of the crowding, chaos and upheaval at many checkpoints, ambulances cannot simply drive up unhindered. Even where an ambulance lane exists (such as at Qalandiya), it is not always open. For people on foot going for treatment or surgery the situation is no better. They must produce not only a permit but also a letter of referral/invitation from their doctor/hospital. As this may well be in Arabic, soldiers frequently will ignore or reject these documents – claiming that they, like IDs, are easily forged. Aya Kaniuk reporting from Huwarra (1 March 2003) writes:

The soldiers told us for instance that they absolutely agree with us that the regulations (like forbidding people from visiting relatives, or passing for anything other than medical reasons) is not because of security but for the plain purpose of making Palestinians' lives miserable. The rationale being that this way they who are 'crushed' will put pressure on the 'bad guys' (i.e. terrorists or radicals). The soldiers also made overtly blasphemous and sexual remarks loudly enough for the Palestinians to hear such as: 'this Palestinian whore [while pointing at a young girl] prefers you [meaning a particular soldier], no, you' (referring to another), or referring to a particular child as a 'prostitute patient', i.e. everybody's sick child for presentation at checkpoints.

Qalandiya, 10 December 2003
Watchers: Aya K, Ivonne M, Ilana H
This was a sick man ... who was shot in the neck a year ago. Maybe an hour earlier he was standing in line with his sister and a few children waiting his turn to cross the checkpoint. He came up to the soldiers, telling them that he was sick and that he wanted to be allowed to pass. The soldiers, besides refusing his request, ordered him to the end of the line. A row erupted of which there are a few versions. The soldiers say the sick man began the fight with a *caffa* (I think a shove, or that his hand touched the soldier's body); he was dragged to the *budke* [small sentry-post], probably beaten – suddenly lost his consciousness, fell, and remained unconscious. The sister ... started screaming ... Due to her screams, which the soldiers called a 'disruption', they closed the checkpoint to pedestrians. They ... didn't

seem concerned, insisting that the fellow struck a soldier first, as if this in some way nullifies the fact he might be dying ... [Finally, a Palestinian ambulance was called and permitted to take the man to a checkpoint nearer Jerusalem, where an Israeli ambulance took him to hospital][23] ... It seems that if you happen to be dying, or giving birth, or just plain sick between A-Ram and Qalandiya, you are doomed.[24] (Aya Kaniuk)

Although the incidents described in this section are often regarded by the military as operational and solders are therefore not called to account, the report below describes one case where the perpetrators were actually punished, thanks to the testimony of Watchers.

Beit Iba, 19 February 2004
Watchers: Menucha M, Dafna B, Vera R., Hannah
Some two hundred people were lined up at the checkpoint but barred from crossing. A table was strategically placed to indicate the point at which people were supposed to stand and wait. People began to advance and a soldier yelled at them to move back, but no one did. After a few minutes the soldier pushed people back, yelling all the while. Among the first transitees was a doctor whom the soldier not only pushed but also struck and threw to the ground. The doctor got up immediately, an older man who tried to separate them was also pushed aside ... We put in a call to the IDF spokesman but this was frustrating since all he had to say was that there were alerts, as if the connection between alerts and violence was inevitable. After intervention by some other soldiers, including a junior commander, the ... situation calmed down. However, the doctor was taken aside and his ID taken from him. As if this was not enough, the officer began to scream at him 'No one hits my soldiers!' The checkpoint is a topsy-turvy world where black is white and day is night. Shortly after this women were allowed to pass with hardly any check. Men were separated by age, with all the older ones being checked on the road and passing there. The rest, mostly students, were left standing there for ages on the grounds that on Thursdays students couldn't leave Nablus.[25]
At around 16.00 the doctor's papers were returned to him, despite the objection of the soldier who struck him. We met him again as we were leaving, returning from whence he came. He told us that a military jeep had stopped him and taken his papers, ordering him to pick them up at the checkpoint. The doctor had gone on a little

way when another jeep drove up and the soldier who had attacked
him jumped out, rushed him, butting him on the head with his own
helmeted head, before returning his ID. The doctor bled profusely
from the wound on his forehead. The soldier's helmet (with his
name) was concealed under a camouflage hood. No other soldier was
so equipped. We saw to it that an ambulance was called, the attacker
hovering near us all the while. The doctor was taken to a caravan
where the owner of a local quarry lived after being evicted from his
home in order for it to be used as an army base.[26] The medic wanted
the attacking soldier to accompany him when he treated the injured
man; however, we managed to prevent this. We were told that the
battalion commander was on his way but after a long wait the injured
man, his forehead swollen, decided to go home ... A few days later
we learnt that the soldier and his commander were charged and
sentenced, respectively, to 35 and 21 days' imprisonment. (Menucha
Moravitz, sociologist, Tel-Aviv)

Violence is endemic at checkpoints, never far from the surface of
routine, inevitable in the encounter between military and civilian. These
encounters take a variety of forms:

Qalandiya, 16 July 2003
Watchers: Ivonne M, Maya B-H, Tammi B, Aya K
... We heard two shots coming from the usual place between the
fence and Qalandiya [the eponymous refugee camp]. Then we saw
two soldiers: one, Rafi, ready to shoot, his gun pointed directly at
a crowd. He was kneeling, his gun placed on a triangular support,
his eye glued to [the sights], and his finger on the trigger ready to
shoot. Behind him another soldier the [notorious] Nadav ... We ran,
shouting 'Don't shoot!' and when it didn't seem to affect them, *we
used more direct means* [emphasis in the original], for which some of
us are now charged for attacking soldiers and disturbing them in the
performance of their duty – their duty being shooting children. They
plainly admitted to the fact they were going to identify the child who
presumably held or threw ... a Molotov cocktail (we saw no sign of it,
no glass, no smoke, nothing) and shoot him with live ammunition ...
'in cold blood'. The distance between the parties was great and nothing thrown would ever have reached the soldiers, who told us that
had we been Palestinians they would have shot us too. However, we
stopped them. (Ivonne Mansbach)

The women were arrested and taken to a local police station to be charged. The 'more direct means'? Standing between the soldiers and their youthful targets.

Yet another aspect of checkpoint violence involves settlers,[27] who, especially in the more isolated and politicized settlements of the West Bank, see themselves both as an arm of the military and as abandoned by it, thus needing to take their security into their own hands. Apart from the daily harassment of Palestinians in the divided city of Hebron where 400 Israeli residents hold 130,000 Palestinians virtually hostage, settlers conduct rampages through Palestinian villages disrupting farming, in particular the harvesting of olive crops (Eldar and Zartel 2004).[28] These pogroms are often conducted under the eyes of the military and are largely treated with indifference by the authorities (B'Tselem 2002a, 2002b). Watchers too have suffered attacks (MaschomWatch 2005: 67).

Jatt Crossroads, 6 May 2004
Watchers: Anat S, Michal B, Menucha M
There were a number of detainees who told us they had already crossed two checkpoints safely and only now had their IDs been taken for checking ... A military jeep arrived with a very hostile officer, perhaps with a personal involvement since he kept referring to the recent terror attack in Haifa ... He warned that there was a [high] alert and because of this, precautions were being tightened. Soon after he left, a private car drew up and two women got out ... carrying an orange-brown flag with a black Star of David. With curses and insults they fell upon Anat. Shortly afterwards Daniella Weiss[29] arrived together with some men. The women were also physically violent towards us. Meanwhile, our driver Na'adim arrived and parked his taxi near me. The [settlers] ran towards the car ... they hit Na'adim in the face and tried to drag him out of the car. At this stage one of the soldiers intervened and managed to separate them but ... [the settlers] blocked our path to Beit Iba ... [Later] we noted that Weiss was following us in her car. (Menucha Moravitz)

Four years of observation have not staled or withered the Watchers' capacity to be shocked by what they see and hear, and it is this that makes their reports so compelling. Through these testimonies the reader will have encountered a range of West Bank checkpoints, as well as those monitoring access to Israel, seeing the routine of humiliation, brutality and the anguish that prevails there. S/he will have begun to

Three

understand that for the Palestinians, checkpoints are not merely a logistic obstacle but rather a paralysis of the autonomous life, fraught with the potential for violence. We now continue our tour of Checkpoint Palestine along the Annexation Wall where the routine and the violent meet, again with equally disastrous effect.

Notes

1 Abu Dis on the edge of Jerusalem is separated from its neighbours El Azariyeh and Ras al Amud by a concrete wall, part of the Annexation Wall around Jerusalem (see Chapter 4). During 2002, Watchers reported that border policemen guarding the tiny, highly unstable, unofficial passage in the Wall, poured oil on it to make transit even more difficult for local residents.

2 As of 2005, some rudimentary toilet facilities are provided at permanent checkpoints monitoring access to Israel. Their maintenance is delegated to a Palestinian contractor.

3 For want of a better term, a transitee is anyone attempting to pass a checkpoint.

4 Watcher Adi Dagan actually witnessed the shooting of young Omar Musa Matar on Friday, 28 March 2003 (see CPW report for that date and Dagan's letter to *Ha'aretz*, 'Eyewitnesses', 10 May 2003).

5 For instance, Abed Rahman al-Ahmar, a well-known Palestinian human rights activist, who had been held in administrative detention by the Israeli authorities several times in the past, was again placed in administrative detention for six months in November 2001 by a military court and released only in late 2003. No charges were brought against him. He was adopted as a Prisoner of Conscience by Amnesty International in 2001.

6 Huge numbers of Palestinians are arbitrarily arrested, held until the end of procedures or placed under administrative arrest. Many are subsequently released with no charges being brought <www.btselem.org/english/statistics/Detainees_and_Prisoners.asp> accessed 26 March 2005.

7 From the beginning of the intifada, on 29 September 2000, until 31 December 2004, 3,101 Palestinians have been killed in the Occupied Territories, among them 614 minors (under the age of eighteen). At least 1,684 of those killed were not participating in fighting at the time. Thousands more have been wounded. <www.btselem.org/English/Firearms/Index.asp> accessed 26 March 2005.

8 Taxis serving up to ten passengers at one time, replacing public transportation in the West Bank.

9 'Occupied Territories' is also a loaded term; on a recent speaking tour in the USA, Jewish communities insisted that I speak only of 'disputed' territories. I did not comply.

10 In July 2002 the Israeli Air Force dropped a one-ton bomb on a residential complex in order to kill Hamas leader Salah Shehadeh, killing thirteen civilians.

86

11 In some places Jewish cars are waved through, Palestinians directed to a separate line for checking. This, on the authority of the duty guards. Some claim 'my eyes/heart tell me' [who is an Arab, who a Jew].

12 Rivlin is responding to criticism of the army by Israeli-Palestinian members of the Knesset (*Ha'aretz*, 6 June 2004).

13 Ultra-Orthodox Jewish men are largely exempt, as are Israeli-Palestinians, though for different reasons. Other minorities, such as the Druze, do national service and many in that community have made the army their career. There is also a small professional standing army.

14 The army is not the only security force at the checkpoints. The BP play a significant role, especially at access points to Jerusalem and the Seam Area. A separate regiment, established in the 1950s to patrol the borders for infiltrators – Palestinians bent on mayhem, or simply trying to return to their lost homes – the BP have a reputation for brutality, borne out by many of CPW's observations. Regarded as a blue-collar regiment, their terms of service are often inferior to those of more elite units (Sasson-Levi 2003b). The civil or blue police may also be present in the vicinity of checkpoints, as stated above, to settle scores, administrative and criminal, with transitees. General Security Service (GSS) operatives are also to be found, supposedly, but not invariably, incognito sussing out suspects and potential informers. Tensions and power struggles between the different security forces are also outside the subject of this book. Only some 25 per cent of soldiers serve at checkpoints. Navy and air force conscripts and reservists do not do checkpoint duty.

15 There is a growing movement of conscientious objection within Israel both among conscripts and reservists (Kidron 2003). Of late there has also been a refusal movement in the Druze community, traditionally a mainstay of Israel's regular army (Ada Ushpiz, *Ha'aretz*, 9 March 2003).

16 Israel's animal-rights organization; the speaker equates Palestinians with animals.

17 There is an active refusal movement among reservists, dating back to the time of the Lebanon war (1982–2000) and they are represented by the veteran organization Yesh Gvul – a play on words for 'there is a border/there is a limit'. Another group of combat soldiers, the Courage to Refuse (2002), also refuses to serve in the territories, while twenty-seven air force pilots, a very elite grouping, have declared refusal to bomb civilian population centres. Reserve refusal, as that of conscripts, may incur prison sentences. The defence establishment does not recognize conscientious objection.

18 By Michael Gal a former CEO of the Jerusalem Municipality; and two reserve officers, Hagai Agmon and Ron Schatzberg.

19 One notable volunteer was the then-Attorney General, Elyakim Rubenstein. In a subsequent meeting with CPW he praised the army for its humanitarian stance, despite 'glitches' that he claimed to address in a report to the senior echelons. However, the report was not published, nor did he address issues raised by CPW.

20 The team's weekly reports which, since mid-2002 onwards, combine

background information on the escalation of the conflict using material from the Arabic press and media, are available at <MachsomWatch@yahoogroups. com>.

21 Lit. Shahidimc (lit. witnesses)– martyrs, including suicide bombers.

22 Ramadan, the holy month of fasting in the Islamic calendar. Lasting from sunrise to sunset, it is a movable occasion and thus may occur during the short winter days, or the long summer ones. Traditionally, Fridays in Ramadan are especially significant and many worshippers head for prayer in the major mosques. Those living in Jerusalem, the third most holy site of Islam, were considered fortunate in being able to pray at the great Mosque El-Aqsa and at other holy sites on the contested Haram-es-Sharif ('the noble sanctuary'), which is also the Temple Mount, former site of the Jewish Temple. In happier times, thousands of Palestinians from all over the West Bank converged on Jerusalem to worship. In recent years, and particularly since the start of the El Aqsa intifada in 2000, entrance to the area has been restricted by the Israeli authorities to children under thirteen and to adults over forty, or forty-five, or fifty according to the order of the day. Similar scenes are reported every year.

23 West Bankers cannot access Israeli medical services unless they are civilians injured by Israeli citizens or the army, as per a military order dating from 2001.

24 A year later, in November 2003, CPWs were approached by the injured man, asking them to testify on his behalf in a complaint against the army.

25 Students are allowed to leave Nablus only on Saturdays and to return only on Wednesdays.

26 Palestinian homes may be taken over by the army and used as observation posts. The family is usually confined to one small room and frequently there is considerable damage to the property. No compensation is given (MaschomWatch 2005: 106).

27 Settlers/Israeli residents of the West Bank have an almost automatic right to bear arms. Settlements, all illegal under international law, have their own security personnel and armouries (Eldar and Zartel 2004).

28 Israeli NGOs Rabbis for Human Rights and Gush Shalom organize Israeli activists each year to help harvest the olive crops in order to protect Palestinian farmers threatened by settlers.

29 Weiss, a prominent settler leader, is notorious for violent activism against Palestinians.

4 | The Annexation Wall

The Court finds that the construction by Israel of a Wall in the Occupied Palestinian Territory and its associated régime are contrary to international law; it states the legal consequences arising from that illegality. (International Court of Justice, The Hague, 9 July 2004)

Rather than create the outlines of a two-state solution, this Wall will kill that idea for Palestinians, and drive them, over time, to demand instead a one-state solution – where they and the Jews would have equal rights in one state. And since by 2010 there will be more Palestinian Arabs than Jews living in Israel, the West Bank and Gaza combined, this transformation of the Palestinian cause will be very problematic for Israel. If American Jews think it's hard to defend Israel today on college campuses, imagine what it will be like when their kids have to argue against the principle of one man, one vote. (Friedman 2003)

As cruel, time- and space-consuming as the checkpoint system is for all West Bankers, it is even more oppressive for the 'People of the Wall'. That is, the 38 per cent of all Palestinians whose livelihoods, lands and lives are irreparably damaged by this obstacle where security–geography–demography dramatically collide.

In June 2002, the government of Israel decided to erect a physical barrier to separate Israel and the West Bank in order to prevent the uncontrolled entry of Palestinians into Israel. In most areas, the barrier is comprised of an electronic fence with dirt paths, barbed-wire fences, and trenches on both sides, at an average width of 60m. In some areas, a wall 6 to 8m high has been erected in place of the barrier system.

The Annexation Wall/Security Fence/Security Barrier/the Wall/ is the ultimate barrier that will, supposedly, protect Israelis against terrorists, while suffocating Palestinians trapped in its meshes, in enclaves that prevent access both to Israel and to the West Bank where their lives and services are found. The dimensions of the Wall, which does not follow the Green Line, and its routes, both actual and proposed, are more than adequately documented elsewhere (B'Tselem, 2003b, 2005; OCHA 2005) and subject to constant change. No compensation is given to the thousands of landowners whose fields are devastated, expropriated or rendered inaccessible, whose olive groves are uprooted and whose orchards are destroyed and daily lives disrupted by its presence. Israel claims that the Wall is a temporary measure, occasioned by the need for defence in wartime. The dimensions and the social, economic and ecological damage caused by the erection of the Wall make it well-nigh irreversible. To point to just one aspect of this damage, health care:

- 32.7 per cent of the West Bank villages will suffer from lack of access to health facilities, rising to 87 per cent in the enclaves [areas surrounded on all sides with no free access to either the West Bank or Israel]
- 10,000 chronic patients suffer from lack of access to essential health services.
- 117,600 pregnant women, of whom 17,640 are at high risk, may suffer from the lack of access
- 133,000 children under the age of five may not be able to get all the vaccinations necessary on time or at all
- 26 local clinics have already been cut off from the general Palestinian health system; upon completion of the Wall, the number of isolated clinics will rise to 71, out of over 500 local clinics throughout the West Bank
- 52 per cent of the doctors working in these clinics are delayed on their way to work, or are not able to reach work at all due to the Wall (Physicians for Human Rights 2004)

The consensus in Israel is that the Wall will reduce, if not fully prevent, terror attacks and that the price paid by the Palestinians for Israeli security is not necessarily a matter for concern.[1] Even some activists say they are not opposed to fences in principle. They want the Israeli government to end the Occupation and withdraw to the pre-1967 borders, with adjustments. A wall marking such a border, they say, might not end terror but Israel would then 'be justified if we hit back'.

However, an intensely active opposition, both national and international, to the Wall per se has had some success in putting the issue on to the public agenda.[2] The activity of these groups is constant and ranges from protest camps, demonstrations within and outside the Green Line, to petitions and legal action by NGOs such as B'Tselem, Physicians for Human Rights, the Moked, Centre for the Defence of the Individual, and the Association for Civil Rights in Israel.

The active opposition, international pressure and negative media representation have combined to force the Israeli government to make changes in the route of the Wall. In June 2004 two legal rulings forced a reconsideration of this, supposedly essential, security barrier. The High Court of Justice at The Hague declared the Wall illegal and hinted at possible future repercussions for Israel. The Israeli Supreme Court, sitting as a High Court of Justice, responded to a petition by Palestinian residents of Beit Sourik, near Jerusalem, and ordered the route to be moved closer to the Green Line, in order to cause 'less suffering' to the Palestinians (ruling HCJ 2056/04). In February 2005, the government approved a new route for the Wall, some of which will now run along the Green Line. Fewer Palestinian lives, and less Palestinian land, a 'mere' 7 per cent, will fall victim to the juggernaut, yet it remains as a terrible indicator of Israel's fundamental disdain for and distrust of the Palestinians.

The story of Jabarra

Since the summer of 2003 when the first stretch of the Wall was completed, CPW has conducted shifts at the so-called agricultural gates/checkpoints that punctuate the Wall. Essentially these differ little from those at other barriers, although the ramifications of disruption reverberate more widely, deeply and intensely there.

Jabarra is a village of 300 people to the south of Tulkarm. Although the new route of the Wall may alleviate some of its hardships, Jabarra's story serves as a model for the ills of the Palestinian population trapped in the enclaves of its sinuous, disputed route, their lands beckoning sorrowfully from the other, forbidden, side.

Jabarra was once a prosperous, middle-class West Bank hamlet. It is connected by ties of family and services to the surrounding villages, as well as to the West Bank city of Tulkarm to the east and the Israeli Palestinian township of Taibe to the west. Residents from surrounding villages own land in Jabarra and Jabarrans worked in the surrounding villages and towns. By 2004, Jabarra had become a ghost town, its thriving poultry and greenhouse industries decimated. Its residents, mostly teachers, doctors, clerks and other white-collar professionals, were unable to reach their work, whether across the Green Line in Israel or in the West Bank. The Wall simply trapped Jabarra in a no-man's-land, without services or access. Its decline is repeated in dozens of villages along its route. The thousands of acres of Palestinian land in the Seam Area (i.e. area between the Green Line and the Wall), enclaves of annexation, are a promise of things to come (B'Tselem 2003b).

Michelina Dank, a Polish-born physicist, has documented the process of Jabarra's demise in a series of reports from the field:

October 2003 Until October 3, the eve of the Day of Atonement, there was free movement across the checkpoint for humanitarian cases and for all residents of Jabarra in all directions. Non-residents require a permit and identifying document or listing on a register held by the soldiers at the checkpoint. This applies mainly to residents of surrounding villages, owners of orchards and greenhouses in Jabarra entering via the agricultural gate, No. 839 and also to children crossing at the 'children's gate' (Gate 753).

October 4–31 There has been a drastic change and the checkpoint has been closed to all commuters in all directions. Simultaneously, the gates between Jabarra and its neighbour A-Ras have been sealed. At first we were told by the soldiers that this was for the duration of the High Holidays; however, it soon became clear that the temporary has become permanent. Residents of Jabarra instead of enjoying free passage are now forced to apply for personal permits, issued by the DCL in Tulkarm. Residents have refused to apply and in response the army has sealed off all the entrances to the village. In this way residents are left without even minimal medical and community services and with no possibility of going to work or school. The army has not relented even though it is clear that the village is without even basic food supplies: bread, milk and baby formula. For the first time humanitarian cases are delayed at the Jabarra checkpoint and residents of surrounding villages are detained. The aforesaid permits are actually permission for Jabarra residents to reside in their own village and require supporting documentation from the Palestinian Authority (PA) verifying the right of the applicant to his residential status. Permits are individual; each family member must apply separately.[3] The army enjoys the right to cancel a permit at will, which means that the individual concerned becomes an 'illegal' or 'infiltrator' in his own home and can be arrested, or banished from his land and made a refugee. The passage of teachers, students and schoolchildren is frustrated ... Either passage is completely banned or transitees are forced to cross back and forth via the checkpoint itself [instead of through the access gates], something that requires a walk of several kilometres in both directions. There are also cases where soldiers searched the children's satchels. In one incident, children were allowed to cross the checkpoint but their teachers were barred. Farmers are almost totally barred from reaching their fields and the agricultural gate is sealed until 28/10 even though this is the height

4 Waiting to cross the Annexation Wall, 2004 (photo: CheckpointWatch)

of the [economically crucial] olive picking season. (CPW Reports of 8, 13, 10, 20 October 2003)

July 2004 We witnessed a considerable improvement [in attitude] at both Tulkarm and Jabarra checkpoints when they were manned by reservists and military police who were patient, business-like and even polite, unlike the previous units (Report, 3 July 2004, afternoon shift). However, after the military incursion into Tulkarm at the end of July, the situation at Jabarra checkpoint changes from day to day. On 26 July Tulkarm residents were allowed to leave their city only in the direction of [nearby] Qalqilya. Jabarra checkpoint was open only for the passage of taxis, cars with special permits and humanitarian cases. On 27 July in the afternoon we received a call from a Jabarra resident to the effect that despite all promises residents are not allowed to enter or leave without a special permit. As a result there was a total lack of supplies to the village and the local grocery store was bare of foodstuffs. The next day our contact notified us that supplies had been renewed and passage to vehicles was permitted, although a limit had been placed on the number of crates of food allowed in. Till now our attempts at clarification have been fruitless.

What emerges very clearly from these reports is not only the disruption of Palestinian life, but also the total indifference of the military (and political) authorities to the well-being of West Bank residents. As the occupier, Israel is obliged under international law to ensure the safety and provision of basic services to those residents.[4] Unfortunately, this indifference, or deliberate abandonment, is not confined to Jabarra but is repeated the length of the Wall and throughout the West Bank.

From day to day the rules of passage change. The so-called agricultural gates, the checkpoints, seldom open at the appointed time, which for farmers often means losing precious work hours in the crucial cool morning hours. Schoolchildren and teachers are often delayed, once again forced to wait in all weathers with no shelter. The massive yellow-painted gates and fences rear up among neglected fields and orchards with surreal bellicosity. As throughout the West Bank, there is a striking absence of activity in areas that once hummed with life. Again, one asks in bewilderment, what purpose is really being served here? Michelina Dank, the faithful witness to Jabarra's sorrows, adds a coda:

> It's true that it is planned to bring the fence closer to the Green Line. About a month ago, the people of Jabarra got maps from the DCL showing the new route according to which Jabarra will be inside Palestinian territory. Since then, though, two things have happened: until now, Jabarra was fenced in from east and south, with the Green Line to the west. Now, they are fenced from the north too. Every day, at 6 p.m., the gate there is closed. To enter or leave, residents need to call a soldier to open it.
>
> Secondly, up to now, the only people allowed to enter Jabarra apart from permanent residents, were Israeli citizens. Some weeks ago, the order was changed and Israelis are forbidden entry except for close family (parents, children, siblings). Now Jabarra really is a ghetto. (personal communication, 26 March 2005)

Mutatis mutandis, under occupation the more things change the more they remain the same. Barring access to the West Bank for Palestinian-Israelis means that community, economic and other significant ties are disrupted, further isolating the West Bank communities in their enclaves and Israeli Palestinians from their family ties (Hass 2005).

At least one reason for the insistence on building this barrier, despite opposition at home and abroad and the enormous cost to the already depleted Israeli exchequer, is indicated in Tom Friedman's remarks above: demography. The realization that within decades Jews will be outnumbered in Israel-Palestine is very frightening for most Israelis, including policy-makers. Nowhere is the alleged demographic threat more threatening than in Jerusalem.

'O Jerusalem! Our feet are standing (outside) your gates!'

'Our feet were standing at your gates, O Jerusalem. Jerusalem built as a city united together.' (Psalm 122)

Enveloping Jerusalem is an attractive line for Israel since it is built on the Zionist ethos of 'taking our fate into our own hands', undertaking unilateral action and creating facts on the ground in accordance with exclusive Israeli interests. This ethos has an enormous attraction in Israel and it has only been strengthened by the assumption, a wrong one in my view, that 'there is no partner for a peace arrangement' or that 'there is nobody to talk to'. This has been the prevalent assumption since the summer of the year 2000. There is a great temptation to use unilateral action as an instrument that will be decisive in determining the wishes and deeds of the other party. (Klein 2003a: 1)

I find it hard to find words to describe this process of cutting Abu Dis off from Jerusalem, which is being effected even without completion of the [Wall]. From week to week the 'wicket' area grows emptier. Cars hardly pass through it; garbage and stones pile up in a place which hummed with people, children, vehicles ... Silence reigns near the gas station, once the centre of the village, and all the shops are shuttered. (Ruti Rosenberg, Swiss-born retiree, 5 January 2005)

In terms of the permit–closure–checkpoint policy, the situation in Jerusalem is even more anomalous, or grotesque, than that pertaining in the West Bank as whole. The construction of the Wall continues apace on its sub-section, known as the Jerusalem Envelope, bisecting and encircling the Palestinian suburbs to the east and north of the city, cutting them off both from its centre and from other parts of the West Bank. Families are separated, services truncated, and huge detours are needed to get children to school, the sick to medical care and even the dead to burial. Urban and rural landscapes alike are ravaged, infrastructures damaged, social fabric disrupted. Crossing the Wall, defying the military, becomes an act of resistance. The situation is compounded by the fact that many inhabitants hold the privileged blue Jerusalem residence IDs while their spouses and children may hold West Bank IDs and are therefore barred from entry to the city, and to Israel as a whole (B'Tselem 2004b).

Even geography is confused and arbitrary: walk down the main street of some neighbourhoods and the western, left-hand pavement may be Jerusalem, while the right-hand one is in the West Bank. The width of a road lies between. In some places the Wall coils in and out among the houses.[5]

Abu Dis[6] is part of a network of villages to the east of Jerusalem,[7] once sharing common medical, commercial and educational services, and bound by ties of family and kinship among the residents. The villages were formerly connected by two roads to Jerusalem, the old Jericho–Jerusalem road, and one running northwards through the neighbourhood of A-Tur. A third road to the east followed a slightly more circuitous route. The average travel time in any direction was between seven and twenty minutes. In the city, residents were able to access a higher level of services where they could bank, get medical care, attend educational institutions, worship at the great mosques and churches, shop or visit family and friends. The villages were definitely satellites of the Holy City and dependent upon it. Not only that, but Jerusalem has the same significance for Muslims and Christians that it holds for Jews: a mystical sanctity, a source of spiritual inspiration no less than temporal convenience.

The Abu Dis Wall, which is also the Azariyeh and Ras al Amud Wall, marks the Jerusalem city limits and Palestinians may no longer enter there for security reasons. This has as much to do with demography as with fear of terrorists. The Wall is not only there to stay but, like some cancerous growth, its ill-effects multiply with time. Here too it leaves families divided, pupils and students cut off from schools and colleges, doctors from their practices, the sick from their medical services; the villages have no medical facilities other than a couple of very basic clinics. Patients in need of emergency hospital treatment, and women in labour, must now take a detour route lasting upwards of forty minutes, with checkpoints and patrols en route, instead of the previous seven-minute trip to Jerusalem. Even the dead need a permit to pass.

Abu Dis, 2 December 2002
Watchers: Amy K, Dina B-E

Almost at the end of our shift we noticed a commotion. People were calling for the jeep and the soldiers. A man approached us in tears and told us that his neighbour ... had died half an hour ago and that the alley was blocked on both sides so that the ambulance couldn't get through. The body was in the alley covered with a blanket. When we approached the soldiers, they were already calling a tractor to lift the cement barricade. However, the neighbours could not get hold of an ambulance and we contacted the Moked [Centre for the Defence of the Individual] to see if they could help. When we left they were still waiting for an ambulance and for the cement barricade to be lifted. (Amy Katz, Chicago-born storyteller, Jerusalem)

The Wall at Abu Dis[8] first appeared, without warning, in August 2002. Watchers turned up for their shift at what had previously been a modest, rather laid-back checkpoint on the eastern edge of Jerusalem. Imagine their surprise when they discovered that not only had the barrier been moved a mile down the road, but now consisted of a row of *bitonnadot* (7-ft-high concrete blocks) down the main street between Abu Dis and its neighbouring villages. Bewildered residents were lined up at a checkpoint, a narrow gap in the blocks, trying to go about their daily business. I visited there myself some hours later. Shock and disbelief were stamped on every face. It was a trauma zone. Despite our naive certainty that this was some mistake, that legal or other protest could remove this impediment, it soon became clear that it was here to stay. Worse than that, in 2004–05 it was to morph into the fully fledged extension to the Annexation Wall. CPW's daily reports from the area since 2002 document, in word and photograph, the continuing trials of local residents since that August day.

In an attempt to alleviate immediate problems, such as the passage of schoolchildren, CPW appealed to M, a Jerusalem city councillor from the dovish Meretz Party, himself a tireless supporter of human rights. The following report, despite its humorous tone, expresses the frustration we all experienced. The frustration and anguish of residents can only be imagined.

Abu Dis, 27 August 2002

We spent the best part of half an hour at Abu Dis. The Border Police post has moved again. Three border policemen were busy detaining about 25 Palestinians. They reported that [the checkpoint has been moved] because in the old location they [the police] were an easy target for sharpshooters ... The disappearance of border policemen has an immediate effect. Youths leap over the fence. Less agile people sneak through gaps between the concrete blocks. The street is busy with pedestrians and a few cars. It seems nearly normal. So much so, that M forms the opinion that things '*are probably not as bad as we [watchers] make out*' ... [emphasis in original].

We pass on to him a summary of problems both existing and likely

97

to ensue. It appears that [M] is only concerned with school kids coming from Jerusalem into [West Bank] Abu Dis; he is satisfied that they have [an appropriate route]. We explain that even this concession means that the children have to change [transportation] on both sides of the check-post, not to mention Qalandiya-like scenes: soldiers searching school bags. We haggle: How about allowing school buses through?

No reply ... We were subsequently informed by the police, lawyers and human rights organizations that the Wall separates Jerusalem proper from the West Bank and that, for security reasons, there is no feasible action to be taken. (Dina Hecht, film-maker, Jerusalem)

The following reports, a few among thousands, although not the most dramatic accounts available, serve to illustrate the routine of life in the shadow of the Wall.

Abu Dis, 29 November 2002
Watchers: Inbal M, Michal Z, Barbara S (one day after terror attack in Beit She'an, Ramadan)

Massive police and border police presence around the old city. Opposite the Rockefeller Museum, as we try to turn right towards the Mount of Olives, our way is blocked ... because of the Ramadan Friday prayers.

As we approach the Abu Dis wall, large numbers of *servis*-taxis without drivers await us at the parking lot – due to the curfew, there is practically no business to be done. A few young men tell us what moments later we'll see with our own eyes: a new and 'improved' wall is being built, blocking all the passages between the two sides of the town ... As always, it is deeply upsetting to see people in the humiliating act of climbing over the remainders of the wall by the mosque, among them women raising their skirts in visible embarrassment in order to make it past the obstacle, under the watchful eyes of the Border Police ... Looking up the hill, we can't believe our eyes: the entrance to Al Quds University's department for Islamic studies is blocked by huge concrete blocks! ... Nobody had deemed it necessary to inform the university about the impending blocking of the entrance! (Barbara Schmutzler, German-born bassoonist, Jerusalem)

Abu Dis, 11 September 2002
Watchers: Daniela Y, Aya K, Ivonne M

The officer ... is very polite with the Palestinians and even asks them whether they have money in their ID [wallet] before checking to make sure they take it out. As we all know, there have been hundreds of complaints of Palestinians whose money has been 'confiscated' by soldiers ... Two children tried to get to Jerusalem through the open field and one soldier wanted to make them go back through the mosque and come back again as an educational stint, but the officer, with our steady presence very close by, forgot the educational part and allowed them to continue on their way ... about 70 Palestinians detained, all of them on their way from Jerusalem to Abu Dis. We found here the same pattern: their ID number was registered and then they were allowed to go. We could not understand the logic of this ... we didn't see the soldiers checking the numbers over the phone but just writing them down. That means they were not looking for suspects going out of Jerusalem [or they would have detained them on the spot]. Are they mapping all the residents of Abu Dis? (Ivonne Mansbach)

Abu Dis and environs, 5 January 2005
Watchers: Rachel M, Levana R, Hava, Ruthi R
We decided to start at Abu Dis rather than, as usual, at Sawahre, chiefly because we wanted to know how things have been going with the schoolchildren now that cabs and buses no longer wait in front of the wicket ... From within the village, near the wicket wall, we were greeted by a strident and frightening siren. And why not? It makes sense that, at 7 a.m., no one should ... sleep peacefully in his own house. The jeep speeds on its way. The street is almost empty of people. A number of detainees stand near the monastery wall. Several Border Police stand nearby. [We are told] that some of the detainees have had blue identity cards as well as work permits taken from them/confiscated. I asked the commanding officer about the detainees and our conversation quickly heated up, partly because of me. He promises to explain later ... he doesn't understand that I mean it when I ask him not to call me *neshama* [honey] then manages to address me as *geveret* [ma'am]. We stand around him and he sounds off: he is considerate of the population. For example, when old women turn up, or someone who really can't walk, he lets them through. They – the Border Police – are in a hard place ... Everyone dumps on them. Everyone, but everyone, complains about them. The residents must use a new crossing-place at a-Za'im, '[only] ten minutes' walk from here'. We decide to go see this new crossing. You reach it by tortuous byways, on a path hard to negotiate by car. Clearly, the way is not short, and it is unpaved as well. (Ruti Rosenberg)

The access point in the Abu Dis Wall known as the *bawabba*, *pish-pash* or wicket, has changed scores of times; it has been extended, fortified, reinforced and shifted – always to the detriment of the residents. Acknowledging, grudgingly, that some access must be provided in this herma-structure, there is usually one point at which people can scramble, climb or squeeze across – a crack in a wall, a pencil-slim opening in between the concrete blocks, a fence to be scaled. Its invariably perilous nature is a clear indication punishment not security is the real motive here.

Beyond Abu Dis lies the village of Sawahre es Sharkiyeh, at the top of the notorious Wadi Nar (Valley of Fire), a treacherously steep and twisting route that leads, eventually, to Bethlehem to the south. This road, slippery in winter and suffocatingly dusty in summer, is now the only route permitted to West Bankers wishing to travel from the south to the central or northern West Bank. Thus, a journey that formerly took thirty-five minutes via Jerusalem, now lasts anywhere from two hours upwards. Even ambulances are not exempt.

There has been a considerable evolution of this checkpoint, dubbed the Container, once consisting of two concrete blocks and a roving jeep. As of the summer of 2004 it is a fully fledged transit station, complete with revolving metal doors, perched perilously on a cliff top. The renovations include rudimentary toilets and some shelter. Now, as then, the line of taxis stretches deep into the wadi. Pedestrians may be seen scrambling up the steep hillsides in an attempt to bypass the checkpoint, often successfully, under the noses of the military. Although in April 2005 reports indicate that the flow of traffic is unimpeded, the potential for the army to use this location to cut off the southern from the northern West Bank at will remains.

Like its fellows on the wrong side of the tracks, Sheikh Sa'ad is also hostage to the Wall. This hamlet of 2,200 residents lies just east of the village of Jabal Mukaber, annexed to Israel in 1967. Sheikh Sa'ad was never part of that annexation and no road was ever built to connect it to Jerusalem. The only access to the city was through Jabal Mukaber. Sheikh Sa'ad, which enjoys no medical, educational or other facilities, has a good reputation in terms of security. Residents are not known for what is termed terrorist activity by the Israeli authorities – anything from flying a Palestinian flag on one's roof to planning or executing attacks on Israelis. Yet, one day, again without prior warning, residents were surprised to find a patrol of border police dumping debris at the one exit to their neighbourhood. No explanation, no apology. Sheikh

Sa'ad was now closed off to the world. The refuse blockade contained hospital beds, lockers, fragments of medical equipment. Rumour had it that that the dump contained contaminated material, polluted medical material and radioactive waste from Hadassah Hospital. Frantic residents complained and protested, but found no redress. A road was supposedly to be built to the east, connecting Sheikh Sa'ad with Abu Dis. As of 2005, this road has not materialized. Twenty-five to 30 per cent of the population has left. Those remaining are trapped, with no transportation or access. They cannot even bury their dead with ease, since their cemetery lies beyond the Wall in Jabal Mukaber, access to which requires permits, mostly denied (B'Tselem 2004b).

Another victim of the Wall is the network of villages between Qalandiya and Jerusalem: A-Ram, Beth Hanina, Bethunia and others. In both A-Ram and Beth Hanina (pop. 60,000), too, the Wall massively disrupts daily life: 70 per cent of schoolchildren and students are cut off from their institutions of learning, the sick from hospitals in East Jerusalem, the dead from the cemeteries.[9] Institutions, NGOs and services all lie on the Jerusalem side of the fence, cutting off employees from their work, managers from their desks and residents from their services. Once again, residents' information regarding these critical changes in their lives came from the press, or after the fact. 'My office is close to my house – I just walk across the street. Now, the Wall ends just before the intersection of where I cross. When its construction is completed, I will have to drive all the way through Qalandiya checkpoint, turn right around, and cross the checkpoint again ... before I can get to my office' ('The Writing on the Wall: Maha Abu Dayyeh', *Jerusalemites*, 2 February 2005).

Not only are A-Ram and Beth Hanina cut off from Jerusalem but also from the neighbouring villages.[10] Beth Hanina and its neighbours are no hotbed of terror, but have always been a docile part of the Palestinian Jerusalem entity. Their presence, however, threatens the demographic balance in the city, the result of Israel expanding the municipal boundaries in every possible direction (Choshen 2003). Maintaining that balance in its favour has long been an avowed campaign of the Municipality, in order to strengthen its claims to sole sovereignty over the city (Liss 2003).

Demography is geography

A long-standing aim of successive Israeli governments has been the E-1[11] plan that would connect the settlement of Ma'aleh Adumim (pop. 31,000) with Jerusalem in one continuous mass to the northeast of the city.

> The ramifications of this [plan] could hardly be starker. E-1 will cut off East Jerusalem from its environs in the West Bank, virtually ruling out the possibility of East Jerusalem ever becoming the national seat of Palestine. Given the topography, it will dismember the West Bank into two cantons, with no natural connection between them. If implemented, the plan will create a critical mass of facts on the ground that will render nearly impossible the creation of a sustainable Palestinian state with any semblance of geographical integrity ... And denying the possibility of a sustainable Palestinian state leaves only one default option: the one-state, bi-national solution that signifies the end of Israel as the home of the Jewish people. (Seideman 2004: 1)

The demographic threat overshadows the security threat in Jerusalem. There are a number of reasons for this. Jerusalem is the poorest of Israel's ten large cities. Employment is heavily dependent on traditionally low-salary public services. There is little industry and little or no attempt by recent governments to create jobs by encouraging the development of new sectors. Unemployment reaches 11 per cent. Housing costs are among the highest in the country. The increase in the numbers and influence of the Orthodox and ultra-Orthodox Jewish communities[12] has caused many young secular professionals to move to the central region of the country (Della Pergola 2001).

As well as those leaving, many Israelis avoid visiting the holy city because of a fear of suicide bombings, of which there have been several over the years. Yet surveys indicate that only 39 per cent of Israelis are willing to concede over even shared sovereignty in the city. Among Palestinians, too, just 44 per cent support such a concession (Palestinian Centre for Policy and Survey Research 2005b). Compromise is perceived by Israel not only as relinquishing a symbol but also as recognizing the legitimacy of the Palestinians' rights to the land and its history. This is something that threatens to undermine the essence of the Zionist narrative that asserts, if not absolutely exclusive, certainly superior, claims to belonging for the Jewish heirs of the Patriarchs. For Israelis, Jerusalem is the symbol of the ancient and unbroken connection that legitimizes the Jewish presence in the Land. For Palestinians, the great mosques are both the symbolic and also the very tangible indications of a similar historic claim. The Wall is the concrete symbol of the impasse between the two. Regardless of the changes in its route, that symbolism remains intact.

§

The Annexation Wall also has its symbolic aspect. Historian Benny Morris, an allegedly leftist pioneer of the new history trend that exposed Zionist myths regarding the war of 1948 (Morris 1989), has this to say:

> [They are] barbarians who want to take our lives. The people the Palestinian society sends to carry out the terrorist attacks and in some way the Palestinian society itself as well. At the moment, that society is in the state of being a serial killer. It is a very sick society. It should be treated the way we treat individuals who are serial killers ... Maybe over the years the establishment of a Palestinian state will help in the healing process. But in the meantime, until the medicine is found, they have to be contained so that they will not succeed in murdering us ... Something like a cage has to be built for them. I know that sounds terrible. It is really cruel. But there is no choice. There is a wild animal there that has to be locked up in one way or another. (Benny Morris, interviewed in Shavit 2004)

What message then is sent to the Palestinian people, perceived as so dangerous that they can only be allowed to exist within the confines of a barbed-wire cage? It is certainly not a message of partnership or peaceful intent. Dispossessed and delegitimized, behind the Wall, Palestinians are designated outcasts whose only hope of a future is to accept the superior spatial, temporal and historical rights of their oppressors. Accept and rejoice. It's a tall order.

Despite military means and might, Israelis still fear the alleged Palestinian threat, whether by the sword or by demography. Ironically and tragically, creating ghetto Palestine has also fashioned ghetto Israel.

Notes

1 In February 2004, 53.4 per cent of Israelis 'greatly supported' the erection of the Wall, while another 30.1 per cent 'considerably supported' it; 70 per cent believed that it would considerably reduce terror attacks and 16.5 per cent felt that it would prevent them altogether. Asked whether the Wall should follow the Green Line or be determined by the government, 66.1 per cent felt the government should decide. Thirty-six per cent felt that the suffering of the Palestinians as a result of the Wall should be a minor consideration in its planning; 20.4 per cent felt that 'considerable' consideration should be

given to that suffering (Tami Steinmetz Centre for Peace Research at Tel-Aviv University, February 2004).

2 Gush Shalom, Anarchists Against the Wall, Rabbis for Human Rights, Israel Committee Against Home Demolitions, Women's Coalition for Peace, Bat Shalom of the Jerusalem Link, Ta'ayush – Arab-Jewish Partnership, have all been tireless in organizing non-violent protests against the Wall. Changes in the route of the Wall continue to be made, as a result of both internal and external pressure, in ways that cannot be foreseen at this point.

3 Residents, briefly, refused to apply for permits as a mark of protest.

4 Fourth Geneva Convention 1949, Section III, Part III, Article 53.

5 As at Bethunia, near Ramallah, where trigger-happy private security guards charged with patrolling the Wall have caused the deaths of several local youngsters (Aya Kaniuk, CPW Report, 17 February 2005).

6 Abu Dis is a small village (pop. around 7,000) some 3 or 4 miles east of Jerusalem. During the Oslo years (1993–2000), Israel proposed it as the capital of a Palestinian state-to-be, the Palestinian Jerusalem, and indeed considerable public building went on there. According to the Accords, and the later Wye Agreement, Abu Dis was due to be handed over to the Palestinians during the stage preceding the final status talks. Ehud Barak, during his term as Prime Minister (1999–2000), unilaterally decided that he would not honour this so-called third stage agreement, but would instead proceed to the all-or-nothing final status negotiations at Camp David (July 2000) in which Abu Dis would be part of the deal. Barak's refusal to honour this commitment contributed greatly to the suspicion and hostility of the Palestinian negotiating team and to Arafat's lack of confidence in Barak. For insights into the possible rationale and agenda of Mr Barak, see Aga and Malley (2001).

7 Ras al Amud, Abu Dis, Azariyeh, Sawahre es Sharkiyeh, Jabal Mukaber, Sheikh Sa'ad and parts of Tzur Baher.

8 I feel a personal stake in both Abu Dis and Sheikh Sa'ad, since I was there on the day when the first barriers appeared in 2002, sharing with residents the frustration and bewilderment of this intrusion into their lives, an intrusion we were powerless to prevent.

9 The Municipality of Jerusalem does not grant planning permission in East Jerusalem and its satellite suburbs. No land has been made available to Jerusalem Palestinians for new building, let alone for new cemeteries. Older cemeteries are located closer to the heart of Jerusalem, just 3–4 miles away, and, of course, closer to the great mosques.

10 In June 2005 the High Court of Justice issued an interim order suspending work on the barrier in Dahiyat al-Barid, a section of A-Ram, until further deliberation of the petitions against it.

11 As of early 2005 the plan is suspended, owing to both internal Israeli and US opposition.

12 The ultra-Orthodox parties, Shas and United Torah Judaism, have long enjoyed substantial representation on the city council. The current mayor (2005), Uri Luplianski, is ultra-Orthodox.

THREE | **The observers**

5 | Dilemmas of witnessing

For me the hardest part was challenging authority, the authority of the army. I was raised in the US to be a good girl so that even though I knew that we [Watchers] were right and the rules of the army were wrong and arbitrary, it was really difficult to be on the side of breaking those rules. (Dr Lauren Erdreich, US-born anthropologist, Ramat Gan, personal communication, July 2004)

I come from a Leftist home and was always politically minded, but going to the checkpoints was a revelation – I knew they were there and what went on there but had brushed it aside. That exposure was like going to an optician and getting your first spectacles, suddenly you see things that had been fuzzy or obscure in clear detail, colours, and sharp outlines. In the case of the checkpoints, it was the end of denial. (Esti Tzal, photographer, Jaffa, personal communication, August 2004)

It's a terrible crisis for an Israeli woman of the founding fathers' generation to discover the dark side of [Israeli] reality. I personally respect [their] attempts to see what goes on, to witness it and at the same time to mourn it. (Irit Selah, producer, January 2004)

Having encountered the checkpoints in previous chapters, the reader will begin to understand their compelling hold on Watchers, the sheer awfulness that draws one back again and again. A picture of Watchers' dedication and valour will also have emerged. For the women quoted in the epigraphs above, this is one more instance of protest and opposition. For others it is a much more conflicted act, illuminating 'the dark side of reality' they would rather not recognize. That dark side, the oppression of the Palestinians over generations, is the side that is denied, not only in current Israeli discourse but in all Zionist narratives where the Palestinians are always perceived, presented and represented as the aggressors, those who 'hit us back first'.

In this chapter I address some of the dilemmas that confront Watchers as they have emerged in CPW's internal discussions on the organization's information and bulletin listing <machsomorg@yahoo. com>. I will focus first on the overall ideological debate regarding political versus humanitarian protest, and then look at two more areas of ambivalence: Watchers' relations with the army and with the Palestinians.

Most of us who grew up in Israel have internalized the Zionist myths, spellbinding as they are: redemption of the 'Land without a People for a People without a Land', the Land that lay neglected and abandoned until Jews came to redeem it by purchase, labour and the blood of the fallen. According to the myth, the War of 1948 was a war of the few (Jews) against the many ('Arabs') and purity of arms was the watchword of Israeli troops. The Palestinians left voluntarily, seduced by their leaders who promised them a swift return at the head of the victorious 'Arab' armies. Since 1948, Israel has consistently held out the hand of peace, this is always rejected by the 'Arabs' and Israel is allegedly the victim of aggression, never the perpetrator.

I myself can vouch for the difficulty of dispelling these myths and accepting the different narratives suggested by modern Israeli and Palestinian historians (Pappe 2004; Kahlidi 1992; Morris 2000, 1999, 1989; Shlaim 2000).

In four years of activity, the membership of CheckpointWatch (CPW) has grown and changed and the feminist-political agenda of the founders is no longer that of the majority. Some members are driven by conscience to oppose human rights abuses, wanting to 'end the Occupation' yet unable to put 'an end to denial' and recognize the checkpoints not only as a deliberate policy of control and dispossession, but also as part of an entrenched ethos. This is the ethos that sanctifies all means in reaching a desired goal. Some women come from the Zionist elite, daughters and wives of the heroes of the myths of '48. To challenge those myths is to challenge their own identity. For CPW as a movement, the task is to try and contain ideological differences without compromising its own position. This chapter will explore how far that task has succeeded.

For all the differences between their various positions, most Watchers describe themselves as left-wing. As we have seen in Chapter 2, 'Left' in Israeli discourse refers almost exclusively to one's position on the Palestinian issue and covers a spectrum of views from conservative to radical. The term elides the significant ideological differences between, say, a member of the non-Zionist, socialist-communist (and largely Israeli-Palestinian) Democratic Front for Peace and Equality (Hadash) Party, and someone from the Zionist, centrist Labour (Avodah) Party.[1] Very broadly, and by no means unanimously, parties of the Zionist Left support the continued Jewish nature of the State of Israel, a peaceful conclusion to the Israel–Palestine conflict based on some variation of a two-state solution in exchange for Palestinian commitment to suppress terrorism and recognize the State of Israel. This implies a mutuality that bears no relation to the imbalance of power in favour of Israel. It implies a demilitarized, vassal Palestinian state.

With the failure of the Camp David talks in July 2000, the so-called Peace Camp declared itself 'disappointed' in the Palestinians. There is an incorrigible belief among Israelis that the intifada of 2000–04 is an existential war with an implacable enemy who wishes to 'drive us into the sea'. The idea, promulgated by Ehud Barak,[2] that the Palestinians rejected his most generous offer, consistent government propaganda, overt and subvert, as well as the suicide bomb attacks, only increase that fear. It feeds into the myth of Israel as the eternal innocent victim. Although the myth is disproportionate to the reality of Israel's military might, it is very potent. It nurtures the self-image of a helpless David facing the Goliath, not only of the Arab world but of the whole international community.

The radical Left, on the other hand, a small but extremely active opposition of largely extra-parliamentary groups, has developed an ideological commitment to the legitimate national aspirations of the Palestinian people in their land. It does not, however, have a unifying ideological position, some members supporting a two-state solution, others calling for a bi-national, secular democratic state. Lacking a power base the radical Left is not widely influential and for the most part has no social agenda.

Support for human rights, the rights of *all* humans *qua* humans, are regarded in Israel as somehow invalid, not realistic, even treacherous. The mildest derogatory term used is *yefe nefesh* – beautiful, rarefied soul unwilling/unable to deal with the harsh realities of life, something considered very un-Israeli! CheckpointWatch's activity contradicts this view by asserting that human rights are absolute, not qualified by national or ethnic belonging. This modest assertion is equated by many with 'being on the side of the Palestinians'. As women who see themselves as an integral part of Israeli society, some Watchers are therefore confronted with painful dilemmas in regard to their own identity as Zionists[3] and as loyal Israelis, hence the desire to depoliticize their activism, as will be shown. This overlooks the fact that under the Occupation, where human rights are abused wholesale, humanitarian activism itself becomes a political act. It is the humanitarian versus the political dilemma that I want to address first.

Humanitarianism versus political activism

Who beat upon the wall/Till Truth obeyed his call (W. B. Yeats, 'An Acre of Grass' (*Last Poems, 1938–39*)

I am [both] an ultimate Leftist and a Zionist ... supporting the two-state solution ... if it were up to the founders [of CPW] there wouldn't be an Israel! (Hagit Back, community activist, initiator of CPW's Southern branch, January 2005)

Zionism? Shoot and cry, that's us: We act like the local Cossack; commit crimes, shoot civilians, lie unashamedly, invade neighbouring sovereign states, expropriate land, destroy homes, and cry again. (Hava Halevi, writer and landscape gardener, January 2005)

During 2004 the tension between mainstreamers and radicals, or Zionists and non-Zionists, within CheckpointWatch, as exemplified in the statements of Hagit and Hava, increased. A dissonance that had always existed as an undercurrent came very much to the fore. There were a number of reasons for this. There were power struggles – new members resisting what was perceived as the dictatorship of the founders – personality clashes and political differences. These tensions reflect the genuine desire of mainstream members to be agents of change, to reach out both to decision-makers and to their own (elite) circles with an acceptable message for 'ending the Occupation'. They want to protest and yet to reassure – and be reassured – that they are still part of the Israeli collective. Radical members see this attitude as robbing CPW of its challenge to the existing order. They feel that moderation in the extreme circumstances of the Occupation is unacceptable.

In July 2004, Tami Shelef of the Northern Branch (17 July 2004) suggested, for reasons both ideological and instrumental, a switch in focus. Rather than stressing the human rights of the Palestinians in public statements, CPW should express concern for the moral well-being of the soldiers. Her proposal generated a chain of discussion that in different guises continues well into 2005.

One of the first to take up the cudgels in support of Tami's suggestion was Dahlia Golomb (Tel-Aviv branch) from the very heart of the Zionist elite. Her father, Eliahu (1893–1945), was a founding leader of the Palmach, one of Israel's pre-state militias, the forerunner of the IDF. Dahlia is a true daughter of the early pioneers in that she thirsts for results and sets about achieving them. Together with a group of co-Watchers, she formed a sub-group (the Forum) within CPW to investigate the subject of presentation and representation, the hiring of a professional PR person, and more. The unilateral nature of this initiative caused a furore in the ranks, a storm that raged for months around procedure and practice, although the underlying issue, again, was ideological.

> *20 July 2004* If we define our ultimate goal as 'Down with the Occupation', everything else will follow from that. We also have operational goals ... (a) bringing the injustice that is going on in the territories to the attention of the Israeli public ... (b) to help as far as is possible to preserve the human rights of the Palestinians and I want to add a third clause: *to protect the soul of the soldier from corruption in the impossible situation in which he finds himself at the checkpoint.* To my mind soldiers are, in spite of everything, part of that society ... which we want to influence ... it's an ongoing fact that the suffering of the Palestinians arouses only the Left ... In a recent conversation on the radio ... *I didn't present myself as coming from [CheckpointWatch], which is controversial. Instead I presented myself as a mother and grandmother* and suggested to [others like me] that they begin to investigate what their children are really doing at the checkpoints and to go there and see the inhuman task with which they are charged ... the injury caused to the soul of every soldier ... If we arouse mothers to the damage caused to [all] our sons (of course because of the damage done to the Palestinians) ... there is a chance we will become ... not four mothers[4] but a growing movement of mothers ... contributing to our major objective: getting out of the territories. (Dahlia Golomb, retired musicologist, Tel-Aviv; italics added)

For CPW's radical wing, Dahlia's position is untenable; for one thing, concealing her membership of the organization. For another, many were affronted by the implication that authority can only be claimed for women through motherhood and by solidarity with soldiers, the executors of oppression, simply because they are 'our sons'. It's worth noting that in these exchanges our daughters are notably absent from the rhetoric, although they too serve alongside their male peers. Sons it seems are the privileged subject. (We will return to this discussion in Chapter 6.)

The radical Left has often been accused, not unjustly, of speaking only to itself. Dahlia posits a need to create a new dialogue with the public, one that will speak to more hearts and minds. She asks not whether to take arms, but what arms to take and how to use them. The debate is a valid and important one that remains unresolved. The tactic of moderating the political message has been tried before, with little result, as was the case with the Peace Now movement. The seeming success of the aforementioned Four Mothers' campaign is a poor precedent. That was about 'bringing our boys home' from foreign territory, Lebanon, where war had already claimed the lives of over 1,000 soldiers.[5] It plugged into an existing consensus, rather than challenging it, and was consistent with Israel's strategic needs. CPW's activity, on the other hand, presents a challenge to our 'our boys', and military and government policy in general. It is a very different protest. Both sides in these disputes passionately claim truth as their exclusive prerogative and are determined that it will indeed 'heed their call'. The exchanges of e-mails are often thoughtful, sometimes acrimonious, but express enormous determination to be heard and to convince.

Protest or resistance

The argument around CPW's goals, strategy and tactics, combined with procedural conflicts, raged for several months during the summer and winter of 2004, fuelled by personal, political, class and regional differences. In early 2005, when this book was almost finished, an incident occurred which once again throws the political versus humanitarian issue into high relief. Inevitably, it involved the army.

On 13 January 2005, Watchers were shocked to hear on the state radio (Kol Israel/Voice of Israel) that a member of CPW had, allegedly, attacked a soldier at Qalandiya checkpoint and that the army was considering stopping CPW observations. Here is the incident in the words of the 'attacker', Aya Kaniuk.

> *12 January 2005* What Happened at Qalandiya
> On January 12 soldiers pounced on a Palestinian youth who was doing nothing (except being a Palestinian). I tried to stop them ... I was as much use as a puff of wind, even less. While shaking the youth with considerable violence they seized and bent his wrists back, held him in a stranglehold and flung me to the ground as if I was no more than a fly. They continued dragging him towards the checkpoint and finally dumped him beneath the awning ...

Only next day did the army spokesman's office respond to Aya's frantic real-time phone calls saying that the youth had no permit and was removed from the checkpoint to ensure the flow of traffic there. A random search of his possessions had allegedly revealed a long knife, although in the video made by Watcher Tamar Goldschmidt[6] it is clear that the youth is not carrying any baggage and is wearing only a light windcheater. He was detained and subsequently released. Aya too was charged with attacking and scratching a soldier. In fact, it was Aya who was scratched, beaten and cursed. Despite its threats, the army did not ban CPW from the checkpoints, although women were subsequently harassed and even arrested by the police at Qalandiya. Press and radio reports made much of the fact that Aya's intervention 'obstructed security' by trying to prevent the arrest of a suspected terrorist.

The prospect of falling foul of the military, of being classed as belligerent, obstructive or, worse, disloyal, fuelled a chain of correspondence to the on-line discussion forum MachsomOrg <machsomorg@yahoo.com>. Some declared it a parting of the ways for CPW; others distanced themselves from Aya's brave, if foolhardy, action, some voiced unconditional support. This was by no means the first time that Watchers, especially Aya, have physically intervened to prevent or stop violence by soldiers, usually in life-threatening cases, as we have seen. Perhaps the difference this time was the 'bad press', or the prospect of others being expected to act in similar fashion.

Although many women consider Aya as having broken a taboo, of acting aggressively towards soldiers, intervention in cases of violent abuse of Palestinians was one of the ground rules of CPW from its inception. Right or wrong, effective or ineffectual, Aya's intervention might classify as resistance as opposed to protest. She challenged the army's undisputed right to use violence wherever it sees fit, and on whomever it sees fit, and she challenged the notion that alleged security needs justify the use of force. Her 'No' violated the most fundamental tenets of Israeli discourse: that, despite aberrations, a fatherly military really does know best. For the army is simultaneously father – the omniscient, authoritarian, yet protective figure – and the son, desirous and deserving of nurturing. As we have seen, women soldiers are subsumed into this patriarchal imagery. The Qalandiya incident, therefore, not only raises serious issues of practice for the organization, it could be indeed a parting of the ideological ways between protesters and resisters. Yet the explicit issue of resistance was hardly raised. A few excerpts from among the many responses shed light on the nature of the debate.

17 January 2005 The pictures [in the Qalandiya video clip] make difficult viewing. However, one cannot overlook the violence of that same woman [Aya] who seized the coat of the arrested youth and obstructed ... his removal by the soldiers ... I think our activity and our viewpoint are very important, but under no circumstances should we breach the boundaries ... disturb the work of the soldiers ... they are first and foremost our sons. Rather we should in good faith explain ... observe the rules, write complaints, photograph. All this is fine and right [but] we have no monopoly on justice, truth and compassion. In my opinion, we are obligated by one thing, the preservation of human dignity for all men: Jew-soldier or Palestinian, and we should behave according to [the dictum] 'Thou shalt love thy neighbour as thy self' and by personal example. (Ofra Makover, school principal, Beersheva)

Ofra expresses identification with the army and a Judeocentric position. 'Personal example', one of the attributes of the ideal officer, is taken straight from the Israeli military lexicon. 'Love they neighbour as thy self' (Lev. 18:19) is an exhortation featured also in Talmudic literature. Tzili Goldenberg responds (18 January 2005): 'Do you mean that we should just stand aside while the occupation army commits these crimes? ... Must we love the brutal soldier? ... What about soldiers who are not Jewish but Bedouin or Druze.[7] Is it OK not to love them?'

Indeed, not all our sons are equal, even in the eyes of the Watchers. For instance, when reporting incidents of violence, Watchers frequently point out the ethnic or class origins of the soldiers/Border Policemen involved. By defining them as new immigrants from the former Soviet Union or Ethiopia[8] or as members of minority groups, it is possible to claim that they do not represent 'us' – Ashkenazi/Jewish Israelis – who are allegedly decent and humane. The racialization of new immigrants, especially those of colour, alongside Palestinians, Mizrachi Jews and foreign workers, is beyond the scope of this book (Lavie 2005).

On 19 January 2005 Iris Bar, a counsellor for soldiers suffering from post-traumatic stress syndrome, asks:

What do you mean we mustn't disturb the soldiers? ... The mere fact of our presence at checkpoints disturbs them ... As regards 'our sons' – so what? Does that mean they are wonderful and beautiful souls? ... There's no such thing as simply documenting. Our presence itself is intervention in the first degree and the army doesn't like it unless we are [merely] complaining that there is no sunshade. Is that what we are there for? Not in my opinion.

Iris sees CPW's goal as exactly that 'disturbance' of the military that Ofra protests. The alleged disturbance is in itself resistance, both physical, Watchers' active presence in the field, and symbolic, questioning the right of the military to immobilize and oppress a whole population.

5 The Annexation Wall at Abu Dis, near Jerusalem (photo: CheckpointWatch)

The concern that Aya's intervention has set a precedent for action is shared by many Watchers. Shula Barr (18 January), from the Northern Branch, detaches herself from any personal criticism of Aya, but sees the incident as a watershed for CPW. She asks whether it is in future to organize militias and whether violent/physical intervention is now incumbent on all Watchers: 'Does the fact that I have never to date found myself in a violent confrontation mean that I am less understanding, identified, faithful, dedicated ... sensitive ... where do we go from here?'

Only one Watcher, Sylvia Pitterman (21 January 2005), asks pertinently how the Palestinians feel about such intervention. Is it followed by vengeful reprisal by soldiers? What happens when the Watchers go home? She adds that the organization needs to be sensitive to CPW's ideological heterogeneity when determining practices and to the fact that members with sons or husbands in the army have obvious concerns for their well-being.

This brings us to a more direct discussion of Watchers' relations with the army in general, fraught as they are with emotion and confusion.

An uneasy alliance

The military have been forced to recognize CPW as a significant player in the field. This is certainly due to the social class and status of many Watchers and their connections to power centres, academic, political and economic. Another factor is the consistency of CPW's work, its growing membership, massive press coverage in Israel and abroad, and the general integrity of its practice. Naturally, the army has its own agenda, one that does not necessarily view the preservation of human rights as its paramount goal but which is very concerned for its public image.

> It seems that the human rights discourse and humanitarian rhetoric were often adopted as external ideas that the IDF had to comply with for a variety of reasons such as public relations, the pressure of the media and social movements, international norms, and public debate within Israel. More concretely, these discourses are often understood by local level commanders as another operational parameter – such as terrain, the weather or forces to be deployed ... taken into account when running their units and that can be, under certain circumstances, ignored. (Maymon and Ben Ari 2004: 10)

Watchers meet not infrequently with senior army officers and commanders, including the IDF Judge Advocate General, and even off-the-record with the Chief of Staff (July 2004). These meetings are another point of disagreement. Some Watchers find them instrumental, others see them as frustrating and pointless. Contacts with the command echelon are undoubtedly flattering. For some they create a feeling of being taken seriously, and of being 'a loyal opposition' rather than a subversive fringe group. As we have seen, the need to balance protest with loyalty lies at the heart of the dilemmas discussed in this chapter.

As one who initiated our first meetings with the command echelon, I can say that these began as a process of clarification of the fluid rules of the checkpoints, a demand for human rights training for soldiers and the alleviation of the mobility restrictions for Palestinians. We regarded these meetings as taking protest into the enemy camp, a call for accountability. I for one was convinced that one meeting with our determined Watchers and the army would do away with checkpoints altogether! With hindsight, I am not sure if the initiative was a wise one. The courteous relations between the army and CPW, like so much else in the strange planet of Occupation, are ambivalent, with the potential to neutralize our work. For instance, members have voiced concerns that certain public statements, such as those opposing the Annexation Wall, will 'annoy the army and put a stop to our observations'. This is yet another difference between mainstreamers and radicals, the latter seeing themselves at the checkpoints by right, not by grace.

The officers listen politely to our complaints about the hounding of Palestinian taxi drivers, confiscation of ID cards, arbitrary detentions, non-issue of permits to civilians, delaying of ambulances and medical personnel.[9] They claim to be limited by government policy as well as, inevitably, by security needs. There is an underlying assumption that, as women, Watchers don't properly understand these needs that must override all others. However, recognition of CPW and its concerns also posits the army as a humane defender, with nothing to hide. As one officer said, where else in the world would an army allow civilians to monitor its operations in the field?

Nevertheless, Watchers have themselves become the bearers of knowledge once regarded as exclusive to the security forces. Despite declarations by the military regarding its humanitarian concerns and the establishment of an emergency humanitarian hotline by the Civil Administration in 2002,[10] possibly inspired by CPW's activities, little has changed on the ground in four years of intifada. At least until mid-2005, the closure–checkpoint policy continues to operate, and while here and there checkpoints are removed or strictures lifted, the reinforcement of checkpoints like Qalandiya as permanent border posts proceeds apace (see Appendix I) while the barriers that obstruct passage between Palestinian villages and towns continue to make the lives of West Bankers impossible and have little, if any, apparent connection to security.

Perhaps it is this knowledge that is perceived as threatening or renders CPW worthy of being courted – or maligned. Some Watchers are uneasy with this assumption of knowledge, feeling they have encroached on a sphere of authority not their own. This goes against everything they have ever been educated to believe in, while the encounter with soldiers at the checkpoints themselves raises yet another set of conflicts.

The silver platter

> ... the people will ask, bathed in tears of wonder, 'who are you?' ... they answer 'We are the silver platter on which the Jewish state was served' and fall ... wrapped in shadows. (Alterman 1974)[11]

Alterman's poem describes a ghostly pair, a youth and a girl, returning battle-stained from war, exhorting the 'people' to remember to whom it owes its nationhood. The Home Front, for all of Israel is so defined, is handed statehood on the silver platter of the (self) sacrifice of young lives. This topos colours much of Israeli discourse regarding the army, soldiers and things military in general. As explained in Chapter 3, Israel's citizen army (an army with a state rather than a state with an army?) is perhaps unique among democracies in its almost universal mobilization. Symbolism, practice and personal involvement at the individual level mean that issues relating to the military are highly emotionally charged, even fetishized (Ben-Ari 2001).[12]

> I found my experience with CheckpointWatch very difficult emotionally, personally. I have loved Israel all my life. I was not born here, I chose it. Part of loving Israel was pride in our soldiers – these young people who make it possible. I live here – I know how awfully we sometimes behave, especially some of our young people. But I also know how wonderfully they can behave ... Suddenly here I am coming to the checkpoints to keep an eye on the soldiers ... to try to influence them to behave fairly and decently. I have nothing against that, and I have nothing against another adult commenting to one of my children about their behaviour. Some of the women who came to the checkpoints spoke of 'writing things down so the soldiers would feel they're under pressure'. I felt uncomfortable with that; I didn't want to make them all, the decent and the not decent ones alike, feel under pressure. Once the 'humanitarian officer' (some of whom are definitely manipulators there to distance the true humanitarians from the soldiers, not to protect the Palestinians) asked us to make a friendly gesture and buy the soldiers bagels, since they are not allowed to. Two of us went off looking for some ... and the head of our group was angry and said, 'We're not here to be nice to the soldiers, that compromises our position with the Palestinians.' I can't agree to be globally hostile, or suspicious of all soldiers. I feel very strongly that they are also victims of our society's evil and stupid policies, and I hate what we as a society are doing to our young people. I want to consider the soldier I see innocent until proven guilty. (Rahel Rokach, American-born psychotherapist, Jerusalem, personal communication, July 2002)

Rahel Rokach, an activist with CheckpointWatch and with Physicians for Human Rights, is strongly committed to principles of justice. She reflects the 'silver platter' metaphor, the feeling that 'these young people make [Israel's survival] possible' by virtue of their 'defence' of the homeland rather than by communal, artistic or scientific achievements. She continues the Israeli romance with its youthful and supposedly innocent army, a romance that is compounded by the sense of existential danger. The notion that society is to blame for what it has done to Israeli youth in placing them at the corrupting checkpoints, elides the requirement that the individual be responsible for his acts. Rahel paradoxically claims that we owe our children unquestioning protection and support, even after they have officially entered adulthood, and in fact are protecting us through their army service. The putative innocence-until-proven-guilty of soldiers, despite all the evidence of brutality and wanton killing to the contrary, is one of the elements that enable a whole society to live in denial of the acts committed in its name. Like no few Watchers, Rahel seems to hope that the viciousness experienced at the checkpoints, the violence of the Occupation, is transitory, an aberration rather than something that is intrinsic to a flawed national priority and ethos, the 'evil and stupid policies' that she herself denounces.

The tendency to view cases of systematic oppression as anomalies is not unusual among Watchers. There is an urge to alleviate the immediate problems of the checkpoints to provide shelter, water, better conditions or to educate the soldiers. Although not dealing with the root of the problem, implicit in this attitude is the understandable desire for an end to the Occupation, for a time of peace as well as a genuine wish to better the lot of human beings in an impossible situation. Nava Eliashar describes with irony a soldier actually being civil to a Palestinian, contrasting this with the routine hostility of other scenes she has witnessed. Her 'wonderful soldier' represents a deep nostalgia for the old Israel, an Israel that perhaps never existed except in our dreams, or perhaps it is a longing for the Israel that may some day emerge from this maelstrom.

> I have seen so many checkpoints, heard so many excuses ... put-downs, humiliations, orders ... But only today, after 900 days of checkpoints, for the first and definitely unique ... time, did I hear a soldier say, 'You can go through, *geveret*' (ma'am). A large-bodied soldier with the face of a baby, with horn-rimmed glasses and awkward movements, a worn-out, tired, lonesome, scared soldier. My wonderful soldier – you rekindled in my heart the flicker of hope that seemed to have been extinguished ... Such a day-to-day, routine, trivial sentence [because] ... there in that other planet, in the planet of the checkpoints, the rights of the other are trampled into nothingness. There, the other

is ... not ... a human being because a human being has rights ... and understandable human needs – while they, the mass on the other side of the checkpoint, are the ruthless enemy, they raise terrorists, they are guilty, guilty, guilty ... How many times have I ... asked [soldiers], 'Would you want someone to talk to your grandmother the way you just spoke to that old woman?' ... [Often they react] with amazement at my audacity ... How dare I compare their family with Palestinians? ... 'They have no rights' ... 'The punishment does not humiliate them – they don't feel anything', or 'I hope they kill you and your children, and then you'll understand what they are made of.' Then today ... it happened just like that, at the Qalandiya checkpoint thronging with people. Suddenly a soldier addressing a heavy-set Palestinian woman ... dust-covered, exhausted, heavily laden, and simply ... [spoke polite-ly]. He [saw] a human being ... Just a woman, like any strange woman you might bump into at the neighbourhood grocery store. Thank you, my soldier, thank you very much. I know you meant nothing by it, and in the crush of people, you never knew that I too would hear what you said. But I did hear ... and was filled with hope. (Nava Elyashar, systems analyst, Jerusalem, personal communication, 13 May 2002)

The perpetrators as victims

My husband is currently serving [on reserve duty] at a checkpoint near Tulkarm ... he talks [constantly] about the hardships of the [Palestin-ians] and does all he can to help, even endangering himself. No one goes to reserves because he feels like it ... I don't understand why the women at the checkpoint threaten [sic] my husband, especially as he's not to blame for the situation. If you really want to help, bring chocolate and drinks for the [Palestinian] children there ... I really feel injured ... My husband is endangering his life for you and for your children too. (letter to CPW from wife of a reservist, 11 February 2004)

The victim theme, as expressed in the above quotation, haunts the soldier–observer relationship. We Watchers are aware that the con-scripts suffer hard conditions, boredom, long hours. We know that, for many, reserve duty is onerous and tough on the family, as the reservist's wife complains in her letter. Those Watchers who are parents and grandparents of soldiers, past and present, are deeply concerned both for the immediate safety and for the future of Israeli youth, undoubt-edly brutalized by the watchdog role forced upon them. We can find connections of language, culture and common fate with many soldiers.

But there can be no comparison between the lot of the oppressor and the lot of the oppressed. For the former the painful option of refusal to serve always remains; for the Palestinians there is nothing they can do to refuse, nor even alleviate, their plight.

Victimhood is a dominant theme in all Israeli discourse, not least among the soldiers themselves, and they frequently ask Watchers, 'What about *my* human rights?' Liran Ron Furer, in his book *Checkpoint Syndrome* (2003) describing his conscription duty at a Gaza checkpoint in the 1990s, also plays heavily on the victim theme. A short-lived *succès de scandale*, the book catalogues abuses against civilian Palestinians and is redolent of a fundamental anti-Arabism. There is a notable lack of any sense of responsibility by the writer for his abusive acts. Furer claims that the checkpoint syndrome, the drive to hurt and humiliate Palestinians, is common to all conscripts and sanctioned by commanders as a sop to the troops. He blames his superiors, the boredom, and the harsh conditions of service, as justification for the shocking deeds described. It is only during his post-army trip to the beaches of Goa that his head clears and he realizes what was done to him: 'You stuck me in stinking Gaza after you brainwashed me with your guns made me a rag … I was afraid of smiles you turned me into something else I was not me … ' [punctuation in the original] (Furer 2003: 3.)[13] It is this sense of being a victim that in part enables the soldiers, and, by extension, the Israeli public at large, to justify the continuing abuses of Occupation (Grant 2003).

The reverse of claiming eternal victimhood is to blame the victims on the other side. In conventional Israeli wisdom and policy not only do Palestinians not have the right to bear arms, but Palestinian civilians have no right to be where the seemingly infinite number of suspects and wanted persons hang out. Anyone familiar with the crowded geography of the West Bank will realize the absurdity of this contention. Suicide bombings are to be condemned as inhuman crimes against both victims and perpetrators, but with regard to Palestinian militias, taking arms against an invading, ruthless, enemy with superior military power is, surely, legitimate resistance.[14] It is the kind of resistance that pre-state Israelis used against the British in far less gruelling circumstances during the Mandate (1922–48) and which is a major component of the state's formation myths. No doubt for the Palestinians, too, heroic sagas are already in the making.

Sympathy for, or identification with, the soldiers on the one hand, and compassion for the Palestinians on the other, are yet another dilemma for Watchers. As we have seen, some lean more to one side than the other, depending largely on political orientation. Readers will be aware of the absence of a Palestinian voice in this work. As an Israeli I cannot claim the right to speak on behalf of the Palestinians nor truly to know how they perceive CPW. From the perspective of even the benign occupier, relations can never be fully equal or neutral.

Between solidarity and patronage

Even on the Left of the political map there seems to be a sense that while the Palestinians are entitled to their rights, their rights are less equal than those of Israelis. For many, the notion of Palestinians as human beings with equal and legitimate claims to life, liberty and the pursuit of happiness still seems incomprehensible. Nowhere does this find more acute expression than in the demand that Israel's security needs, real and imagined, be not only recognized but also fulfilled *by the Palestinians* before any real 'peace' can be concluded.

The term peace assumes a non-existent symmetry between the sides, given Israel's superior political and military might. Palestinian militancy is not seen as a struggle for liberation, like that of Israel in 1948, but *ipso facto* as a desire to destroy Israel.[15] It is a fear entrenched in Israeli thinking and political policy. Historian Benny Morris declares: 'in certain situations expulsion is not a war crime. I don't think that the 1948 expulsions were war crimes ... There are historical circumstances which justify ethnic cleansing. I know this term is utterly negative in 21st century discourse, but when the choice is between ethnic cleansing and genocide, your own nation's genocide, I prefer ethnic cleansing' (Morris in Shavit 2004: 2).

Many, though by no means all, Watchers, had never met Palestinians other than as employees – cleaners, builders and other 'hewers of wood or drawers of water' (Joshua 9:21) – before their checkpoint watches because, even before September 2000, casual relations, as equals, between Israelis and Palestinians seldom occurred as a matter of course. Outside of activist circles, prejudice and fear are obstacles to friendly contact between the communities. From the 1980s until 1993 and the signing of the Oslo Accords, it was actually illegal for Israelis to have contact with members of the PLO, not to mention the more radical factions, on penalty of imprisonment. One had to go out of one's way to make contacts, often by such formal means as dialogue groups or political meetings abroad. This is not to say that no real inter-community friendships existed, simply that these were the exception rather than the rule. During the Oslo years (1993–2000) there were a number of Israeli–Palestinian joint ventures, such as scientific, infrastructure and educational projects, funded by the international community. Restrictions on Palestinian movement have made face-to-face meetings almost impossible, while barriers of language, culture and circumstance seem insurmountable. With the outbreak of the Al Aqsa intifada, the Israeli centre-left, including the intelligentsia, declared its disappointment with the Palestinians as allegedly reneging on their commitment to peace. Accepting Ehud Barak's presentation of the failure of the Camp David talks as resulting from Palestinian intransigence, they saw no point in continued dialogue.[16] Even Watchers question the sincerity of Palestinian intentions with regard to peace. For instance, one complains bitterly of a banner flown at a peace rally that, allegedly, says 'No to the Wall, Yes to War'. Another declares the incident inexcusable, and describes how she left a rally where similar cries were heard, because, 'With all our anger and criticism at [Israel's] conduct its existence is still dear to most of us'. Within the feminist movement, too, where Israeli–Palestinian contacts were relatively strong, there has been a break in relations (Lentin 2000).[17] The same is true for grassroots dialogue groups.

For many Palestinian activists, too, 'normalization' of relations with Israelis for the duration of the continuing occupation is ideologically unthinkable, to say nothing of logistically impossible. While for radical Israelis these inter-community contacts were both political and personal, for at least some of the Palestinians they were purely political, functional and therefore often disappointing. There was a tendency to prefer high-level contacts with Israeli NGOs rather than with activists in an attempt to influence policy and public opinion, attempts that were mostly disappointed. Here, too, the potential for Mizrachi-Arab Jewish women to build bridges was blocked by Ashkenazi-white dominance (Lavie 2002). As Lavie, somewhat harshly, points out elsewhere:

> The feminist peace camp is almost 100% upper middle class Ashkenazi (European Jewish) ladies ... [It] ... opens up an interpolated borderland for either the upper class, English speaking Palestinian woman peace and co-existence activist, or for the proverbial Palestinian refugee. Such a spellbinding act of discursive charity allows the Palestinian woman space between her 'nation' and 'race'. (Lavie 2005)

However, there has recently been a revival of meaningful grassroots contact through the many joint Palestinian–Israeli protests against the Annexation Wall. New and different ties of solidarity may perhaps form here both between individuals and with organizations, the sides working more as equal partners than as patron and client.

At the checkpoints things are more complex. Here, Watchers come face to face in common cause with a wide spectrum of Palestinian society, neither workers nor threatening enemies but human beings in need, women, men and children. Regardless of their political views, many Watchers devote considerable time and effort to helping individual Palestinians at checkpoints whether the latter are denied passage, detained, arrested or abused. As we have seen in previous chapters, Watchers passionately engage with the military and its attendant bureaucracy despite the endless time consumed and the all-too-frequent lack of results. There are considerable differences in practice. Some women will try to obtain passage only for 'legal' transitees, namely those with permits, or for emergency cases. Others make it their business to act on behalf of all those trying to cross, or even circumvent, the checkpoint. Inevitably, this assistance takes on the taint of patronage, since Palestinians have no agency in dealing with the Israeli authorities that control their lives (as we have seen in Chapter 3). Even the acquisition of rudimentary spoken Arabic by many Watchers is a gesture encompassing both solidarity and condescension, however well-intentioned.

Palestinians are sometimes moved by the solidarity and concern expressed by Watchers by their very presence in the threatening arena of the checkpoints. They see Israelis sharing their fate, even if only for a few moments, as Mr Bassem Khoury says:

> I would like to thank you for your wonderful effort. I know how dif-
> ficult it is for one to leave the confronts [sic] of his home on a cold
> and rainy day to go help his 'enemy' in an area where his personal
> security is not hundred percent generated [sic]. Your actions embody
> the true meaning of humanity. Thank you very much and please do not
> give up. Both, Israeli and Palestinian civilians trapped in this cycle of
> madness, must do much more for the sake of their children's future.
> (9 September 2002)

Mr Khoury, like the majority of Palestinians, is a civilian whose movement between home and work has been disrupted by a check-point. Implicit in his letter is a sense of the rarity of Israeli solidarity with Palestinians – the 'enemy'. Note that Mr Khoury also speaks of a future, perhaps a future in which both sides will have returned to sanity.

Five

124

Friendships have formed between Watchers and Palestinians at the checkpoints, whether between taxi drivers acting as guides and mentors or with local residents. People will ask for some Watchers by name if they are absent for long periods from their shifts.

However, as the political situation and that on the ground deteriorate, a frequently heard comment is that the checkpoints breed suicide bombers. Watchers are also reproached by Palestinians for being ineffectual. At Beit Furiq (28 July 2004) several transitees railed at me that our presence benefited only ourselves: we were appeasing our consciences without bringing them any relief. By and large, though, Palestinian culture requires civility, especially to strangers, and overt hostility has been rare. Not uncommon is the kind of situation reported by Michaela Rahat (21 April 2004) who, having laboured long and hard to ensure the passage of ambulances at the Wadi Nar checkpoint, complained that while she doesn't expect gratitude she is irked by the lack of acknowledgement in subsequent Palestinian reports, such as that of the Palestinian Medical Relief Society (PMRS), where no mention is made of CPW's assistance, nor that of Physicians for Human Rights (PHR). Galling as this lack of acknowledgement is, it may be an attempt to redress the imbalance of power and to assert some measure of Palestinian agency.

At the end of our shifts we Watchers return to the normal lives denied to all Palestinians. For some women, the awareness of this privilege leads to intensive activity: phone calls and consultations, complaints to authorities, escorting Palestinians through the maze of military bureaucracy; visits to harassed or bereaved families. Sometimes this help is effective. Sometimes, despite all good intentions, it is counterproductive.

At Huwarra (July 2003) two Watchers decided to investigate permit-granting, or withholding, procedures. They accompanied two Palestinians, Ali and Raja, whose applications for magnetic cards had been rejected without explanation, to the local Civil Administration office (DCL). A long line of people waited and, when finally ordered to enter the building, each man was commanded to lift his shirt as proof that he was unarmed. When their turn came, our intrepid Watchers decided in 'a mixture of humour and solidarity' to lift their shirts too. Pandemonium ensued and the women were ejected from the DCL and threatened with arrest, though not before they had managed to hear a whole list of complaints from the waiting applicants whom they promised to try and help. Ra'a'd, commander of the DCL, after threats to close the office

125

altogether, relented and invited the women to meet with him. The two Palestinian men, however, were forbidden entry to the base and were returned to the checkpoint to await the decision regarding their fate.

Ra'a'd's concern was that the army not be accused of ordering the women to lift their shirts. He assured them that not even Palestinian women are asked to lift their garments, much less Israelis(!). Watchers admitted their initiative, Ra'a'd's anxiety was allayed and the conversation concluded civilly enough with an invitation to return incognito to observe that DCL procedures are fair. 'We resisted telling him that in our opinion no orderly implementation of procedures could make this unfair, unjust place fair and just.' The report concluded:

> The individual requests we had collected ... were rejected, according to Ra'a'd for good reasons that he did not, however, explain. It was hard to see the despair on the faces of Ali and Raja waiting for us at the checkpoint. 'I've got two kids and I haven't worked for three years. What will happen to me and my family, how long can we go on like this?' (name withheld)

This desire to help, the (illusory?) feeling of power that we as Israeli activists enjoy and the urge to exercise that power, are hard to resist, as is the 'mixture of humour and solidarity' that caused the women to lift their shirts. It is a very Israeli conferring of dominance: a mix of good-will and arrogance, both towards the Palestinians and towards the soldiers. The women ignored the provocative effect of their behaviour on the latter and are ignorant of, or oblivious to, the taboos against exposure of the female body in Palestinian/Arab society. Their understandable willingness to listen to the Palestinians – who often ascribe to Israelis powers that most of us don't have – and the promises of help, arouse expectations which when disappointed only cause more frustration and grief. This is the dilemma for all activists/relief workers, knowing that the little one can do is never enough, arousing expectations that can never be met. Yet the alternative of abandoning the attempt is unthinkable.

The situation also posed a dilemma for the commander in question, whose name indicates that he may be a member of the Druze community. He found himself in a double-bind. Army regulations were violated and he could not overlook that without losing face. Yet he had to contend with two assertive, middle-class, Israeli-Jewish women, who might well be in a position to lodge complaints against him even though it was they who had broken the rules. He managed to navigate these tricky straits rather well and, for the Israelis, civilians and soldiers alike, the incident ended in a draw. For Ali and Raja, whose surnames and professions are not recorded, this is yet another defeat and humiliation.

A happier outcome in a more dramatic situation was reported from Qalandiya checkpoint on 29 January 2002, long predating Aya Kaniuk's disputed intervention described above.

Qalandiya, 29 January 2002
Watchers: Nurit L, Vivi S, Michal S, Nina M
Today we saved a Palestinian taxi driver from death?, imprisonment?, detention of many hours?, severe beating? Car confiscation? (one of these for sure). But we were there and he went free ... We saw a transit driver arguing with a soldier and many Palestinians gathered around. We learned that the driver was told to leave his vehicle because he had allowed passengers to alight too near the checkpoint area. The driver refused and swore at the soldier. He claimed that his ID had been taken away and not returned. The soldier struck [the middle-aged man asserting that the Palestinian hit him first]. The latter was ready to die but not to lose his pride. We all went into action: one of us tried to calm the men, the other pulled the soldier's gun from the rear (he was on the verge of killing the driver) ... Meanwhile, another one of us persuaded the reinforcements who arrived on the scene that the Palestinian was innocent ... An officer, seeing us and the crowd, calmed things down ... moved the soldier away and let the Palestinian go.

The women's action was spontaneous and as dangerous to themselves as to the threatened driver – they, and he, were saved by the element of surprise: Israeli women physically defending a Palestinian man. Their Israeliness marks them as unassailable, privileged to defend the proud man, and him no stripling, who may not, by virtue of his Palestinianness, defend himself. Despite their frequent impotence in the field, Watchers, as Israelis, are empowered to protest and to complain, another luxury denied the Palestinians.

Palestinian women suffer the same tribulations and indignities as their men folk, as reports quoted elsewhere in this book have shown. We suspect that many suffer sexual harassment, certainly verbally, but because of a culture of silence on such matters, there is little hard evidence. Politically active in the first Intifada (1987–93), Palestinian women now seem to take a back seat, attempting to keep home and family together in the impossible conditions that prevail in the West Bank and, even more so, in Gaza.

Watchers, and other women activists, are often treated as honorary men by Palestinians, perhaps because our status as Israelis seems to invest us with traditional masculine qualities: initiative, agency and independence. Or perhaps because as emancipated females in a male-dominated zone we challenge traditional gender roles. This is just one more example of the emasculation of the Palestinian male. The checkpoint situation with its attendant public humiliations and denial of independent action has robbed Palestinian men of their ability to protect and provide. Not only are they and their dependants totally vulnerable to the military, but in accepting help from Israeli activists they must also be grateful to those who, despite all good intentions, benefit from the Occupation. In Palestinian society, where pride, status and honour play such a major role in the individual and collective self-image, the disempowerment of the Occupation is devastating and its effects will be felt for generations. Conversely, in Israeli society a dominant self-image, paradoxical to that of the eternal victim, is one of both strength and moral rectitude. When this image is deflated, for instance by vulnerability to suicide bombers or by revelations of army brutality, the devastation is no less. British journalist Linda Grant writes of a 'new generation of Palestinian and Israeli young people [whose] ... collective memories and stories are being filled with anger and a deep desire to see the other side suffer' (Grant 2004). Young soldiers in the field have more than ample opportunity to fulfil that desire. The Palestinians, with no voice and no rights, who in different circumstances would be conducting lives of autonomy and initiative, are reduced to the status of pieces on a game board. Watchers, too, are trapped by the rules of the game, mediating between oppressors and oppressed from the wrong, dominant, side of the checkpoint.

§

The dilemma for Watchers is, as we have seen, not whether, but how, to take arms against the sea of troubles brought about by the Occupation. The issues of relations with the army, with the Palestinians and the underlying reassessment of our identity as Israelis, and what that stands for, are substantive and deeply painful.

The issues discussed are fundamental to Israeli society, or at least its centre-left. There are conflicts of loyalty to the collective, balancing the concern for Israel's moral stature with a more tribal concern for the nation's youth. For Watchers there is also the conflicted attitude to the army command, many of whom share class identity and, supposedly, a common ethos; there is the ambivalence in confronting soldiers, the nation's sons, as well as those considered outsiders: members of minority groups and new immigrants. Last but by no means least, there are relations with the Palestinians, a contradictory blend of empathy, sympathy, guilt, distrust and, inevitably, dominance. It's a heady mixture. The tensions created have remained ideologically and procedurally unresolved. Yet the work of observation and reporting continues and, to date, few women have left CPW on ideological grounds. This says a great deal about the way Watchers feel about the importance of their activism, regardless of whether they see this is political or humanitarian.

In a positive development, the Forum, referred to above, has evolved into a separate NGO, Yesh Din (There is Law), focusing on settler violence against West Bank villages, gathering evidence from residents via an interpreter. The evidence will be used in legal actions against the perpetrators. Using their considerable connections, the group raised a significant amount of money, hired a professional strategist to train them and a prominent civil rights lawyer, Michael Sfarad, to represent them. Yesh Din members continue with their CPW shifts and there is an exchange of information between the two organizations. The procedural irregularities that preceded the formation of Yesh Din and the refusal of the more radical group to expand the mandate of Checkpoint-Watch, have left a certain amount of ill-feeling, although, as of mid-2005, a threatened split has been averted. Although muffling CPW's ideological message, keeping political debate alive has meant the possibility of change, a broadening of positions, rather than their fossilization.

All Watchers are changed by their activism. No woman who has stood at the checkpoints will ever forget what she has seen there. However she qualifies her experience, however great her sympathy for the nation's warrior sons, she can never again fully take refuge in denial, never again submit to the myth of 'enlightened occupation'. The big question here is how that change in perception is conveyed, not only to today's public but to future generations. Who will have the last word? Or rather, which version of history will be canonized? Will it be the narrative of the Occupation as the continuation of a historical process that began a hundred years ago when the early Zionists claimed 'A Land without People for a People without a Land', or that of an aberrant episode in Israeli history, redeemed by the courage of those who spoke out? Will it be the history of those who submit to their sympathy with the sons, or of those who wish to redress the sins of the fathers?

These questions bring us to the vexed question of media representation of CPW.

Notes

1 For an in-depth discussion of Zionism, post-Zionism and the debate surrounding these concepts readers are referred to Kimmerling (1983, 2001), Silberstein (1999). Suffice it to say that Zionism here refers to the concept that the Jewish people in colonizing Palestine and establishing the State of Israel are returning to their historic land by right under the Law of Return (1950) that provides for any Jew wishing to settle in Israel to acquire immediate citizenship including voting rights. The definition of who exactly is a Jew is problematic and contested. While this discriminatory law is considered by many to be justified in the post-Holocaust period, it raises serious questions regarding the democratic nature of the Jewish state, denying as it does the right of return for Palestinians forced from their homes by the war of 1948 and again by the Six-Day War in 1967.

2 When the Camp David peace talks collapsed in July 2000 with Chairman Arafat's refusal of Israel's supposedly generous offer, Israeli premier Barak declared that there was 'no partner for peace' and that the refusal was tantamount to a declaration that the Palestinians wanted to reclaim not only the West Bank and Gaza but also the State of Israel. It is worth noting that at the Taba talks, in late 2000, the two sides were able to come much closer to agreement, but Barak had no mandate, Clinton's term had ended and Israel's war on the Palestinians was well under way (Aga and Malley 2001; Klein 2003b).

3 In this instance I use the term only in its plain sense of identification with the Jewish state, its goals and institutions, not least of which is the army.

4 A protest movement initiated by four women in the wake of the death of seventy-three soldiers in a collision between two helicopters ferrying troops across the border into Lebanon (February 1997). The movement enjoyed the backing of powerful, albeit controversial, establishment figures such as Dr Yossi Beilin, then Deputy Foreign Minister.

5 A similar campaign, Shuvi (Return), supports Sharon's plan for disengagement from Gaza. On its website the group identifies itself as 'mothers, wives, sisters and friends' (of soldiers).

6 The video was made accessible through MachsomOrg <www.psifas. blueorange.net/data/Qalandiya12.1.2005.wmv>. Kaniuk, who is of course unarmed, is seen struggling with the soldiers who are manhandling the prisoner. Subsequently she is seen being thrown to the ground.

7 Founded in the early eleventh century, the Druze faith is a breakaway from Shi'a Islam; communities are found in Lebanon, Syria, Israel and Jordan. Druze men are conscripted to the Israeli military, and many of them become career soldiers. Their inclusion, and the exclusion of Israeli

Palestinians, is part of Israel's divide and rule policy. As native Arabic speakers, Druze often serve in Border Police units, roles that bring them into conflict with the Palestinians.

8 *Ha'aretz* (4 February 2005) reports that 75 per cent of IDF fatalities are from so-called peripheral groups, immigrants and minority populations.

9 A committee to study checkpoint conditions was established in 2002, headed by the Secretary-General of the Ministry of Defence, Baruch Spiegel (Spiegel Committee 2003). The very moderate recommendations for removal of some checkpoints and humanizing of procedures there have never been fully implemented.

10 In practice, neither the Palestinians nor the soldiers are aware of the hotline's existence. In some cases it has been of help, but only in that everyday needs have had to be treated as 'special cases', dealt with as matters of mercy rather than of law.

11 Nathan Alterman (1910–79), Polish-born Israeli lyric poet.

12 For example, the army has voiced doubts about its role in the proposed forthcoming evacuation of Israeli settlements in Gaza, and proposes that the police should instead be charged with this task. The Chief of Staff and officers of the General Staff feel that by carrying out what, if it takes place, will be a matter of government policy, they will forfeit public support, including the support of settlers and their supporters who are increasingly in evidence in command positions (Amos Harel, 'The Army Cannot Evacuate Settlements', *Ha'aretz*, Hebrew edition, 2 August 2004). More and more there are calls from religious leaders and public figures alike for soldiers to refuse to obey commands to evacuate settlements. These calls base themselves on the obligation to refuse a 'patently immoral order'.

13 Interestingly, Furer claims not to have changed his (right-centrist?) political views. His goal seems to be absolution and to call the military to account for its sins against its sons.

14 For instance, are heavily armed settlers, living in highly defended and armed settlements, civilians or paramilitary personnel? (Eldar and Zartel 2004).

15 In this context, compare the surveys of Palestinian public opinion before and after the death of Yasser Arafat with the prospect of Israel's disengagement from Gaza and a cessation of hostilities. Support for suicide bombings dropped from 77 per cent to 29 per cent between October 2004 and March 2005 (PCPSR poll, 15 March 2005).

16 For one of the many critical reappraisals of the failure of the Camp David negotiations and after, see Hussein and Aga (2002).

17 Exceptions are members of the Coalition of Women for a Just Peace, who continue to demonstrate for an end to the Occupation and work with Palestinian women within Israel and in the Occupied Territories.

6 | Representation

In the previous chapter, I reviewed the diversity of political opinions and the ongoing debates these have generated in CheckpointWatch. No matter what the presenting issues in these discussions, an inevitable subtext is CPW's place within the Israeli collective. Some women choose to step outside this collective with which they no longer identify. Others try to bring their protest back into the fold, into the Zionist embrace. But how is CPW seen by that collective? In particular, how is the organization represented in the media? This chapter examines some dominant media discourses in relation to MachsomWatch/CheckpointWatch (CPW) and to human rights activism as a whole.[1]

Since its inception in 2001, CPW has generated great media attention, at first in the international press and media and latterly within Israel. The international press focused on the political stand of Watchers against government and military policy, praising Watchers for their physical courage at the checkpoints. The Israeli media, on the other hand, have stressed Watchers' identities as grand/mothers and do-gooders, neutralizing their political significance. Watchers have tended to play into this depoliticized representation, whether for tactical reasons or because they genuinely believe that they are non-political. I argue that this representation is counterproductive to putting CPW's message across and that it diminishes the real achievement of the organization. I question whether taking the political sting out of our work will minimize or excise the validity of our testimony in the future. In the production of collective memory, will CPW be cited as yet another example of the world's 'most humane nation's' humanity?

While discussing CPW's media appearances in general, I will look in detail at three newspaper articles. Two of these, by Tom Segev writing in the liberal daily *Ha'aretz*, and Sima Kadmon in the mass circulation *Yediot Achronot*, demonstrate the aforesaid depoliticization. The third article, by Gil Ronen in the National Religious[2] weekly *BeSheva*, on the other hand, sees CPW in a very political, almost subversive, light.

A love-hate relationship

The Israeli public enjoys a love-hate relationship with the media. On the one hand, there is hostility and suspicion, on the other a desire to play the game and provide newsworthy, tantalizing, material, and in so doing not only to consume, but also to become, news.

An exhaustive review of the Israeli media is beyond the scope of this book, so a brief description must suffice: Israel enjoys a relatively free press, with censorship ostensibly limited to security issues.[3] For so small a population, just over 6 million souls, there is a plethora of publications, including three major daily Hebrew-language news-papers: *Ha'aretz*, *Yediot Achronot* and *Ma'ariv*; two English newspapers, a flurry of widely read local papers as well as a considerable press in Arabic and Russian. As happens elsewhere, in times of war and national disaster, the media tend to rally round the flag, to construct the news rather than simply report it. This is due less to control from on high than to emotional responses, fear, ignorance and jingoism. Above all, there is the desire to sell in a highly competitive field (Dor 2004; Tsfati and Livio 2003).[4] Inevitably, this led to an all-time low in the media representation of Israeli–Palestinian relations during the El Aqsa in-tifada. The three mainstream dailies eventually resumed publishing radical voices such as the poet Yitzhak Laor, journalists Amira Hass, Akiva Eldar and Gideon Levi, publicists Uri Avneri and Tanya Reinhart, alongside more mainstream and right-wing journalists, but these are somehow marginalized among the centrist-right correspondents who make up the staple diet of the Israeli press and for whom the voice of the IDF spokesman is law.

The Israel Broadcasting Authority (IBA) is the organ of state broad-casting, with one TV channel and several radio stations. It offers pro-grammes in Arabic, English, Russian and, for Ethiopian immigrants, Amharic. The Second Authority is a commercial enterprise, with two TV channels, one broadcasting in Russian. The army has its own radio station, Galei Zahal – the IDF Wavelength, run largely by conscripts. This is an energetic and extremely popular station with varied pro-gramming geared both to soldiers and to a wider audience. Funded by the Ministry of Defence, many a journalist cut his teeth at Galatz, as it is known. There is a vibrant opposition press and media,[5] such as Indymedia-Israel and the Alternative Information Centre, both sub-ject to periodic harassment by the authorities. There are a number of independent radio stations, commercial and/or sectarian, as well as numerous pirate stations such as the popular settler-run station Arutz Sheva (Channel Seven).

The mainstream press and media privilege Jewish suffering, motherhood and motherland, frequently resorting to family imagery, particularly in relation to the army. Israel is seen as holding the high moral ground, threatened by the sea of barbarism around. This imagery is almost always contrasted with that of the Palestinians who are equated with terror and an existential threat to Israel's survival (Steinitz 1999: 39–43). Palestinian militants are depicted as terrorists desiring to cause suffering to Jews *qua* Jews, rather than as resistance to oppression. They are also shown as inducing their own suffering by their intransigence to Israeli needs and aspirations. Palestinian mothers (the fathers are absent from this discourse) allegedly send their children to die, purportedly caring less than Israeli mothers about their children. Palestinian attachment to the motherland is seen as spurious, a claim trumped up to invalidate legitimate Jewish claims.[6]

At the same time, the Israeli reader or TV viewer has access to a multiplicity of foreign press and media channels, some of which are conduits for more critical reporting about the Occupation. These tend to be discounted as not objective or as anti-Semitic. Not only that, but within Israel itself there is vigorous public debate around soldier testimonies and reports from the field by left-leaning journalists and independent film-makers. These revelations and testimonies are not a new phenomenon but began to appear as early as 1948–49, continuing during the Lebanon war (1982–2000) and the first intifada (1987–93) up to the present.[7] Each revelation is greeted with shock and disbelief then fades into oblivion. It is not that the public is uninformed or that information is suppressed; it is at best regretted, more often excused or denied.[8]

The media

Israel enjoys a culture of debate and dispute. No social gathering, or even business meeting, is complete without a good argument, preferably around politics or religion, but almost any issue will do as well. Voices are raised and tables thumped as a matter of course. In the UK, embarrassed colleagues left the room when another Israeli and I began a political argument, by our standards in very measured tones. Many Israeli TV interview/talk-show programmes reflect this cultural norm and are notorious for the hectoring of participants, particularly members of the public anxious for their moment in the limelight. It is worth noting that politicians gracing these shows are usually allowed to get away with outrageous evasion and demagoguery. The purpose, after all, is not elucidation of truth but the scoring of points, the more contentious the better – providing of course that they remain within the consensus. The exceptions to this rule are Palestinian-Israeli parliamentarians, who will find themselves harassed, interrupted, insulted and silenced on prime time, to no protest from viewers. But then Palestinian-Israelis are not considered part of the collective; their legitimacy as loyal citizens of the state is constantly challenged by parliamentarians, police, media and the public at large. Palestinian politicians or speakers from Gaza and the West Bank fare even worse.

And what of Watchers? Not unnaturally, we were initially thrilled with being courted by the media as an opportunity to get our message across. However, this proved to be problematic. Daniella Yoel says: 'I spoke on both Channel One [IBA] and Two in early 2002. On Channel One the technicians wanted to stop the broadcast in real time, saying that I obviously had no children in the army ... My son was actually on reserve duty at the time. On Channel 2 both the interviewers and the crew were simply hostile' (personal communication, 7 December 2004). The accusation that she has no son in the army was intended to undermine Daniella's credibility as a witness, supposedly rendering her unable to identify with security needs or claim to be part of the collective. She herself refutes the allegation, thus asserting her right to testify. In the wake of the programme she actually received several death threats.

In December 2003, Daniella appeared again, this time on a popular prime time, very mainstream, talk show hosted by Yair Lapid, son of the then Minister of Justice, Tommy Lapid. She reports: 'I was [first] interviewed for two hours by [Lapid's] assistant, so he knew exactly what I would say. [Yair] cut me the minute I tried to say that Occupation goes hand in hand with terrorism and guerrilla warfare. Yet he was congratulated in [the press] for finally having something meaningful on his show' (personal communication, 7 January 2004).

Despite Lapid's censorship, Daniella conveyed a dignified message of conscience. In terms of public opinion, there was growing concern with the effect of the intifada on Israeli youth and these factors, combined with Lapid's authorizing celebrity status, contributed to the explosion in membership of CPW that occurred during 2004. CPW was seen to be not only positive but also 'in'. By this time, three years into the intifada, frequent reports of so-called aberrations, at checkpoints and during military operations, had alerted the public to a sense that the morality of the army was being compromised. There was a feeling that Israel was not living up to its own ethical claims. Joining CPW was one way of redeeming those claims.

When Hanna Barag, former secretary to David Ben Gurion, appeared

135

on the Channel 10 (3rd Channel) Russian-language programme *Mabat Nashi* (A Feminine Viewpoint), addressing an audience traditionally right-wing and nationalist, her co-interviewee was Manuela Dviri, a bereaved mother, speaking about the physical and moral well-being of soldiers. The presenter was, if not hostile, certainly challenging to Hanna. Her tone and what she said indicated her concern that Zionist values were being betrayed by CPW. 'You say you are doing this for the sake of the mothers – what about Palestinian mothers who send their sons to be martyrs?' or 'If we give back the settlements in the West Bank, next they will want Haifa, how do you relate to the motherland?' or, again, 'Why don't you worry about your own people?' Hanna, caught between Manuela Dviri and the presenter's patriotism, felt obliged to assert her Zionist credentials. She worded her message in accordance with a mainstream lexicon, insisting that the Occupation was the greatest risk to Israeli national security; but even this moderate statement was curtailed as the credits rolled (personal communication, July 2004). This is one more example of how the media are not out to expose truth or provide information but rather to comply with, and shape, consensual opinion. It requires considerable skill, experience and determination on the part of interviewees not to be drawn into this ploy.

The element of media pandering to the lowest common denominator was also clear in the following incident. During her shift at the Beth Iba checkpoint (24 July 2004), Naomi Lalo witnessed an incident in which a soldier ran amok, beating and shooting a young Palestinian music student, Muhmad Kna'an. Naomi was interviewed at length for both radio and television by leading current events commentators as well as by the press. Although she was the heroine of the day, none of the journalists involved was interested in the checkpoints or in CPW. What they wanted was a description of blood, guts and a perpetrator to blame, preferably an outsider. Naomi was pressed to describe the soldier's ethnic origin. Was he an immigrant? Not one of the collective? She refused to cooperate with this. Word was that the soldier was temporarily or permanently mentally disturbed, distressed by his checkpoint duty and family concerns. The issue of checkpoints, and the inevitable brutalization of all the soldiers who serve there, were scarcely touched upon. Certainly there was no mention of the endangered Palestinian collective, hardly of Muhmad himself (personal communication, Tel-Aviv, September 2004).[9]

The iniquities of the checkpoints are well known and documented in the Israeli press. During the summer of 2004, hardly a day passed

8 Jubarra checkpoint, 2005 (photo: Esti Tsal)

without some checkpoint report, often featuring CPW. Journalists Amira Hass and Gideon Levi (2000) in particular have long been drawing attention to ongoing abuses such as the delay of medical emergencies and women forced to give birth at the checkpoints, often with fatal results for mother and/or child. Hass in particular has brought checkpoints to the forefront of her writing (Hass 2002a, 2002b, 2003b). Recently, dramatic incidents, such as the one described above, have drawn more general media attention and the army is increasingly forced to take measures against these supposedly aberrant soldiers (B'Tselem 2005; MaschomWatch 2005).[10]

In most media stories, though, there is detachment from these acts. The racialization of aberrant soldiers, those resorting to violence and abuse beyond the inherent violence and abuse of the checkpoints themselves, has already been mentioned. The soldiers involved are represented as emotionally disturbed, unable to withstand the checkpoint pressures; or they are characterized as members of minority groups, immigrants not trained in the Israeli ethos.[11] To paraphrase Liran Furer (2003): It is not us, we are not ourselves. Israel claims to be the most humanitarian of nations and its army the most humane in the world. Yet one of the outstanding *topoii* of Israeli discourse is the dismissal

Representation

137

of human rights as a luxury, one not admissible for a country beset by, and at war with, terrorism. So endemic is this *topos* that many of even the most liberal of journalists fall prey to it lest they be accused of being *yeffe nefesh*, beautiful souls – the signifier for wimps.

Balanced perspectives? A popular cliché claims that Jewish Israelis are 'The People of the Book'; perhaps they are better called 'The People of the Newspaper'. While there is much hostility and suspicion towards the press as leftist, treacherous and altogether not a very good thing,[12] newsprint is one of the most significant factors in shaping Israeli public opinion. If it is in the paper, it exists.

Tom Segev is a respected left-of-centre historian and journalist who has written a number of critical books on Israeli history (Segev 1986, 2001, 2002). He has consistently dared to attack sacred cows, including the army. He wrote a purportedly objective article following a CPW shift that he accompanied. However, a careful analysis of the text reveals the ambivalence of his attitude.

The headline 'Women of the Checkpoints' (*Ha'aretz* English edition, 10 August 2002) is indeed neutral enough. Segev assumes the role of the anonymous narrator that is, of course, also the voice of male, hegemonic authority: 'They describe themselves ... as Women for Human Rights and Women Against the Occupation ... They call their vigils CheckpointWatch.'

According to Segev, then, CPW is self-styled as a human rights group without the sanction of any (male? establishment?) authority. He then proceeds to define the group for himself: 'No longer young, most of them are academics; some of them are also active in the Women in Black organization,' positioning the organization as a group of elderly women cut off from harsh reality in an ivory tower and associated with an allegedly radical fringe group, Women in Black (see Chapter 2; Helman and Rappaport 1997; Shadmi 2000).

Segev goes on to describe an encounter with a verbally violent soldier, not omitting to mention the latter's heavy foreign accent, again positioning him in Israeli terms as an outsider. Even when describing the checkpoint, a scene that usually outrages even the most casual observer, Segev's tone remains objective. '[Watchers] document routine bureaucratic hazing in surroundings that recall a border crossing between two hostile countries somewhere in the Third World – something like India and Pakistan, say.' 'Bureaucratic hazing' is an understatement for the callous, brutalizing conduct of the checkpoints. The latter are consigned by Segev to some unknown geographical 'somewhere', rather than to the doorstep of every Israeli, and Palestinian, wherever they may live. Segev also implies that the checkpoint is 'between two hostile' entities, whereas it is Israel that controls both sides of the barrier.

'Three or four of those who wanted to enter Jerusalem were held up for a few minutes but were allowed through. Only one woman was turned back. She tried to cajole the policeman, pointed to the bundle she was carrying, implored him. He raised his voice: "Yallah!" The woman left.' The situation, surely, cannot be so bad if only three or four are held up and one person fails to 'cajole' or 'implore'. The problem seems to be merely that the soldiers cuss and raise their voices to insistent old ladies, and not that a whole people are imprisoned in a series of Bantustan-like enclaves, subjected to endless humiliations and detention for hours in all weathers; not to mention expropriation of their vehicles, car keys or vital documents, let alone beatings and shootings. There is also no mention of the fact that some soldiers feel it part of their patriotic duty to impound money, telephones and other items from those they detain. As to what Watchers actually do:

> The idea is not for [Watchers] to intervene in what goes on: they are the eyes of the nation. Sometimes, though, they are unable to restrain themselves. One of the reports relates, in English, how they interceded to bring about the release of *a few Palestinians* who were being detained by soldiers and also gave one of them NIS 100 so he could get home. (italics added)

A 'few Palestinians' are detained, just a few; the situation therefore cannot be so bad. A hundred shekels is worth about £13/$20 and might represent a significant proportion of a Palestinian labourer's daily wage. The Watcher concerned could thus be seen not only as overdoing the generosity, but as enabled to do so by virtue of her class and standing.

Watchers, then, are allegedly well-meaning and unable to restrain their motherly instincts. The fact that the report quoted is in English again marginalizes the group as, supposedly, not truly Israeli but rather what is known in Israeli vernacular as 'Anglo-Saxon', that is, from an English-speaking country with liberal notions unsuited to Middle Eastern realities.

Nor does Segev bother to discuss what the Watchers' activism might mean in the context of the Palestinians deprived not only of freedom of movement in the supposed interests of Israeli security, but of their own security, physical and economic. Checkpoints are not nice; they

139

are Third World intrusions, manned by youths with foreign accents. The checkpoint for Segev is a duel between elderly, soft-hearted women and the military. The Palestinians hardly figure.

> The Border Policemen have a heavy responsibility; the checks at the barrier cannot totally stop terrorists from entering [Jerusalem]. There was a shooting incident outside the Damascus Gate in Jerusalem that day [of the shift]. Little wonder that the women of the checkpoints irritate the policemen although [one claims] their presence has a restraining effect on the police.

The suggestion is that the attitude and behaviour of the police are understandable in the wake of a terror attack. What are the women doing there, despite their claims to effectiveness? They irritate the soldiers who have to deal with the reality of terrorism as well as alleged Palestinian deceit and corruption.

> In the meantime, Chief Inspector Shimon Amor, a hefty 40-year-old, a 13-year veteran in the Border Police, came over. He behaved as though he had just completed a course on how to deal with human rights activists. Grim-faced, as befitted his position and the situation, he was also very polite: No, there is no reason why the women should not observe what was going on from both sides of the checkpoint, if they wished ... 'We are here for the good of the citizen,' Amor stated with a certain solemnity. Many of the papers that the Palestinians show the police are false, he said, and you can buy documents for NIS 2,500. 'You have no idea how corrupt they are there, in the Palestinian Authority,' he added and remarked in a philosophical tone that 'their culture is not our culture'.

Amor, as is evident from his name, of Mizrachi/Arab-Jewish origin. His pomposity therefore becomes a butt for mild sarcasm, as does his claim to cultural superiority. Yet he emerges as the hero. He reprimands the violent Yoni, of the heavy accent, in 'fatherly' fashion. Is Segev suggesting that checkpoints are better left to the fathers, while mothers and grandmothers merely distract from the heavy responsibility of the military? He concludes with a distinctly paternal pat on the shoulder:

> The women of the checkpoint are part of a fairly large number of human rights activists, both Israelis and foreigners, who are in the territories in the hope of easing the plight of the residents. There is no better way these days. As long as Palestinian terrorism continues,

the media is less and less inclined to report the adversities being experienced by the residents of the territories and the Supreme Court generally refuses to protect their rights ... and thus would seem to be hastening the need for a higher instance, such as the International Court at The Hague.

There is indeed 'no better way'. But note: 'easing the plight of the residents', not political protest against the Occupation, 'adversities' instead of oppression, gross human rights infringements and abuses; 'residents of the territories' and not Palestinian civilians in the Occupied Palestinian Territories. The word 'occupation' is not mentioned. In this way the real nub of CPW, and human rights work generally, as political protest is diminished. A mere tut-tut about these abuses suffices and some distant international court can deal with them. Segev writes with a kind of casual indifference about matters of crucial moment. His important point, the condoning of human rights abuses by the Supreme Court, is lost in the casual sweep of the reference. Perhaps Segev regards women's activism as negligible, insignificant? What is missing in his article is the recognition of the political nature of human rights protest, that and the outrage that elsewhere characterizes his writing.

While Segev sets out to give a neutral picture of checkpoint life, from at least two sides of the CPW–Palestinian–army triangle, Sima Kadmon is supportive and engaged on the Israeli side.

§

These women's names will not be familiar to you from petitions and political ads in the papers; they are not political activists. They are women who one day woke up with the realization that they needed to do something besides griping and whining. Many of them are over sixty, from established families, with sons and daughters that served or are serving in the army. Quite a few have grandchildren. (Sima Kadmon, 'Many Mothers', *Yediot Achronot*, 21 November 2003)

Kadmon is a political commentator writing for *Yediot Achronot*, *Ma'ariv* and other media outlets. She accords CPW a generous spread which delighted Watchers. This was the first exposure in a truly mainstream paper. This article also resulted in a huge recruitment of mainstream, largely non-political, women to CPW.

The title of the article is a play on the name of the Four Mothers group (see Chapter 5, note 4). From the outset CPW is positioned as part of the normative collective: 'their names will not be familiar to you from petitions and political ads in the paper; they are not political activists'. This is by no means true of many Watchers, including some of those interviewed, dedicated demonstrators and petition signatories that they are. Kadmon is reclaiming CheckpointWatch for the consensus. Her subjects are presented as the women next door, people of conscience, with sons and daughters in the army. One is 'an attractive grandmother of a soldier'. Another 'has no defect in her biography that can explain what happened to her recently'. 'Happened to her', the awakening to the iniquities of the Occupation, is apparently akin to falling in love, or being mugged; 'established families' is code for Zionist.

Kadmon accompanied the women on a shift to the notorious Huwarra checkpoint near Nablus. Unlike Segev, her response was visceral and she was obviously disturbed by what she saw. Her article does not narrate or editorialize but mostly allows Watchers' own voices to be heard. Many of the testimonies reported in the article involve the suffering of the vulnerable, the non-threatening: Palestinian women, children, old men, the sick. Interviewees, too, talk about their own pain, the nightmares caused by what they witness. One weeps and Kadmon assures us, 'she is not the only one among the women who choke back their tears when they describe their experiences'. We are speaking here of tender-hearted souls, on the model of 'merciful mothers' as the Hebrew phrase has it.

Another dominant theme in the article is the impeccable paternal lineage of the Watchers. Some are characterized as descendants of Israel's 'Mayflower' or pioneer generation; one is the daughter of a well-known writer. The husband of another 'sat on the knees of Jabotinsky and Begin'.[13] This heritage indicates not only indisputable patriotism, but also implies the blessing of the founding fathers for their daughters' activism.

The women speak about their relations with the soldiers and the desire to save the soul of Israeli youth, stressing their own status as mothers/matriarchs. Perhaps the interviewees are here downplaying CPW's political role in the hope of influencing public opinion. Many of the women who joined in the wake of the article took them at their non-political word.

Kadmon's lack of editorializing robs the subject of political potency. For instance, the word 'occupation' is mentioned only three times – never by Kadmon herself – though some of the more radical statements are allowed to creep through. The representation reinforces the image of Watchers as naive and well-intentioned, bleeding hearts. 'Women, who only recently used their mobile phones to chat with friends and family, have become the nemeses of the commanders in the area.' This description belies the considerable academic and professional credentials of many Watchers, including the women interviewed here, long before they became CheckpointWatchers! (At least they are depicted as a nemesis rather than being in cosy collusion.)

Kadmon depicts a group not to be feared as politically subversive, but welcomed as a humanitarian role-model. Watchers are, supposedly, committed to a Zionist world-view, redeeming the 'aberrations' of violence and brutality that sully our national image. As descendants of the pioneers, their activity is reassuringly in line with supposed Zionist ideals. Middle-Israel can rest in its bed because where else in the world would an army permit its citizens to monitor its actions in the field? Truly, we have/are the world's most humane army/nation – inseparable as these two concepts are.

The article is warm, admiring and positive, but it is just that admiration that rankles. It plays on many of the tropes already mentioned: the national collective; the army, as family; the warrior sons and fathers supported by a home guard of nurturing mothers, concerned not only for the physical, but also for their moral welfare. In neutralizing the political significance of CPW and reclaiming it for the consensus, Kadmon also reclaims the checkpoints, and the Occupation itself, as humanized by CPW.

§

In contrast, Gil Ronen ('The Association Against the Soldier', *BeSheva*, 20 May 2004) is not fooled by the seeming innocence of Watchers. As his title indicates, he has the organization pegged:

> As if the reality of the checkpoints was not dangerous and frustrating enough, the women from the extremist-Leftist organization, MachsomWatch/CheckpointWatch, come and disturb the soldiers in their duties. The leaders of the organization, which doesn't accept men in its ranks, hold extreme feminist views behind which lurks a Marxist ideology. Senior IDF officers meet with them, the Association for Civil Rights has awarded them a prize[14] but the experience with the Jibril deal and the withdrawal from Lebanon, proves how much this feminist defeatism is effective and dangerous.[15]

'CheckpointWatch is allegedly another human rights organization, like B'Tselem,[16] it documents not-nice behaviour of IDF soldiers towards unarmed Arabs and reports them.' Here we have it: an exposé of extremist/leftist/traitors who inform on soldiers. 'Not-nice' may include all the familiar ills of long delays, verbal and physical abuse of unarmed 'Arabs'. For Ronen, clearly, all 'Arabs' are the enemy, though some of them may happen to be unarmed. 'Arabs' for Ronen are an indistinguishable mass, not particularized as Egyptians, Syrians, or, in our case, Palestinians.

We now discover that CheckpointWatch Amazons work in a 'quasi-military manner', a statement which heightens the image of a sinister fifth-column threatening the already beleaguered military. After all, says Ronen, complaints are issued against soldiers, and the reports published on CPW's website 'serve mainly anti-Israeli organizations abroad'. Watchers intervene 'when it seems to them that Arabs are being badly treated'. Presumably, in Ronen's eyes, 'Arabs' can never really be badly treated because they deserve everything they get. The complaints are therefore a function of subjective perception. He quotes from reports (Qalandiya, 2 and 3 March 2004; Huwarra, 6 and 9 May 2004) in which 'not-nice' soldiers were reported to their officers. Ronen notes with approbation that one officer scolds: 'My first concern is for the safety of the soldiers.' The women, whom Ronen has disowned ('not my grandma!'), claim to be Zionists, lecturing, or hectoring, the soldiers for their own good. But the truth of what really lurks behind that innocent, feminist, façade is about to be revealed.

Watchers may at worst appear to be misguided nuisances but don't be fooled: this is merely a front for the real purpose of CPW. Ronen explains that, after the fall of the Soviet Union, the international Left has dropped its pretence of championing the proletariat and now hides behind the skirts of feminism. He castigates the power of women, 'especially in the areas of politics and security'. Adi Kuntsman, Ronnee Jaeger and I are 'the Marx, Engels and Lenin' of the organization, our sins itemized for all to see. Ronnee and I had signed a petition against the bombing of Serbia, while Adi, a 'militant Lesbian', has referred in interviews to her 'immigration', instead of her *aliyah* (ascent), the term used to mark Jewish immigration to Israel as national homecoming. (Recognition as a Marxist ideologue might have been more flattering in a more serious context.) Ideological antecedents and goals aside, CPW presents an immediate danger to the nation.

The direct contact between CPW and senior and junior officers is a very bad thing. In an age where the generation of 1948[17] is dying out *... where the prestige and standing of the Prime Minister is fading, no new leadership has yet emerged and central government is weakened, the importance of each and every officer in the field is vital.* As the Arab population of Judea, Samaria [sic] and Gaza becomes more barbaric, IDF officers are required to be more aggressive, sometimes not nice, tough and determined. That's how it is in war. If these officers get used to listening to lesbian Marxist grandmas every morning their ability to make hard military decisions will be impaired. (italics added)

One may laugh at Ronen's feminist conspiracy theory but the suggestion that the army is the alternative to weakening central authority is disturbing, as is the notion of increased 'not-niceness' – how much more brutality and oppression must be wielded in this all-out war against the Palestinian people? The 'weakness' Ronen refers to is Sharon's unilateral disengagement plan from Gaza authorized by the Knesset (October 2004) despite massive lobbying by the Right and resignations from government by the nationalist parties.[18] The views expressed by Ronen are common currency within the settler movement. Although by no means all settlers are ideologically motivated, there is a hard core whose goal of redemption of all the Land of Israel, messianic aspirations and greed for land and water are intertwined with racism and xenophobia. This is a closed, often lawless, society, some of whose members have lost touch with geopolitical realities (Eldar and Zartel 2004).

Unlike Segev, Ronen does not pretend to be an impartial observer but is himself a combatant. CheckpointWatch must be overcome! Gleefully he quotes from one CPW report: 'We had to flee from [settler women] as from an enemy' (6 May 2004). He exhorts Women in Green, a tiny rightist fringe group, to come to the checkpoints and challenge CPW. His call to arms did not go unheeded and subsequently groups of right-wing women appeared at checkpoints during CPW shifts. Often accompanied by their menfolk, they attacked both Palestinians and Watchers, while sometimes bringing snacks and treats for the soldiers. Soldiers usually do not intervene in these clashes and often seem to find them entertaining, appropriate revenge for the disturbing presence of CheckpointWatch.

In conclusion

The three articles quoted above, by Segev, Kadmon and Ronen, the objective, the positive and the negative, were selected because, despite the differences between them, they reflect general Israeli public discourse and debate regarding the place of women in the political sphere. This discourse positions and idealizes women as mothers and grandmothers as a support network for the real work of politics and security, reserved for men. Through these mothers, Israeli society as a whole can reclaim its high moral ground, eroded by the supposed obligation of oppression (Rosenfeld 2003–04). Women stepping outside that role are dismissed as eccentric, foolish meddlers in matters that don't concern them. Worse still, they may be lesbian non-mothers, subversive agents using their feminism as a front for treachery.

The very title of Sima Kadman's article, 'Many Mothers', privileges the motherhood discourse, displaying throughout the motherhood/daughterhood of Watchers. The interviewees themselves seem eager to emphasize their maternal credentials as authorizing and sanctioning their human rights activities.

Tom Segev hardly mentions mothers. What he does do is to stress the median age and academic nature of Watchers with the effect of neutralizing their political significance. He uses the family analogy in the depiction of the fatherly officer who is able to contain the wayward son/soldier, whereas the women only 'irritate' and exacerbate the situation. He, too, seems to imply that Watchers have stepped outside their designated role, encroaching on the important security function of the army/BP. He fails to accord political significance to their work.

Gil Ronen is unequivocally right-wing, writing for an audience that shares his views, or even more extreme versions of them. Like Kadmon and Segev too, he must play to his own gallery. Yet, by his very radicalism, he illuminates the elements in normative discourse against which the mainstream Left must battle. Strip away the extreme accusations, the racist language, and you have themes endemic to Israeli thinking: the identification with the military as a defensive, not an aggressive, institution of unchallengeable authority; the demonizing of Palestinians as barbaric terrorists; the depiction of women activists as abandoning their appropriate roles as grandmothers and mothers, actual or potential. In Chapter 5 we saw how these themes, in a different way, pose serious dilemmas of belonging and legitimization for Watchers themselves. These dilemmas surface again and again in Watchers' self-representation, reflecting both outrage at the abuses they witness and a certain defensiveness for daring to take action against them.

What is it, then, that is so profoundly threatening in women's activism? Is it that it challenges the established order? Women in Black, defying convention, used their bodies to challenge the Occupation – an abstract concept, despite its very concrete manifestations. This challenge generated outrage, as the often sexually-loaded abuse hurled at them by passers-by indicates: 'Whores of Arafat', or 'What you need is a man ... ' (Helman and Rappoport 1997; Shadmi 2000). How much worse, then, proactively to criticize the military establishment. How do Watchers dare take responsibility for possibly allowing a terrorist to pass? How do they dare to know better than the Chief of Staff or Minister of Defence? If those hegemonic bearers of knowledge can be challenged, where will it end? Where is the omniscient voice on which we can rely?

Another threatened element is that of fidelity. Watchers are often perceived, and not only by the extreme Right, as giving aid and comfort to the enemy, and as such they are misguided, if not treacherous. The collective must either expel them (as in Ronen) or find a way to neutralize them. Segev does this by marginalizing Watchers as harmless, well-meaning. Kadmon removes CPW's political sting by declaring CheckpointWatchers to be non-political, with impeccable Zionist pedigrees.

What is at stake here is not merely the media representation of CPW, as important as this is to the organization and its goals. The real issue is the state of Israeli society as a whole, a society condoning and supporting the oppression carried out in its name. As I have shown, the ills of the Occupation are well known, if not acknowledged, through the press, the many testimonies of Watchers, soldiers and, indeed, the Palestinians themselves. Analyses of Israeli policy fill the daily newspapers. Yet each testimony is hailed as a revelation of aberration, an exception that proves no rule. The crying and the shooting continue, side by side. There is here a wholesale denial that CheckpointWatch, for all its vigour and will, has not succeeded in breaching, nor even addressing in its moderately toned media appearances.

The journalism of today will form an important part of the collective memory of tomorrow. The question, unresolved, of whose voice will be recorded and dominate that memory is crucial. Will the good grandmas become part of a new myth of a national struggle for survival against a cruel enemy, yet another example of morality maintained under stress? Or will the true face of occupation be exposed, leading to a more genuine confrontation with Israel's violent past?

147

Notes

1 I would like thank my partner and colleague, Adi Kuntsman, for suggesting this chapter and for her insights in analysing the articles quoted here.

2 The National Religious Party, formerly a moderate, centrist party, has since the early 1990s become more and more radically nationalist, becoming the political representative of a growing settler population. Today it is part of the ultra-nationalist National Unity grouping with a hard-line policy opposing the establishment of a Palestinian state and openly supporting a policy of transfer of Palestinians.

3 The relations between press and government in Israel are somewhat unusual for a democracy. Although there is supposedly no censorship, editors are very much aware of the bounds of reporting on security matters, while the director of the Israel Broadcasting Authority is a political appointment, sometimes a direct appointment by the prime minister. Members of the IBA are chosen according to a political key, with representation from the major parties. The Israel Government Press Office is responsible for authorizing the credentials of every journalist, Israeli or foreign, and has been known to refuse accreditation to foreign journalists writing material deemed critical of Israel. As of 2004 there is a move within the Ministry of Defence to tighten the censorship rules (*Ha'aretz*, 6 March 2005).

4 'Israeli Journalists Flunk the Israeli Media', a survey commissioned for the *Seventh Eye*, a journal 'for and by journalists' published by the Israel Democracy Institute. The survey covered journalists from the written and electronic media, including the Hebrew, Arabic, English and Russian-language press. Of those interviewed, 26 per cent agreed that the media must exercise care regarding topics that might harm Israel's image in the world, while 32 per cent agreed that the media must emphasize positive aspects of society and state; 24 per cent defined the public as the greatest influence on their work.

5 A recent innovation (2004) is the *Kibush* website where a daily selection of the Israeli and international press critical of the Occupation may be found (<www.kibush.co.il>).

6 A favourite trope in Israeli discourse claims that the name Palestine dates only to the Roman conquest of the Holy Land/Eretz Israel/Canaan (c. 1st century BCE to 3rd century BCE) and is therefore, supposedly, invalid. Palestinians have countered this by claiming descent from the Canaanites whose presence preceded the Israelite conquests (c. 1100 BCE).

7 See: <http://soldiertestimony.org/Israel/>, accessed 26 March 2005.

8 For instance, in the spring of 2004 an exhibition of photographs entitled 'Breaking the Silence' was mounted by reservists documenting their tour of duty in the divided city of Hebron, where 130,000 Palestinians are virtually held hostage to the small Israeli settlement in their midst. The exhibition, documenting the mostly routine abuses perpetrated or witnessed, generated tremendous public and media response and was followed by a wave of additional soldier testimonies. 'Breaking the Silence' has evolved into a public education project and archive. The group dissociates itself from refusal,

describing itself as non-political, patriotic, and concerned with what is 'happening to us'. It is not clear whether the testimonies are merely 'shooting and crying', a means of absolution, or whether they indicate a deeper change in the soldiers concerned (<www.breakingthesilence.org.il>).

9 The army opened an immediate inquiry into the incident and the soldier was removed from checkpoint duty.

10 At the time of writing 1,694 Palestinian non-combatants have been killed by army fire since September 2000, including 536 minors. Only ninety investigations have been initiated, twenty-nine indictments filed and only one soldier convicted (B'Tselem February 2005). A committee has been set up in the Ministry of Defence to investigate whether the morale of soldiers in the second millennium falls short of IDF tradition, or at least the myth of IDF tradition (*Ha'aretz*, 24 November 2004).

11 As a country of immigration, Israel has in the last fifteen years absorbed over a million newcomers, mostly from the former Soviet Union and Ethiopia. The newcomers acquire instant citizenship under the Law of Return (1950), permitting all Jews automatically to acquire Israeli citizenship on immigration. Nevertheless, newcomers may find themselves marked by culture, accent and physiognomy as Other, and struggle to be regarded as fully Israeli.

12 A popular right-wing car sticker carries the slogan 'The People are against hostile media'.

13 The nationalist Revisionist movement led by Ze'ev Jabotinsky (1880–1940) supported armed struggle against the British and opposed the Partition plan of 1947, demanding the whole Land of Israel for Jewish settlement. A slogan of the movement was 'Two banks to the Jordan, this one is ours and so is the other!' Jabotinsky was succeeded as leader by Menachem Begin, later Prime Minister of Israel (1977–82).

14 Association for Civil Rights in Israel awarded CPW the Emile Greenzweig Prize for Civil Rights for 2003.

15 Ahmed Jibril, head of the leftist rejectionist group PFLP, with headquarters in Damascus. In 1986 a deal was struck with the organization for the release of three Israeli POWs in exchange for the release of over 1,000 Palestinian prisoners. This was the subject of considerable controversy in Israel. The unilateral, and controversial, withdrawal from Lebanon in July 2000 is attributed here to the activities of the Four Mothers organization. Its timing was motivated by Ehud Barak's desire to show political results, possibly to reach some agreement with Syria. It was considered by the Right to be withdrawal under fire, endangering Israel's northern border.

16 For the Israeli Right, 'B'Tselem' is a code-word for treachery.

17 The legendary generation of Israeli pre-state warriors, founders of today's army, fighters in the War of Independence.

18 The proposed disengagement has generated massive opposition by the Right, and a wave of refusals to evacuate settlements by right-wing/religious soldiers.

149

7 | Conclusion

I am there because I want to protest the existence of ... checkpoints. They are the sharpest, most intense metaphor for the Occupation. (Aya Kaniuk, quoted in Sima Kadmon, 'Four Mothers', *Yediot Achronot*, 2 November 2003)

This book is about speaking out, about bearing witness to injustice. Specifically, it is an exposé of Israel's curfew–closure–checkpoint policy and the bureaucracy that supports it, illustrated by excerpts from the daily reports of CheckpointWatchers, Women Against the Occupation. These reports are an Israeli testimony to the Occupation as it is experienced by the Palestinians who suffer it day by day, year in, year out.

The abuses at checkpoints that we have witnessed daily over the last four years and recorded in the early chapters of this book are not isolated cases by individual miscreants; they are part of a system which is in itself deliberately abusive. More than any other aspect of the Occupation, checkpoints symbolize the absolute power of the Israeli state over the Palestinians. Checkpoints not only physically control mobility, time and space, but also determine, or rather deny, the boundaries of Palestinian national autonomy, for individuals and the collective alike. CPW by its civilian, humanitarian – and yes, political – presence challenges that absolute power.

Giving a context for the Watchers' activism, I have presented some of the dilemmas that arise between those Watchers who see their activism as political and those who wish to present it in purely humanitarian terms. I have shown the motives that bring women to the difficult task of checkpoint watching. The ambivalence of the group as both feminist and yet also playing into the trope of motherhood, so beloved of Israeli discourse, is also discussed. An analysis of media representation of CPW and the Left generally adds a further dimension of understanding to the complexity of what it means to be Israeli, in particular left-wing Israeli.

Looking back

Checkpoints are the tangible culmination of a historical process of dispossession, oppression and control of the Palestinians in their land, which began long before the present intifada, before the Occupation and long before 1948, from the very start of Zionist settlement of the Land in the nineteenth century. This is a statement of fact and in no way invalidates the powerful historic Jewish connection to the Land, nor the achievements of Zionism on behalf of its own adherents. Zionism is not an evil ideology. For the Jewish people it was a liberation movement, a chance for normality – an end to wandering, persecution and marginalization. The failure to realize the desire to be 'normal' lies in the persistent ethnocentric and exclusive nature of Zionism, its origins in the colonialist *Zeitgeist* of the nineteenth century and its aggressive territorial expansionism. The history of persecutions and, undeniably, the Holocaust have added strata of trauma that are reflected in the current conflict. Despite the political manipulation of the Holocaust in Israel, that trauma is very real. To overlook that, and to overlook the real hostility of some of the Arab world, especially during the early years of the state, is to deny fact. That said, Israel has never outgrown its colonialist and guerrilla past, never fully accepted the limitations that accompany the privileges of sovereignty. It has adopted a deliberate policy of expansionism and belligerence towards its neighbours, and has disregarded overtures for peace (Shlaim 2000). As for the desired normality for the Jewish state, this book demonstrates the abnormality of Occupation, both for the oppressed and for the oppressor. The oppressor has, of course, the option to mend its ways. The oppressed can, at best, resist; at worst, succumb.

Most Israelis feel threatened by the prospect of genuine political recognition of Palestinian rights, with its enormous implications for the re-reading of past Israeli-Zionist history. Together with the alleged demographic nightmare, or bound up with it, is the fear that historical fictions and errors will be exposed, of looking in the mirror and asking what has been done in our name, whether things might have been done differently, with less cost in lives and suffering, for Israelis and Palestinians alike. Perhaps it is not easy to relinquish an enemy, for the enemy, the 'Arabs' and the alleged danger they represent, have largely defined Israel over the fifty-seven years of its existence. What is more, Israeli society is largely held together by the conflict; deep ethnic, religious and social divisions bubble just below the surface. These divisions are conveniently shunted aside in favour of a spurious national unity in the face of the supposedly implacable enemy. As we have seen, the Left, too, has failed to address these divisions as part of a coherent strategy of opposition.

Some will doubtless say that reassessing history is a two-way street.

151

I would, however, contend that the Palestinians have paid the price, many times over, for their resistance to Zionist settlement and their refusal of the 1947 UN Partition plan. They have paid not only by the *Naqba* (disaster) of 1948, and the Occupation, but also in their abandonment by both the Arab and Western international communities and the delegitimization of the Palestinian national struggle. Israel, on the other hand, enjoys international recognition and the almost unqualified support of the world's only current superpower, the United States, and is itself a significant military power. It can afford the risk of reassessment.

Many Watchers would not agree with these analyses but rather look back with nostalgia to a golden age, an age that can be reclaimed by 'ending the Occupation'. But that is not enough if the Occupation continues by other means, such as Israeli control of Palestinian economy, borders, air space and roads. It is not enough partially to adjust the route of the Annexation Wall along the Green Line while still continuing to enclose large numbers of Palestinians in ghettos, whose access to the world is monitored via armed barricades. Nor will more 'humane' checkpoints resolve the conflict. For the Occupation to end, Israel must first of all recognize the validity of Palestinian self-determination and its own responsibility in perpetuating oppression for the sake of territorial gain.

Looking forwards

We leave the checkpoints, as we leave CheckpointWatch, and indeed the Occupation itself, at a watershed, with uncertainty as to what the future holds.

Although some checkpoints have been dismantled and others provide relatively free passage for those fortunate enough to be granted permits, the limitations on freedom of movement still exist. There is considerable use of the mobile or flying checkpoint and strategically placed internal barricades (see Appendix III). Palestinian access into Israel is still strictly controlled. The transformation of some of the larger, strategic, checkpoints, such as Qalandiya, into quasi border-crossings still allows the army the option of closing all, or part, of the West Bank at will. The mechanism of the checkpoints having been established and proven, it remains a potent weapon of control over territory and human lives alike.

In spite of ideological dissent and organizational challenges, CPW has held together and is in process of restructuring, formalizing its

7 Huwarra checkpoint, 2004 (photo: Esti Tsal)

decision-making process and creating a firmer ideological platform. This will give clear guidelines for CPW's mission and conduct at the checkpoints. It is to be hoped that this platform will be broad enough to accommodate a wide spectrum of ideological commitment, yet without compromising the political message that underlies its humanitarian activism.

Not the least of CPW's achievements has been to create an internal dialogue between the radical and the mainstream Left, despite the impassioned and often dissonant nature of that dialogue. As I have shown, the possibilities for debate, as opposed to argument, are rare in Israel and the level of denial regarding the evils of occupation is high. These exchanges within CPW are therefore salutary. Mainstream women hear a point of view to which they have hitherto not been exposed and radical women too are confronted with the need to

Conclusion

recognize mainstream concerns. We have seen the painful process for women confronting their own denial. They are seeking a framework for their experience that will enable them to reclaim their history and ideals while protesting the deviation from these ideals. It is from some of these women that valuable new activities have emerged – such as Yesh Din (There is a Law), which combines the taking of testimonies of settler violence[1] in Palestinian villages with legal action to bring offenders to justice. Although a separate project from CPW, there is an overlapping membership between the two organizations. It remains to be seen whether or not CPW will rise to the challenge of becoming a true opposition or resistance movement in whatever new form the Occupation takes in the future.

At the level of the conflict, there have been considerable changes in the political arena and it would be foolish to forecast what the future holds. Whatever develops at the international and national levels, there will need to be ongoing reassessment of needs and strategies for the protest organizations.

Meanwhile, activists remain alert and critical not only to declared government policy but also to what actually happens on the ground, to whether agreements are viable, and whether they are honoured in practice. The challenges and protests continue unabated. As we have seen, the Israeli Left is primarily an activist/protest force, each group addressing specific issues. An overall strategy of resistance/opposition has yet to develop. This is not because of a lack of leadership; on the contrary, it is a function of too many highly individualistic leaders with an inability to put egos and ideological nuances aside and combine forces.

The last word

In writing the book my own interest, or obsession, not only with checkpoints and the Occupation but also with the phenomenon of denial in Israeli society, came increasingly to the fore. Like many CheckpointWatchers, and particularly as the daughter of refugees, I am influenced by Holocaust history, and by the complicity of silence in the face of iniquity and injustice. Although the study of collective memory and its formation was not the subject of this book, the theme surfaced during the writing. Were I now at the beginning of my task, that would be a bolder *leitmotif.* Israel's collective memory, the redemption of the Land without People for the People without a Land by purity of arms, hard cash and the blood of the fallen, were necessary for survival, for the consolidation of nationhood. Conversely, the sense of victimhood, the reduction of the Palestinians to 'present absentees', or simply 'absentees', have created the climate in which their demonization and de-humanization have come to be axiomatic, part of the story. This perceived innate enmity is not the province of a few diehard bigots but of the decent, law-abiding majority. This is what makes it so dangerous.

Preserving the multiplicity of voices within CheckpointWatch, therefore, is not only vital to the viability of its protest and the strength of its message. Truth is a multifaceted concept, and all those voices are needed both for the authenticity of our testimonies and in forming the collective memory that will emerge from these years of struggle through those testimonies. Yet the question remains: whose voice will dominate? Will the memories of protest focus on the Occupation and its evils and even courageously review the whole trajectory of Zionist settlement in the Land of Israel/Palestine? Or will the protest become part of collective self-congratulation, yet another proof of our, Israel's, moral superiority as though to say that although there was no partner for peace, despite the terrorist attacks, merciful mothers went to succour the 'enemy'. And perhaps that, too, is part of the complexity of truth.

It seems that the beginning and the ending of this story are not so different. CheckpointWatchers, regardless of political persuasion, are still trying to create the just society of which so many of us dreamt. The willingness to protest, to speak out against iniquity to ensure that truth 'heeds our call', even if that truth is different for each one of us, is important in itself. It takes real hopefulness to act even when the outcome of action is unclear and there seems no end to the struggle. What matters is to keep on with that struggle. Sometimes, the journey is more important than the arrival.

Note

1 The issue of settlers, their violence and their symbiotic relationship with the army, are outside the scope of this work. Suffice it to say that the violence is widespread and conducted with impunity (B'Tselem 2003b, 2002a, 2002b; Eldar and Zartel 2004).

Appendix I: Checkpoints observed, 2001–05[1]

The army and Ministry of Defence usually talk about a few dozen permanent checkpoints staffed by soldiers or Border Policemen. However, apart from these barriers there are hundred of physical blockades in the West Bank, each one of which represents severe infringements of freedom of movement for Palestinians. Sometimes these blockades are more difficult than the staffed checkpoints themselves. OCHA, United Nations Office for Human Rights Affairs, coordinates information on a range of subjects connected to the Occupation and from time to time issues reports about checkpoints and other physical obstacles. These include: permanent and temporary checkpoints, blockades to access routes, closed gates, earthworks, ditches and watchtowers. In November 2004, the OCHA counted 719 checkpoints and blockades throughout the West Bank (this figure includes permanent checkpoints and earthwork barricades, both staffed and unstaffed). These can be easily seen at the roads leading to Palestinian villages by anyone driving along West Bank highways. Those listed here are mainly in the southern West Bank but they are representative of the picture throughout the area. All these checkpoints and blockades exist in a region approximately one-quarter the size of Wales.

The fluid nature of the checkpoints should be noted. When the authorities declare 'alleviations' it means (relatively) free passage across permanent checkpoints, although within a short time the open checkpoint is once again closed, not with a bang but with a whimper. For instance, in the wake of 'alleviations' in July 2004, CPW received from the Chief of Staff's bureau a list of checkpoints and blockades that had been demolished. During field observations we noted that for the most part the listed checkpoints had not been demolished at all or were subsequently re-erected *in situ* or close by. It seems that the changes were intended to leave the Palestinian population in a perpetual state of uncertainty, with no real future prospects but perhaps with a false hope of better things to come. Simultaneously, the Annexation Wall was closing in and it was crystal clear that when that happens passage will be dependent on the whim of security forces, and largely forbidden.

There follows a detailed list of the checkpoints regularly observed by CheckpointWatchers. We indicate whether each of the forty or so obstacles is internal, that is between one Palestinian area and another, or monitors access to Israel. At the latter, transitees are often checked both on entry and on departure.

Anata: Monitors entry to Jerusalem, blocks passage to those coming from Anbata and the Shuafat refugee camp that is within the extended municipal boundaries, close to the French Hill neighbourhood and the Hebrew University.

Anbata: An internal, permanent, unstaffed blockade, consisting of a locked iron gate preventing vehicular passage to the main Tulkarm–Nablus road. The gate is on Route 57 a few hundred metres from the crossroads with Route 557, near the settlement of Einav and the Palestinian village of Anbata. At the end of March 2005, the gate was removed when Tulkarm was handed over to Palestinian jurisdiction.

A-Ram: Monitors entrance to Jerusalem from the north. Those passing from Qalandiya to the capital must pass here too. With the construction of the Annexation Wall, A-Ram will increase in importance.

Atara: Internal checkpoint. Lies north of Ramallah and close to Bir Zeit University and the Surda crossing, situated on a bridge that crosses the settler road 465. This is a blockade, operated periodically, preventing access to Route 60 and the northern West Bank.

Awwarta: Internal checkpoint east of Nablus, for back-to-back transfer of goods. Near Huwarra checkpoint.

Azariyeh: Internal checkpoint at the southeastern approaches to the large settlement of Ma'aleh Adumim, on Route 417, the old Jericho road. The checkpoint is open only till 9 a.m. Is the purpose to reduce the pressure of morning traffic at the eastern entrance to Jerusalem? A similar checkpoint functions near the settlement of Mishor Adumim, near Jericho.

Barta'a: Monitors access to Seam Line Area (the area along the Annexation Wall on the Israeli side containing land expropriated for the building of the Wall, while the owners of the land remain on the West Bank side) between the Green Line and the northern West Bank. It lies south of the Israeli Palestinian city of Um el Fahm. It was closed in August 2004 when a checkpoint was opened at Rihan settlement (see below). Until 1967, the 1949 Armistice Line (Green Line) divided the village into two. With the erection of the Annexation Wall, Barta'a East (West Bank) is stranded in the Seam, between the Green Line and the Wall.

157

Beit Furiq: An internal checkpoint at the eastern entrance to Nablus, at the junction between routes 557 and 5487. In March 2005 the checkpoint at the village of Salame was blocked by earthworks and residents of the village and of nearby Azmuth and Dir el Hatab were forced to make a detour via Beth Furiq. Settlements: Itamar, Elon Moreh and their satellites.

Beth Iba: An internal checkpoint, west of the Palestinian city of Nablus on Route 558, close to Route 60, it lies in what was until recently an active quarry. Settlements: Shavei Shomron, Qedumim and Upper Qedumim.

Beth Jala: An internal checkpoint also known as the DCL checkpoint; lies at the southern outskirts of Jerusalem at the western entrance of the township of Beth Jala. Settlements: Gilo, Har Gilo.

Bethlehem: Monitors entry to Jerusalem, also known as checkpoint 300. Lies at the northern exit from Bethlehem. It is slated to move slightly south and be incorporated into the Annexation Wall. Once the busiest of checkpoints, as of March 2005 it was virtually deserted.

Blockades of Southern Mount Hebron villages: A rural area dependent on small-scale agriculture and herding. There are three central towns nearby, Halhul and Yatta under Palestinian control (Area A) and Hebron which is a divided city, part of which is under Palestinan control and part under Israeli control. All the villages in the area are isolated and almost completely closed off by earthworks across their access roads. Vehicular access is prevented between the villages and the towns as well as to Route 60, leading to Bethlehem and Jerusalem, and routes 35, 356 and 317. On these major arteries passage is forbidden to Palestinian vehicles without a permit. As a result most of the traffic in the area is limited to licensed *servis*-taxis, and that only on designated stretches. Pedestrians and donkeys are permitted. Traffic is mostly very sparse; crossing these roads is for the most part limited to pedestrians.

Children's Gate: An internal checkpoint. Also known as the Agricultural Gate or Gate 753. Like the dozens of other gates in the Annexation Wall it is supposed to allow passage to civilians. The gate is on the outskirts of Jabarra.

Cliff Hotel at Abu Dis: A small border police base for detaining 'illegals' (those entering Israel without a permit) and others. Detainees are held in the courtyard for long periods while their IDs are checked with the General Security Services, or for interrogation. There have been numerous reports of beatings and abuse.

Efrat: An internal checkpoint also known as Wadi Rachal and Checkpoint 131, it lies east of the settlement of Efrat, close to Noqdim and Teqoa, on Route 3167, in the heart of the West Bank.

Ein Yael: Monitors entry to Jerusalem near the Palestinian village of Wallajeh on a road leading to a major shopping mall.

El-Hadr blockade: An internal blockade west of Bethlehem, just off Route 60 junction with 375 to Husan and the settlement of Mevo Betar. Three banks of earthworks and refuse lie across what was once the entrance to the town of El Hadr and beyond to the western entrance of Bethlehem. In the past, this checkpoint was staffed periodically. Settlements: Efrata, Eliazar.

El-Hadr South: An internal blockade, used for 'back-to-back' transfer of goods to Bethlehem.

Etzion DCL: Local office of the Civil Administration responsible for the issue of magnetic cards and mobility permits.

Etzion: An internal checkpoint on Route 60, near a major crossroads with Route 367 leading to the Etzion Bloc settlements. Following a wave of 'alleviations', the checkpoint was removed but as of early 2005 is still operated occasionally.

Halhul Blockade: An internal checkpoint at the northern entrance to the town, beside the road leading to the settlement of Karmei Tzur.

Halhul–Hebron Bridge: An internal checkpoint crossing Route 35 and connecting the town of Halhul with the city of Hebron. Settlements: Karmei Tzur, settlements in Hebron, Givat HaHarsina, Kiriat Arba.

Hebron: The city of Hebron suffers not only from being divided between Israeli and Palestinian jurisdiction, but also from the fact that 130,000 Palestinians are held hostage there to a tiny Israeli settlement of 400 souls, as well as the nearby settlement of Kiryat Arba. Both these settlements are known for their radical religious-right ideology and for the violence frequently perpetrated by a number of their residents against Palestinian civilians. As indicated in Chapter 1, there are no fewer than twelve internal checkpoints in this troubled city, whose Palestinian citizens have suffered record numbers of curfew days.

Humanitarian Checkpoint: An internal checkpoint in South Hebron area giving access to humanitarian vehicles only. Lies at the crossroads between routes 60 and 35.

Huwarra: An internal checkpoint at the southern entrance to Nablus on Route 57 close to the branch of 557. This is a system of two checkpoints: north where those leaving Nablus are checked, and south where those entering Nablus are checked. The walking distance between the two is 450m. The southern checkpoint has recently (2005) been cancelled and those *entering* Nablus are checked only infrequently. The checks on those leaving Nablus continue as usual. Settlements: Elon Moreh, Bracha, Yitzhar, Itamar, and outposts.

Irtach: Entry point to Israel, also known as Checkpoint 700, Tulkarm checkpoint, Tul Karm Gate, South or Checkpoint Sha'ar Efraim. Located at the southern entrance to the town of Tulkarm, it is some half kilometre east of the Green Line, near the village of the same name.

Jabarra: There are three transit points, one an entry to Israel, the second an internal barrier and the third a gate marking the entry to the village of Jabarra and the Seam Line area. Also known as Kafriat, it is situated at the crossroads on Route 574 leading from Tulkarm to the village of A-Ras and southwards, along a rough road, impassable in winter, about 3km from the Green Line. In early 2005, work began on a tunnel under Route 557 to the Tulkarm crossing. The tunnelling has uprooted olive trees and destroyed the landscape (see also Chapter 4).

Jalameh: Entry to Israel. In the northern West Bank, north of Jenin, the checkpoint is close to the village itself, on Route 60. It is part of the Annexation Wall, at this point coinciding with the Green Line.

'Jatt Junction: An internal blockade at the meeting point of Route 60 with Route 55, close to Qedumim settlement. There is an almost permanent mobile checkpoint; soldiers in a jeep stop pedestrians and motorists for a spot-check of IDs.

Qalandiya: An internal checkpoint north of Jerusalem, south of Ramallah, close to the airfield of Atarot and Qalandiya refugee camp. With the completion of the Annexation Wall's Jerusalem envelope section, the checkpoint will be moved westwards and will become one of the permanent gates monitoring entrance to Jerusalem. (NB: The geographical definitions around Qalandiya are confusing: the refugee camp is part of the West Bank while the neighbouring suburb to the north of it, Kufr Aqeb, is part of the extended municipal boundaries of Jerusalem.)

Rihan: Monitors entry to the Seam area of the Wall, also known as checkpoint 45, south of the Israeli-Palestinian city of Um el Fahm. This is a new checkpoint located on Route 598, southeast of Rihan settlement, erected after the closure of Barta'a (see above). It is about 4km from the Green Line and traps residents in the Seam Line area between the Green Line and the Annexation Wall. Nearby settlements include Rihan, Shaked, Henanit and Tal Menashe.

Sansana: Monitors entry to Israel. Opened in September 2004, in the southern West Bank. Located on Route 60 where this crosses the Green Line close to the Israeli settlement of Metar.

Shaked: Monitors access to the Seam Line area via the Annexation Wall, east of Shaked and Rihan (see above). It blocks access to and from a number of small Palestinian villages that have been swallowed up by the Seam Line area and numerous nearby settlements

Shavei Shomron: An internal checkpoint on Route 60, five minutes' ride from Beth Iba (see above). Those reaching Nablus from the north are compelled to pass here and through Beth Iba as well. Often a mobile checkpoint checks the transitees between one checkpoint and the other, so that after a long delay at one there is another delay at the mobile checkpoint. Dismantled in December 2004, periodic spot checks continue.

Shema'a: Monitors entry to Israel far from the Green Line in the south Mount Hebron area. It was dismantled in September 2004 when Sansana (see above) was erected. Situated on Route 60 close to the Shema'a junction with Route 317 and close to the settlement of the same name.

Surda: Internal checkpoint north of Ramallah, on the way to Bir Zeit University. This is not a permanent checkpoint but a series of earthworks some 2km distant from each other. The earthworks have been removed and replaced several times during 2004 and in previous years. At times when the passage at Qalandiya has been limited, those Palestinians wishing to reach the southern West Bank were sent the long way round, north to Surda. As of March 2005, Surda is open. Settlement: Beth El.

Tapuach Junction: An internal checkpoint on Route 60 at the crossroads with Route 505 from the settlement of Ariel, descending to the Jordan Valley settlements. Neighbouring settlements include Tapuach, Rahelim, Eli, Ma'aleh Lavonah, Ariel, Midgalim and Ma'aleh Efraim.

Tarkumia: Monitors entry to Israel, some 5km east of the Green Line, on Route 35 close to the junction with the road leading to the township of Tarkumia. The Oslo Accords specified that that Tarkumia would be the main crossing between Gaza and the West Bank, but for the most part this was never implemented.

Tunnel Road: Monitors the entrance to Jerusalem, south of the city on Route 60. Only vehicles travelling towards the capital are checked; there are no pedestrians.

Tzara: An internal checkpoint close to 'Jatt crossroads and the Qedumim settlement. The checkpoint was dismantled in late March 2005 but at night passage is still blocked by a chain.

Wadi Nar: An internal checkpoint, aka the Container. Located at the top of Wadi Nar, the only route linking the southern and northern West Bank, enabling the army to disconnect the two areas at will. Settlements: Qedar and Ma'aleh Adumim.

Walajeh: An internal checkpoint, south of Jerusalem, that operates periodically.

Wicket at Abu Dis: Monitors entry to Jerusalem, also known as the Pishpash/Bawaba, located at Abu Dis, to the east of the capital. This is not exactly a checkpoint but rather an improvised breach in the Annexation Wall over which people clamber or jump. Checking of IDs is sporadic. Settlements: Qedar, Ma'aleh Adumim.

Z'atrah: An internal checkpoint at the foot of Mount Herodion, south of Jerusalem on Route 356, bypassing Bethlehem to the east. The route serves traffic coming from the northern West Bank via Wadi Nar. Settlements: Noqdim, Teqoa.

Other locations visited from time to time: Beth Awa, Nialin, Dir Balut, Zawieh, Jericho, Hamra and Tiassar. The DCLs visited periodically include: Hebron, Beth El, Tul Karm, Karrawa and Salem.

Note

1 Source: CounterView, Checkpoints in 2004 (MachsomWatch, 2003).

Appendix 2: Complaints filed in 2004

During 2004, MachsomWatch sent over 100 complaint letters to the IDF, the Border Police, the Israeli Police, the Civil Administration, the District Civil Liaison offices, the Ministry of Defence, to Knesset Members and to others.

Of these, 13 per cent of the complaints were answered in full; 30 per cent of the cases received an unsatisfactory answer; 5 per cent of the cases received a letter confirming receipt of the complaint, while 52 per cent of the complaints went unanswered.

Complaint letter statistics

Topic	(%)
Violence: shooting, beatings, use of tear-gas	19
Delaying ambulances	4
'Stop all Life' procedure: total cessation of movement	2
Restrictions on movement: barricaded villages, 'forbidden' roads, populace denied movement	19
Inappropriate conduct by the security forces: harassment, bullying, arbitrariness, humiliating attitude	15
Confiscation of papers: identity cards, vehicle licences and keys	7
Physical conditions at the checkpoints: narrow turnstiles, limited opening hours, lack of shade, lack of water, lack of toilets, luggage-checking counter	15
Settlers: causing damage to Palestinians' property; violence towards MachsomWatch/CheckpointWatch women	4
Other: 'grass-widows'[1], use of checkpoints to extort taxes, issuing of nitpicking traffic tickets, policy of the District Coordination Offices, requests to cancel unjustified fines, requests for removal from blacklists of the GSS, harassment of MachsomWatch/CheckpointWatch shifts	15

Note: 1 The impounding of civilian Palestinian homes by the army for military purposes.

Source: CounterView, Checkpoints in 2004 © MachsomWatch, 2005

8 Poster reading: 'Danger MachsomWatch – collaborators with the Arab enemy!' Jerusalem 2005 (photo: Nora Orlow)

Appendix 3: Monthly Digest, November 2004[1]

Machsomwatch observations during November 2004

The violinist at the checkpoint On 9 November a Palestinian violinist, Wissam Tiyam, arrived at the Beit Iba checkpoint. He was asked to remove his violin from its case to be checked, and played a short piece. The incident was recorded on video by a member of MachsomWatch/CheckpointWatch. Our footage set off a storm and overshadowed incidents occurring every day at the checkpoints. 'The Jewish past' hit the headlines, and the incident soon was labelled an 'exception' to the high standard norm of the IDF. Public debate in Israel focused chiefly on the insignificant question, whether the violinist was requested to play, or did so 'of his own free will'. Anyone familiar with the situation at the checkpoints knows that no Palestinian, crossing a checkpoint, enjoys the luxury of 'free will'.

Violence and abuse Abusive, violent behaviour at the checkpoints is widespread. When harsh behaviour and verbal violence are the prevailing norm, it's a short road from there to physical violence.

- The men who had waited for a long time left in great anger. One of them, an Arab citizen of Israel, shouted something to a soldier, who reacted by pushing him. He blew up and shouted at the soldier, 'Who are you to push me?' and returned the push. Within minutes, a bunch of soldiers fell upon him, dragged him to the checkpoint, roughly pushed his face against the fence and beat him mercilessly. He kept shouting, 'Leave me. I am sick and on dialysis. I will die.' But the soldiers continued. They did not listen to him nor us and continued with their beating. They put him in handcuffs and dragged him to the shed, newly covered with netting, that is at the end of the line for cars. He was detained there until the police arrived and investigated him, and freed him to his home, following the intervention of the health coordinator of the Army's Civil Administration. (Dahlia Bassa, Qalandiya, 1 November)
- A soldier screamed at me: 'They're not human beings. They are monkeys. They only understand when you shoot at them and kill them! They are baboons! Jews would never act like they acted at Arafat's funeral!' ... and so on. (Huwwara North, 17 November)

Particularly notable cases of abuse are the *medical cases* when passage is denied and people are only allowed to proceed on their way after arbitrary delays.

- A three-year-old boy accompanied by his father needed to reach a neurologist in Nablus. They had medical documents, but the commander didn't think them sufficient and tried to check whether there really is a doctor of that name in Nablus … Meanwhile, father and toddler waited. After MachsomWatch interceded, they were allowed to pass. (Beit Iba, 3 November)
- A couple on their way to fertility treatment; the husband was denied passage. When MachsomWatch intervened, they were 'granted' the right to pass through. (Beit Iba, 4 November)
- An ambulance arrived at the checkpoint with a woman heart patient, accompanied by a doctor and a nurse, on her way to hospital in Ramallah. Checking took an hour-and-a-half: all ID cards were sent for checking, the equipment on the ambulance needed to be removed. The nurse spread a sheet on the ground and took out everything, including sterile gloves, oxygen masks etc. Then the patient was asked to undergo a body search behind a curtain by a woman soldier. The equipment was returned, but now the driver was told to open the engine cover. The only thing not checked was the air in the tyres … And after all that, they were not allowed through. (Huwwara North, 6 November)

Detention as a penalizing procedure People are detained at the checkpoints for periods well beyond the time needed to check papers, and this has become a penalizing method. Cutting around the checkpoint, or a smile that's interpreted as impudence – are all 'justified' reasons for punishment.

- Among a group of students caught in the hills was a young man who, the soldiers said, had run amok. He has been put in the solitary confinement cell, his hands and feet fettered, with a rag tied over his eyes … and that was how he stood, unable to sit or to move, from 08.00 (according to the Palestinians) until 16.00 (we arrived at 12.00, when he was already in this condition). At 16.00 when he was released, he received a special 'parting gift' from a soldier, who *pushed his head against a wall*. During our shift, we saw the checkpoint commander pointing his gun at him and ordering him to stand with his face to the wall. (Beit Iba, 6 November)
- A high alert was received about a woman suicide bomber. 'Nobody crosses, not even a corpse,' the commander announced. For an hour,

women were forbidden to cross. Close to 200 women and children were squashed into the Nablus line, which became more and more crowded. Children were being trampled in the crush, babies were crying, and there were old and sick women in the crowd, some on the verge of collapse. The commander handed out sweets to the children, then contacted his superiors and explained that this couldn't go on, because these were *people, not animals*. Finally a woman soldier arrived and started checking the women and letting them through. (Beit Iba, 18 November)

• The detainees' 'pen' was crammed with people (close to sixty), who had been detained for over four hours. Two old people were punished because they had diverged from the 'official line'. Many of the detainees were released when it grew dark, around 17.00. (Beit Iba, 11 November)

Closure and encirclement The day before Ramadan ended, a closure and an encirclement were imposed on the cities and villages of the West Bank. On Jewish holidays, closure is imposed. On Muslim holidays – closure. If Jews are killed, a closure follows, and if a Palestinian leader dies, then a closure is announced too, but for security's sake – both a closure and an encirclement, so that heaven forbid any Palestinian leaves home. The buzzword seems to be: a Palestinian outside his home endangers the state's existence.

• At the checkpoint it was announced that the permits issued from 27 October for three months (until 27 January 2004) are no longer valid. A closure is in force, and the permits must be renewed. An Israeli building contractor who employs seven labourers was waiting there; he had come to renew the licences. He has employed them all for a considerable time. His labourers waited inside while the contractor went in to renew the licences, but he came out empty-handed. (District Coordination Office, Ezyon, 24 November)

• There has been an almost month-long closure, and during Ramadan as well Palestinians with Israeli ID cards were unable to visit their families on the West Bank. (Rihan, 14 November)

• Arabs (citizens of Israel) are prohibited from entering the West Bank. The prohibition is enforced across the board: 'a few people arrived, wearing their best holiday clothes, only to be sent back in their tracks'. (Rihan, 15 November)

• An Arab citizen of Israel, living in Ar'ara and working for years in a Jenin hospital, was unable to cross through. (Jalama, 27 November)

'Local rules' regarding the entry of Arab citizens of Israel to the Occupied Territories There is a lack of clarity and arbitrariness in the instructions soldiers receive; illegal orders are enforced.

- Arab citizens of Israel are forbidden to enter the Occupied Territories. According to the soldiers, only *Jewish Israelis* are permitted. Nevertheless, MachsomWatch representatives were held up. They argued that this decision is illegal, and were allowed to continue on their way. But the line of cars driven by Arab citizens of Israel was at a standstill and they were all denied entrance. (Jubara, 27 November)

Life overshadowed by settlers Settlers and their supporters come to the checkpoints to incite, using an aggressive, racist style. Substantial physical and verbal violence are levelled at MachsomWatch women, in front of the soldiers, who refrain from intervening, even though it's their lawful duty to do so until the police arrive. Neither are the police quick to intervene.

- Two settlers yelled at us 'May you burn in hell', and then drove off. (Ezyon, 1 November)
- A truck stopped on Route 60 and two thugs got out. They cursed and spat at us. As they were leaving, I took photos of them. The soldier told them about it, and they shouted: 'Let's smash her camera!' I moved back. Not a single soldier tried to intervene. The thug then slapped the soldier amicably on the shoulder and drove away. (al-Khadr, 11 November)
- Another escalation incident: a violent assault by 'Blue & White' women. It ended at the Ariel police station, and, as a result, two MachsomWatch women were banned from Huwwara checkpoint for two weeks, as were the 'Blue & White' women. (Huwwara, 29 November)

Different strokes by different folks

- The checkpoint, staffed by reservists, was functioning efficiently. The checkpoint commander worked calmly, politely and with good-will; the traffic flowed; the soldiers were also helped by a representative of the District Coordinating Office (DCO). (Beit Iba, 15 November)
- They relate politely and with concern to the people crossing through the checkpoint, and even chat with them. With my own ears, I heard a soldier wishing people 'have a good day'. (Huwwara South, 24 November)
- The DCO representative at Tarqumiya was highly praised by MachsomWatch observers. It was a pleasure to watch his attitude to the Palestinians, and he also got compliments from the Red Crescent representative and the bus drivers. He told us that he'd changed his ideas about the

Palestinian issue and the Palestinians themselves during his job – his attitude towards them has become more and more humanitarian. (Tarqumiya, 10 November)

Recently sighted – posters in eye-catching colours have been put up in the Occupied Territories and Jerusalem, warning:

Danger! MachsomWatch – collaborators with the Arab enemy

Note

1 *Source*: MachsomWatch Matria, November 2004.

References

Abu Dayyeh, M. (2005) *The Writing on the Wall* <www.miftah.org/Display. cfm?DocId=6418&CategoryId=20> accessed 8 May 2005.

Aga, H. and R. Malley (2001) 'Camp David, the Tragedy of Errors', *New York Review of Books*, 9 July 2001.

Alterman, N. (1974) *The Silver Platter* [1948] (Tel-Aviv: Ministry of Defence) (in Hebrew).

Ben-Ari, E. (2001) 'Tests of Soldierhood, Trials of Manhood: Military Service and Male Ideals in Israel', in D. Maman, Z. Rosenheck and E. Ben-Ari (eds), *War, Politics and Society in Israel: Theoretical and Comparative Perpsectives* (New Brunswick, NJ: Transaction Books).

Benziman, U. and A. Mansour (1992) *Sub-Tenants: Israeli Arabs and the Policy Towards Them* (Jerusalem: Keter) (in Hebrew).

B'Tselem (2001) *Rules of Engagement and Lack of Accountability Result in Culture of Impunity for Palestinian Civilian Deaths*, January (Jerusalem).

— (2002a) *Foreseen But Not Prevented: The Israeli Law Enforcement Authorities, Handling of Settler Attacks on Olive Harvesters*, Case Study no. 16, November (Jerusalem) (in Hebrew).

— (2002b) *Standing Idly By: Non-enforcement of the Law on Settlers: Hebron, 26–28 July 2002*, Case Study no. 15, August (Jerusalem) (in Hebrew).

— (2002c) *Lethal Curfew: The Use of Live Ammunition to Enforce Curfew*, October (Jerusalem).

— (2002d) *Palestinian Life Continues to be Cheap*, January (Jerusalem).

— (2002e) *Trigger Happy: Unjustified Gunfire and the IDF's Open-Fire Regulations during the al-Aqsa Intifada*, March (Jerusalem).

— (2003a) *Injury to Medical Teams: Detention, Humiliation, and Abuse of Medical Teams by Security Forces*, December (Jerusalem).

— (2003b) *The Bad Fence – Human Rights Abuses as a Result of the Separation Obstacle*, March (Jerusalem) (in Hebrew).

— (2004a) *Facing the Abyss: The Isolation of Sheikh Sa'ad Village – Before and After the Separation Barrier*, November (Jerusalem).

— (2004b) *Forbidden Families: Family Unification and Child Registration in East Jerusalem*, Joint Report with Hamoked – Centre for the Defence of the Individual, January (Jerusalem) (in Hebrew).

— (2004c) *Forbidden Roads: The Discriminatory West Bank Road Regime*, Information Sheet, August (Jerusalem).

— (2004d) *Through No Fault of Their Own: Israel's Punitive House Demolitions in the Al-Aqsa Intifada*, Information Sheet, November (Jerusalem).

— (2005) 'Take No Prisoners: The Fatal Shooting of Palestinians by Israeli

Security Forces during 'Arrest Operations', Information Sheet, May 2005.

CheckpointWatch/Physicians for Human Rights – Israel (2004) *The Bureaucracy of Occupation* (Tel-Aviv: CheckpointWatch and PHR).

Choshen, M. (2003) *A City in Transition – Population and Boundaries* (Jerusalem: Jerusalem Institute of Israel Studies).

Della Pergola, S. (2001) 'Jerusalem's Population 1995–2020: Demography, Multiculturalism and Urban Policies', *European Journal of Population Studies*, 17(2).

Dor, D. (2004) *Intifada Hits the Headlines: How the Israeli Press Misreported the Outbreak of the Second Palestinian Uprising* (Bloomington: University of Indiana Press).

Dugard, J. (2005) *Questions of the Violation of Human Rights in the Occupied Arab Territories, Including Palestine* (United Nations Economic and Social Council Commission on Human Rights).

Eldar, A. (2003) 'Carving Up Jerusalem for Security of Course', *Ha'aretz*, 19 August.

Eldar A. and I. Zartel (2004) *Lords of the Land: The Settlers and the State of Israel, 1967–2004* (Or Yehuda, Kinneret, Zmora-Bitan, Dvir) (in Hebrew).

Enloe, C. (1983) *Does Khaki Become You? The Militarisation of Women's Lives* (London: Pluto Press).

Friedman, T. (2003) 'One Man, One Vote, One Wall', *New York Times*, 14 September.

Furer, L. R. (2003) *Checkpoint Syndrome* (Tel-Aviv: Gvanim Press) (in Hebrew).

Gazit, S. (1995) *The Carrot and the Stick: Israel's Policy in Judaea and Samaria, 1967–68* (Washington, DC: B'nai B'rith Books).

Ginzburg, R. (2003) 'The Suppressed Subject Returns the Look', Paper presented at the 2003 Annual Conference, Israel Anthropological Association (in Hebrew).

Goldschmidt, T. (2004) Video: *Reports of DCL Offices Etzion, 4 November 2003/ Bethlehem/Nablus 5 February 2004* (Jerusalem: MachsomWatch).

Grant, L. (2003) 'What This War is Doing to Us', *Guardian*, 29 November.

— (2004) 'Inside the Bubble', *Guardian*, 8 April.

Haraway, D. (1997) *Modest_Witness@Second Millennium: FemaleMan© Meets_OncoMouse™* (New York and London: Routledge).

Harel, A. (2003) 'IDF Gave False Information on Nusseirat, for "Operational Reasons"', *Ha'aretz*, 2 November.

Hass, A. (2002a) 'Israel's Closure Policy: An Ineffective Strategy of Containment and Repression', *Journal of Palestine Studies*, 31(3).

— (2002b) 'Israel Forces Internal Movement Permit on Palestinians', *Ha'aretz*, 19 May.

— (2003a) 'Clarifying the Occupation Lexicon', *Ha'aretz*, 11 June.

— (2003b) 'A Babe in Arms: At the Age of 13 Hours Zina Meets the IDF', *Ha'aretz*, 27 March.

— (2005) 'Arab Israelis Barred from Using Route 557 to Enter West Bank', *Ha'aretz*, 28 March.

Helman, S. and T. Rappoport (1997) 'Those are Ashkenazi Women, Alone, Whores of Arabs, Don't Believe in God, and Don't Love the Land of Israel', *Theory and Criticism*, 10: 175–92 (in Hebrew).

Human Rights Watch (2001) 'Israel: Palestinian Drivers Routinely Abused', *Human Rights News*, 27 February <www.hrw.org/english/docs/2001/02/27/ isrlpa254.htm> accessed 28 February 2004.

— (2005) *World Report* (New York: Human Rights Watch).

Jiryis, S. (1976) *The Arabs in Israel* (New York: Monthly Review Press).

Kadmon, S. (2003) 'Many Mothers', *Yediot Achronot*, 21 November (in Hebrew).

Kaminer, R. (1996) *The Politics of Protest: The Israeli Peace Movement and the Palestinian Intifada* (Brighton: Sussex Academic Press).

Khalidi, W. (1991) *Before Their Diaspora* (Beirut: Institute for Palestine Studies).

— (1992) *All That Remains: The Palestinian Villages Occupied and Depopulated by Israel in 1948* (Beirut: Institute for Palestine Studies).

Kidron, P. (2003) *Refusenik* (London: Zed Books).

Kimmerling, B. (1983) *Zionism and Territory: The Socio-Territorial Dimensions of Zionist Politics* (Berkeley: University of California Press).

— (1993) 'Patterns of Militarism in Israel', *European Journal of Sociology*, 2: 1–28.

— (2001) 'The Twilight of Colonialism', in A. Ofir (ed.), *Real Time – Al Aqsa Intifada and the Israeli Left* (Jerusalem: Keter) (in Hebrew).

Klein, M. (2003a) 'Israel's Jerusalem Policy, Sparta and Apartheid', *Jerusalemites*, 5 November <www.jerusalemites.org/articles/press/69.htm>

— (2003b) 'Shattering the Myths of Camp David', *Ha'aretz*, 8 August.

LACC (Local Aid Coordination Committee) (2003) *The Impact of Israel's Separation Barrier on Affected West Bank Communities*, Report for the Mission to the Humanitarian and Emergency Policy Group (HEPG), 4 May.

Lavie, S. (2002) 'Mizrahi Feminism as Multiculturalizing Israel', Lecture delivered at the Kol HaIsha Women's Centre, Jerusalem.

— (2005) 'De/Racinated Transcendental Conversions: Witchcraft, Oracle and Magic Among the Ashkenazi-Israeli Feminist Peace Camp', Paper presented to the Second Christina Conference on Women's Studies, Helsinki, 2–5 March 2005

Lentin, R. (1998) 'Israeli and Palestinian Women Working for Peace', in L. Lorentzen and J. Turpin (eds), *Women and War Reader* (New York: New York University Press).

— (2000) 'The (Self) Silencing of the (Feminist) Lambs: Israel and Palestinian Women Struggling to Come to Terms with the Lost Possibilities of Peace in the Middle East', Paper presented at the Euro Forum, EUI, Florence, 22 November.

— (2003) 'Feminism and Military Gender Practices: Israeli Women Soldiers in "Masculine" Roles', *Sociological Inquiry*, 73(3): 440–65.

Levi, G. (2000) 'Sacrified on a Feast Day', *Ha'aretz*, 31 March.

Liss, J. (2003) 'The Municipality is Preparing for an Arab Majority in Jerusalem by 2040', *Ha'aretz*, 10 December.

Lomsky-Feder, E. and E. Ben-Ari (eds) (1999) *Military and Militarism in Israeli Society* (Albany: State University of New York Press).

Lustick, I. S. (2000) 'Yerushalayim and Al Quds: Political Catechism and Political Realities', *Journal of Palestinian Studies*, 17.

MachsomWatch (2005) A *CounterView: Checkpoints 2004* <www.machsomwatch.org/docs/Counterview.pdf> accessed February 2005.

Maoz, A. (2000) *State Cults: The Celebration of Independence and the Commemoration of Fallen Soldiers in Israel 1948–1955* (Sde-Boker: Ben-Gurion Heritage Centre) (in Hebrew).

Maymon, M. and E. Ben Ari (2004) Paper presented at the Conference on Soldier Testimony and Human Rights, Hebrew University, Jerusalem, 29 February to 1 March 2004 (in Hebrew).

Moked, Centre for the Defence of the Individual (2004) *Annual Report, 2003* (Jerusalem: Moked) (in Hebrew).

Morris, B. (1989) *The Birth of the Palestinian Refugee Problem: 1947–1949* (Cambridge: Cambridge University Press).

— (1999) *Righteous Victims: A History of the Zionist–Arab Conflict, 1881–1999* (New York: Alfred A. Knopf).

— (2000) *Correcting a Mistake – Jews and Arabs in Palestine/Israel, 1936–1956* (Tel-Aviv: Am Oved Publishers) (in Hebrew).

Nirgad, L. (2004) *Winter in Qalandia* (Tel-Aviv: Chargol Press) (in Hebrew).

OCHA (United Nations Office for the Coordination of Humanitarian Affairs) (2005) *Review of the Humanitarian Situation in the Occupied Palestinian Territories, 2004* (Jerusalem: OCHA).

Palestinian Centre for Policy and Survey Research (2005a) 'Joint Palestinian Israeli Press Release', 18 January.

— (2005b) 'Poll no. 15', 10–12 March.

Pappe, I. (1994) *The Making of the Arab–Israeli Conflict* (London: I.B. Tauris).

— (2004) *A History of Modern Palestine: One Land, Two Peoples* (Cambridge: Cambridge University Press).

Palestine Monitor (2005) 'Poverty Fact Sheet' <www.palestinemonitor.org/new_web/factsheet_poverty.htm> accessed 27 March.

PHR (Physicians for Human Rights) (2003) *At Will He Binds, at Will He Loosens – Israeli Policy Regarding Mobility Permits During Encirclement* (Tel-Aviv: PHR) (in Hebrew).

— (2004) *Medicine under Attack* (Tel-Aviv: PHR).

PRCS (Palestinian Red Crescent Society) (2005) on-line <www.palestinercs.org> accessed 6 March

Project on Soldier Testimony and Human Rights (2005) *Israel* <www. soldiertestimony.org/Israel> accessed 27 June.

Pundak, R. (2001) 'From Oslo to Taba: What Went Wrong?' *Survival*, 43(3): 31–45.

Rappoport, M. (2005) 'Following a Government Decision Residents of the West Bank Lose Their Property in West Jerusalem', *Ha'aretz*, 20 January.

Reinhart, T. (2002) *Israel/Palestine: How to End the War of 1948* (New York: Seven Stories Press).

Ronen, G. (2004) 'The Association Against the Soldier', *BeSheva*, 20 May (in Hebrew).

Rosenfeld, M. (2003–04) 'Sunday Morning at the Checkpoints: The "Compulsory Pleasures of the Ruler, the Compulsory Resilience of the Ruled"', *Politika, Israel Journal of Political Science*, 11/12 (in Hebrew).

Sasson-Levi, O. (2003a) 'Feminism and Military Gender Practices: Israeli Women Soldiers in "Masculine" Roles', *Sociological Inquiry*, 73(3): 440–65.

— (2003b) 'Military, Masculinity and Citizenship: Tensions and Contradictions in the Experience of Blue-Collar Soldiers', *Identities: Global Studies in Culture and Power*, 10(3): 319–45.

Sasson-Levi, O. and T. Rappoport (2003) 'Body, Gender and Knowledge in Protest Movements', *Gender and Society*, 17(3): 379–403.

Segev, T. (1986) *1949: The First Israelis* (New York: Free Press).

— (2000) *One Palestine Complete: Jews and Arabs Under the British Mandate* (New York: Metropolitan Books).

— (2002) 'Women of the Checkpoints', *Ha'aretz*, 10 July.

Segev, T., J. Shainin and R. Carey (eds) (2002) *The Other Israel: Voices of Refusal and Dissent* (New York: W. W. Norton).

Seideman, D. (2003) 'Erecting a Barrier to Peace', *Washington Post*, 14 August.

— (2004) 'Letting Israel Self-Destruct', *Washington Post*, 27 August.

Shadmi, E. (2000) 'Between Revolution and Conformism, Feminism and Nationalism, Women in Black in Israel', *Women's Studies International Forum*, 23(1): 23–4.

Shafir, G. and Y. Peled (2002) *Being Israeli: The Dynamics of Multiple Citizenship* (Cambridge: Cambridge University Press).

Shapin, S. and S. Schaffer (1985) *Leviathan and the Air Pump: Hobbes, Boyle and the Experimental Life* (Cambridge, MA: Princeton University Press).

Sharoni, S. (2000) 'Homefront as Battlefield', in T. Mayer (ed.), *Women and the Israeli Occupation: The Politics of Change* (London: Routledge).

Shavit, A. (2004) 'Survival of the Fittest? An Interview with Benny Morris', *Ha'aretz*, 8 January.

Shenhav, Y. (2003) *The Arab Jews: Nationalism Religion and Ethnicity* (Tel-Aviv: Am Oved Publishers) (in Hebrew).

Shlaim, A. (2000) *The Iron Wall* (New York: W. W. Norton).

Shohat, E. (1988) 'Sephardim in Israel: Zionism from the Standpoint of Its Jewish Victims', *Social Text*, 19–20: 1–35.

— (1999) 'The Invention of the Mizrahim', *Journal of Palestine Studies*, 1: 5–20.

Silberstein, L. J. (1999) *The Post Zionism Debates: Knowledge and Power in Israeli Culture* (New York: NYU Press).

Steinitz, Y. (1999) 'When the Palestinian Army Invades the Heart of Israel', *Commentary*, 108: 12.

Tsafati, Y. and O. Livio (2003) 'Israeli Journalists Flunk the Israeli Media', *The Seventh Eye: Journal of the Israel Democracy Institute* (Jerusalem).

World Bank (2002) *27 Months of Intifada, Closures and the Palestinian Economic Crisis: An Assessment* <www.lnweb18.worldbank.org/mna/mena.nsf/> accessed 10 April

Yeats, W. B. (1983) *The Poems: A New Edition* (New York: Macmillan).

Index

bribery: accepted by Israeli military, 69; at checkpoints, 58
Brit Shalom/Tahalof Essalam, 3
Bronfman, Roman, 47
B'Tselem, 27, 90, 144
Buber, Martin, 3
bureaucratic hazing, 138
burial of the dead, prevention of, 101

Camp David, 109; failure of, 123
Checkpoint 300, 34
checkpoint syndrome, 121
CheckpointWatch organization, 1, 5, 32, 33, 62, 155; accused of attacking a soldier, 112–14; all-women's activity, 35; as danger to the nation, 144; checkpoint toolkit, 38; commitment to non-violence, 37; daily reports of, 37, 38, 150; dilemmas of, 8, 107–31; explosion in membership of, 135; Forum, 110; hostility to, 34, 167, 168; humanitarian role model, 143; integral part of Israeli society, 43; media representation of, 8, 129, 132–49; motivation of participants, 39; non-political tendencies in, 132, 147; organizational structure of, 37; paternal lineage of participants, 142; perceived as comforting the enemy, 147; praised for courage, 132; profile of participants, 45–6; proposed shift in focus of, 110; relations with Israeli military, 108, 115–17; relations with Palestinians, 108, 123–8, 129; self-representation of, 146; solidarity of, 124; source of empowerment, 40; study of, 7; tactics of, 38
checkpoints, 15; as collective punishment, 57, 75, 77; as metaphor for Occupation, 150; as system of control and oppression, 35, 55, 150; as theft of time, 16; bypassing of, 23, 34, 100; dismantling of, 152 (and re-

erection of, 156); endemic violence of, 84; fluid nature of, 156; mobile or flying, 152, 161; numbers of, 57, 156; obsession with, 6; procedure for CheckpointWatch participants, 58; upgrading of, 14 *see also* curfew-closure-checkpoint system
Checkpointspeak, 60–3
Children's Gate checkpoint, 158
Citizenship and Entry into Israel Law, 26–7
closure, 22, 74, 82, 80; as punishment for stone-throwing, 58; declaration of, 15; for hot alerts, 61–2; for no apparent reason, 75
Coalition of Women for a Just Peace, 46
collaborators, Israeli, 59; recruitment of, 18
collateral damage, 62
Corrie, Rachel, 55
curfew, in Hebron, 159
curfew-closure-checkpoint system, 32–3, 150; as collective punishment, 15–16

Dank, Michelina, 91–5, 94
dark glasses, used by Israeli military, 62
Democratic Front for Peace and Equality (Hadash), 108
demographic 'threat', 95, 101, 151
denial in Israeli society, 147, 154
detention, as harassment, 58
District Coordination and Liaison (DCL), 18, 20, 23, 26, 60; monitoring of, 21
donkeys, used as transportation, 15, 158
Drukker-Tikotin, Ilana, 32–3, 42
Druze, 126
Dviri, Manuela, 136

E-1 plan, 101–2
Edelstein, Mickey, 24
Efrat checkpoint, 159

Index